Building Single Application Using ASP.NET Core and ANGULAR

Rahul Sahay

BPB PUBLICATIONS
20 Ansari Road, Daryaganj, New Delhi-110002

FIRST EDITION 2018

Copyright © BPB Publication, INDIA
ISBN: 978-93-8655-190-0

Distributors:

BPB PUBLICATIONS
20, Ansari Road, Darya Ganj
New Delhi-110002
Ph: 23254990/23254991

BPB BOOK CENTRE
376 Old Lajpat Rai Market,
Delhi-110006
Ph: 23861747

COMPUTER BOOK CENTRE
12, Shrungar Shopping Centre,
M.G.Road, Bengaluru–560001
Ph: 25587923/25584641

DECCAN AGENCIES
4-3-329, Bank Street,
Hyderabad-500195
Ph: 24756967/24756400

MICRO MEDIA
Shop No. 5, Mahendra Chambers,
150 DN Rd. Next to Capital Cinema,
V.T. (C.S.T.) Station, MUMBAI-400 001
Ph: 22078296/22078297

Published by Manish Jain for BPB Publications, 20, Ansari Road, Darya Ganj, New Delhi- 110002 and Printed by at Repro India Pvt Ltd, Mumbai

Foreword

Building Single Page App using ASP.NET Core and Angular is a great book both for students and industry professionals who have been developing applications. The author does a good job by focusing on concepts that are quite essential for progressing through the book. I can see a book being a good resource for beginner and intermediate level. Advanced professionals can also get benefitted by the code samples and advanced concepts covered later in the book. I do want to add a disclaimer that if you are a fresher who has no experience in developing applications, this book may not be for you.

What I like about Rahul is that he actually codes and also pays attention to where the industry is going. He is very active in the community. The perspective he brings is usually industry standard. This book uses all industry standard conventions for building any quality single page application. Angular has been the de facto leader when it comes to the enterprise SPAs. ASP.NET Core is the primary server side framework fully supported by Microsoft. Combination of ASP.NET CORE and Angular makes this book perfect match for developers who are looking to develop application for futuristic web.

On the journey to be an expert, I think this book is one of the first steps.

CHANDER DHALL
CEO
Cazton Inc

Preface

Building Single Page App using ASP.NET Core and Angular is written in such a way, that while reading you will be building fully functional End-To-End app which you will be starting from basics to advanced concepts in every area. This book uses tons of concepts like Solid Principles, Repository Pattern, Unit of Work Pattern, Entity Framework, Design Principles and many other things to name a few. One point to note here that Author expects to have basic knowledge around these technology stacks to understand the book completely. This book is all about building industry standard application by coupling variety of technologies together. Hence, readers are expected to have basic knowledge on the same.

Angular is used as Single Page Framework for client side. Soon after Angular creation in 2009, AngularJS grew like widely popular framework for building Single Page Application. It started with AngularJS, where in AngularJS still exists and it will remain for the years to come. Now a days it's also known as Angular 1. In order to make this framework more robust and lightning fast, google overhauled this framework completely and decided to change the architecture. They re-written the entire framework in Typescript, which means type system is baked into its core. Angular is wholly different component written for futuristic web. It is written on the top of ES6, web components, web workers, reactive programming and Typescript to name a few. Modularity is the key concept in Angular on which everything is built around. It also offers bountiful collection of configuration and tooling which makes an Angular app very fast.

How this book is structured?

This book is divided into broad sections, and comprising several chapters. First part of this book is structuring the project in and then introducing server side components first and then client side components.

Chapter 1, "Getting Started", helps you to get the feel of overall book. Here, you will understand, what you are going to build throughout the book. You will also get to see what technology, you will be using through. You will also get the glimpse of the finished project.

Chapter 2, "Creating Solution from the Blank Slate", in this chapter, you will be creating solution from scratch. Here, you will be doing all tooling and project setup to get started with application. Here, you will also add necessary library references to other class library projects.

Chapter 3, "Creating Data Context", in this chapter, you will be implementing data technology part of project. First you will be creating models here, then for filling the same, you will be using Entity Framework approach. Here, you will also learn variety of different concepts like data seeding, implementing Repository Pattern, applying database constraints etc.

Chapter 4, "Implementing Web API", in this chapter, you will be implementing

Web API. You will start with simple API design, then you will be writing complex API designs for custom queries. Lastly, you will be adding couple of more controllers for custom based query.

Chapter 5, "Getting Started with Angular", in this chapter, you will be starting with Frontend design like Angular Implementation. We will start with simple Angular component creation. Further we will delve into routing techniques followed by simple Form design and service implementation.

Chapter 6, "Deeper into Angular" in this chapter, we will delve further and look into the guts of application. Here, we will start with client side validation. In that course, we will refer third party libraries like toasty. We will also see how to handle errors in Angular. We will be using cloud based logging scheme in this case.

Chapter 7, "Adding More Features using Angular", in this chapter, we will continue from the last section and extend the application further. Here, we will begin with listing reviews and implementing CRUD pattern for reviews. Here, we will be fixing some crucial navigation issues as well.

Chapter 8, "Adding More Features to the App", this is the bonus section of the book; I can say as all mandatory application based functionality is over by this time. Here, we will be extending the same by adding features like image upload and rendering the same using angular. We will also see how to work with tabbed view in angular.

Chapter 9, "Authentication & Authorization", in this chapter, you will begin by learning the concepts of authentication and authorization. Here, we will be using third party library like Auth0 for the same. Once completed, then you will learn how to use JWTs bearer token for the same. Here, you will implement complete authentication cycle. Here, you will also learn how to create custom login pages. Apart from that, you will see how to implement rules, roles, protect routes etc.

Chapter 10, "Introduction to Azure and CosmosDb", in this chapter, you will begin by learning the concepts of CosmosDb. Cosmos DB is a NoSql database that provides strong consistency. It's scheme free, supports sql-like querying, even has stored procedures, triggers and UDFs (User Defined Functions) written in Javascript. It's Microsoft'sanswer to MongoDb, Cassandra, Couchbase and others. According to Cosmos DB, "Azure Cosmos DB guarantees less than 10 millisecond latencies on reads and less than 15 milliscecond latencies on writes for at least 99% of requests." With that kind of performance guarantees, cosmos DB is set to take over the world. Here, you learn how to get started with Cosmos DB.

Project Download:

GitHub Link: **https://github.com/rahulsahay19/MovieReviewSPA-NG4.** You can download project from here for your reference. In case, if you find any discrepancies, you can report the same in issues' link on git page. In case if you like to provide suggestions, you can mail at bdg@bpbonline.com. You can also download asp.net core plugin for VS Code from **http://bit.ly/ASP-NET-CORE-Ext**. if you are doing asp.net core project using code, then that link is must have tool for that.

Contents

Getting Started

Introduction

In this section, I am going to introduce this whole new story of building a Single- Page Application right from scratch. Here in this context, I am going to talk about a bunch of different client/server-side technologies and demonstrate how these small pieces come together and create a robust End-to-End application. However, I do expect readers to have basic working knowledge of ASP.NET Core and Angular 2 or 4. Then, only you will be able to grasp the techniques comfortably. Hence, without wasting time let's get started.

What is SPA ?

Single Page Application is all about user experience. People will love your app if you give them a nice user experience which not only fits nicely on your laptop or desktop rather it goes nicely with many devices such as tabs, phones, etc. Without breaking any single functionality. As shown in the following diagram, these are the basic requirements for building any SPA.

○ **Reliability:** People know that it's reliable and it's going to work. This kind of reliability only comes with positive experience.

○ **Responsiveness:** Responsiveness means it's going to work quickly for them. Quick is the key thing which any user expects to have in the app which he is using.

○ **Reach:** Reach is often substituted with mobility. Mobility is again one of the key ingredients which every user is looking for. They always want to have the data handy irrespective of what device they are on.

○ **Available:** Availability is really important when it comes to working offline. Hence, delivering a good user experience is a must while building SPA.

"Therefore, in a nutshell, a Single Page App is a web application which fits in a single page providing a fluid UX by loading all the necessary data in a single load."

Now, apart from this, there are many other attributes linked to SPA. They are as follows:

○ **Maintain History:** When you flip between pages, it maintains your history in the same order you visited them. Actually, it does not go to different pages but loads different information on the same page. It looks as if it's presenting different pages to them.

○ **Persisting Information:** Persisting information is also a very important aspect of the SPA. This doesn't mean that you need to save each and every thing in the cache but you can store important things in the cache to improve the performance.

○ **Mostly loaded on Page Load:** Mostly loaded on the page load means a majority of information a user requires gets loaded initially to avoid a round trip back to the server.

○ **Dependent Elements:** As and when a user needs to access different features of the application, the app will download the features for the user.

Technologies Used to build SPA

Movie Review App is built using tons of different client-side and server-side technologies. Some of these are listed below:

Client-Side Technologies

○ HTML 5
○ CSS 3
○ Modernizer & LESS
○ Responsive Design
○ Media Queries
○ Angular 4
○ Toastr JS
○ Bootstrap Templates
○ Font Awesome Icons

Server-Side Technologies

- ✪ ASP.NET Core
- ✪ SQL Server
- ✪ Entity Framework Core – Code First Approach
- ✪ Repository Pattern
- ✪ Unit of Work Pattern
- ✪ Web API
- ✪ JSON & AJAX
- ✪ NuGet
- ✪ IOC
- ✪ POCO Models

Design Techniques

- ✪ Solid Principles
- ✪ Factory Pattern

Tools Used

- ✪ Visual Studio 2017

Glimpse of Movie Review APP

I think it would be a great idea to show you the finished application before directly jumping to creating the same. The following figure shows a glimpse of the finished product in the best possible way. Once you download the app and run it, it will look like this.

Here, I have different options like Login and Movies. The other two options are from the scaffolding project; you can skip those. I have not removed the menus. We will come later to the Login menu. Let's first check Movies' menu. Once, you click on Movies, it will show you the following screen:

Here, Filter Movie is a drop down which shows the following:

Therefore, if I select Avatar, then my Movies List will filter out other movies, as shown below:

Now, if I click on the Reset button or if I select the Blank option from the drop-down menu, then the list will get reset. Next, when I click on Movie Reviews link, then it will show the following screen:

Once the review is fetched successfully, the following toast message will appear on the screen.

We can also filter by review rating by selecting the Filter Reviews by Rating option.

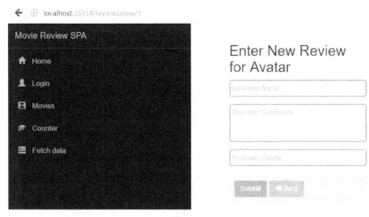

This is the same filter concept we had seen earlier. After this screen appears, we can go ahead and add new reviews as well, as shown below:

You will notice that the Submit button is disabled here, which means you can't submit the form until you fill the valid details. Once I fill in the details, the Submit button gets enabled, as shown below:

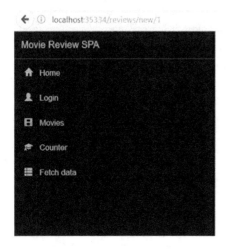

Now, I can submit the form. Once I click on the Submit button, it will show the following toast message:

And then it will get redirected to Movies' page.

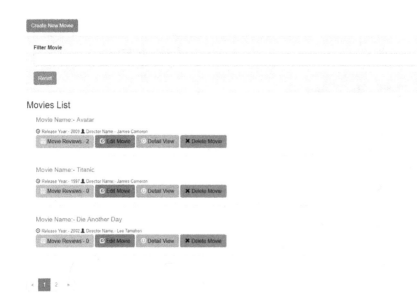

Here, I can see that Movie Reviews has now changed to 2. Similarly, I can Edit Movie as well, as shown below:

On the edit screen, it will show the existing movie, which I can modify, as shown in the following screenshot:

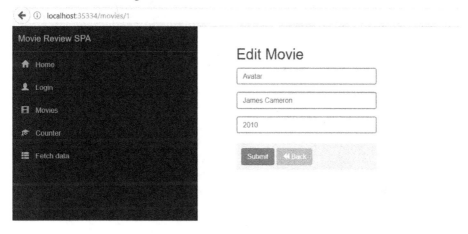

Once I click on the Submit button, it will show the following toast message and get redirected to the Movies' page.

Let me change the year back to 2009. Now, when I click on Detail View, it will appear like this.

This is a tabbed view, which by default is Movie, which basically shows the movie details in read-only mode. Here, I have one button "**View All Movies**" to go back to the Movies' page. The second tab is for images. Therefore, when I click on the Pics tab, it will fetch the images corresponding to the movie.

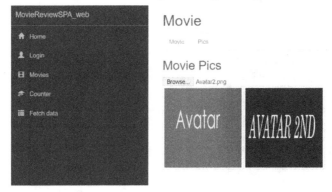

By clicking on the Pics tab, we can browse the movie images as well upload them one by one, as shown in the following screenshot:

Upon successful upload, it will display the following toast message:

And a new image will also appear on the page, as shown below.

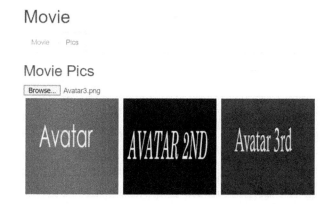

We now go back to the Movies page. Here you can see the Delete Movie tab. When you click on the Delete Movie tab, it will show you a prompt as shown below.

If you click on OK, then it will delete the movie; else it will remain on the same page like normal delete functionality. Now, Click on the "Create New Movie" link as shown below.

It will get redirected to login page as shown below. Here, you can either sign-up with Google or you can create a new user with auth0 Site. I have discussed about auth0 in detail in the next chapter.

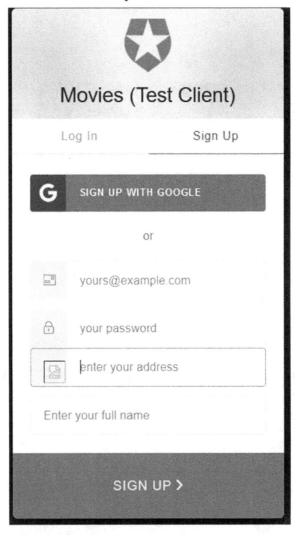

Here, I have logged in with my ID and I am the admin here. I have created rules in such a way that only admin users can create movies. This is just for demonstration purpose; you can extend this feature to expensive operations like delete, update, etc. Once you log in successfully, you will notice that the New Movie option for creating the movie appears on the screen.

Once I click on the New Movie tab, the following screen will appear:

Here, I can create any movie, as shown below.

Here, when I click on the Submit button, a new movie will be created and will show the below toast message.

Now, I can see the new movie I just created on the Movies page, as shown below.

Similarly, I can add/update/delete reviews. We have already seen that.

Glimpse of Movie Review Solution

Let me go ahead and show you the solution structure of a finished app. In the following screenshot, you can see four different projects. Each of them has its own dependency and responsibility.

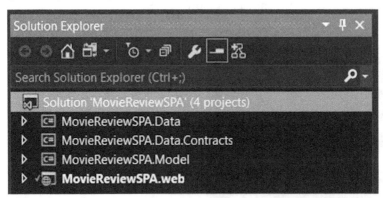

Here, the highlighted one is the web project which is dependent on other infrastructure projects like **Data, Contracts,** and **Model**. The **Data** project is a place where you can maintain the initial seed data, Entity Framework DbContext and many other things that interact directly with the database. **Data Contract** is the place where in you can manage your repositories and apply the **Unit of Work Pattern** on repositories like **Movies** and **Moviereviews**. **Model** is the section where you will have your **POCOs** (**Plain Old CLR Objects**). This is also a place where you can maintain all properties attributed to the tables. Here is a glimpse of all the projects in their expanded form

MovieReviewSPA.Data
- ▷ Dependencies
- ▷ Helpers
- ▷ SampleData
- C# EFRepository.cs
- ✓ C# MovieReviewDbContext.cs
- C# MovieReviewUow.cs

MovieReviewSPA.Data.Contracts
- ▷ Dependencies
- C# IMovieReviewUow.cs
- C# IRepository.cs

MovieReviewSPA.Model
- ▷ Dependencies
- ▷ C# Image.cs
- ▷ C# ImageSettings.cs
- ▷ C# Movie.cs
- ▷ C# MovieReview.cs
- ▷ C# Pager.cs

MovieReviewSPA.web
- Connected Services
- ▷ Dependencies
- ▷ Properties
- ▷ wwwroot
- ▷ ClientApp
- ▷ Controllers
- ▷ Migrations
- ▷ ViewModels
- ▷ Views
- .angular-cli.json
- .gitignore
- ✓ appsettings.json
- global.json
- package.json
- C# Program.cs
- C# Startup.cs
- tsconfig.json
- web.config
- ▷ webpack.config.js

Summary

In this section, we saw the bits and bytes of the Single-Page Application that we used while building the application. We also saw a glimpse of the app and solution. In the next chapter, we'll create the application right from scratch. I recommend that you download the app from **GitHub URL,** which will help you while building, **https://github.com/rahulsahay19/MovieReviewSPA-NG4**. This will enable you to quickly check and fix any issues you face while building the app.

CHAPTER 2

Creating Solution from the Blank Slate

What do you find in this Chapter?

Introduction

In this module, we will begin with a blank solution. Now, in this blank solution, we will add couple of different projects to complete the solution structure of our movie app. Then, we will complete the necessary references of projects to each other. After resolving all project dependencies, we will begin by installing the necessary **client/server**-side components using **Nuget** and **NPM**. Basically, in this section, we will create a framework structure of our entire app.

Solution Creation

In this section, we'll create the complete architecture right from a blank slate. Hence, without wasting time let's get started. In order to scaffold the project, I'll be using **DOTNET CLI**. I'll execute the command given below to install the SPA services in the command line. Also, I am using Cmder here. It's a free command line tool. You can also download it from **http://cmder.net/** or you can use the usual built in command line tool.

```
dotnet new --install
Microsoft.AspNetCore.SpaTemplates::*
```

On successful installation, it will show you the complete template list, as shown below.

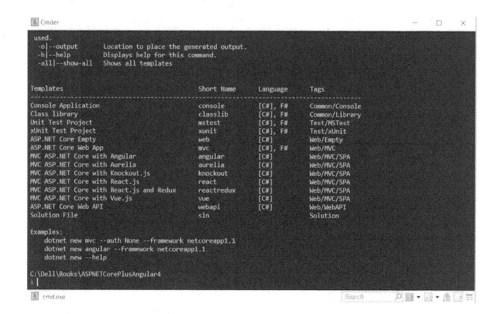

I have created the root folder with the name **MovieReviewSPA.web**.

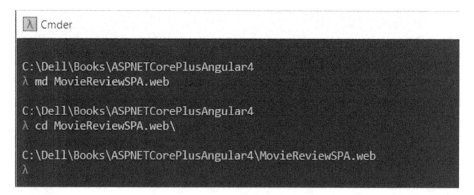

Here, I can go ahead and create a project with any of these available templates. However, in this case, I'll choose angular. Hence, I'll type **dotnet new angular**.

er

```
\Books\ASPNETCorePlusAngular4\MovieReviewSPA.web
t new angular
 generation time: 651.2822 ms
plate "MVC ASP.NET Core with Angular" created successfully.

\Books\ASPNETCorePlusAngular4\MovieReviewSPA.web  (MovieReviewSPA_web@0.0.0)
```

I now need to restore the project so that all the required dependencies get pulled in. I need to type the **dotnet restore** command.

```
Cmder                                                                    —  □  ×

C:\Dell\Books\ASPNETCorePlusAngular4\MovieReviewSPA.web
λ dotnet new angular
Content generation time: 651.2822 ms
The template "MVC ASP.NET Core with Angular" created successfully.

C:\Dell\Books\ASPNETCorePlusAngular4\MovieReviewSPA.web  (MovieReviewSPA_web@0.0.0)
λ dotnet restore
  Restoring packages for C:\Dell\Books\ASPNETCorePlusAngular4\MovieReviewSPA.web\MovieReviewSPA.web.csproj...
  Generating MSBuild file C:\Dell\Books\ASPNETCorePlusAngular4\MovieReviewSPA.web\obj\MovieReviewSPA.web.csproj.nuget.g.
props.
  Generating MSBuild file C:\Dell\Books\ASPNETCorePlusAngular4\MovieReviewSPA.web\obj\MovieReviewSPA.web.csproj.nuget.g.
targets.
  Writing lock file to disk. Path: C:\Dell\Books\ASPNETCorePlusAngular4\MovieReviewSPA.web\obj\project.assets.json
  Restore completed in 2.71 sec for C:\Dell\Books\ASPNETCorePlusAngular4\MovieReviewSPA.web\MovieReviewSPA.web.csproj.

  NuGet Config files used:
      C:\Users\hp\AppData\Roaming\NuGet\NuGet.Config
      C:\Program Files (x86)\NuGet\Config\Microsoft.VisualStudio.Offline.config

  Feeds used:
      https://www.nuget.org/api/v2/
      C:\Program Files (x86)\Microsoft SDKs\NuGetPackages\

C:\Dell\Books\ASPNETCorePlusAngular4\MovieReviewSPA.web  (MovieReviewSPA_web@0.0.0)
λ
```

I can go ahead and build the project now with the dotnet build command.

```
Cmder                                                                    —  □  ×

C:\Dell\Books\ASPNETCorePlusAngular4\MovieReviewSPA.web  (MovieReviewSPA_web@0.0.0)
λ dotnet build
Microsoft (R) Build Engine version 15.1.548.43366
Copyright (C) Microsoft Corporation. All rights reserved.

  MovieReviewSPA.web -> C:\Dell\Books\ASPNETCorePlusAngular4\MovieReviewSPA.web\bin\Debug\netcoreapp1.1\MovieReviewSPA.w
eb.dll

Build succeeded.
    0 Warning(s)
    0 Error(s)

Time Elapsed 00:00:04.94

C:\Dell\Books\ASPNETCorePlusAngular4\MovieReviewSPA.web  (MovieReviewSPA_web@0.0.0)
λ
```

I can also type "**start .**" in the command prompt to explore the folder structure as shown below.

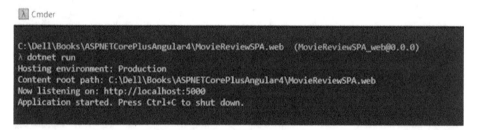

I can also go ahead and run the project from the command line using the **dotnet run** command.

```
C:\Dell\Books\ASPNETCorePlusAngular4\MovieReviewSPA.web  (MovieReviewSPA_web@0.0.0)
λ dotnet run
Hosting environment: Production
Content root path: C:\Dell\Books\ASPNETCorePlusAngular4\MovieReviewSPA.web
Now listening on: http://localhost:5000
Application started. Press Ctrl+C to shut down.
```

Here, it shows that the application is running by default in the production mode. It also shows Content root path, from where all static files get served. Apart from that it shows the current running port. Quite informative! We will dive into these settings and information in the upcoming section. For the time being, we will just navigate to http://localhost:5000.

This is the default view of the app. Now, let's open the same in Visual Studio 2017. A glimpse of the solution is given below. Here, I have made one more change in order to make the solution consistent. Actually, I have created one more parent directory with the name **MovieReviewSPA** and moved my

MovieReviewSPA.web project there. Also, I have renamed my solution in Visual Studio to **MovieReviewSPA,** as shown below.

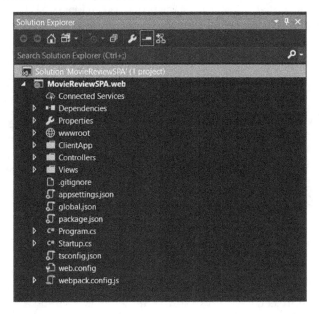

Project Structure

Project structure is almost similar to what we have seen in the general MVC app. Let me start with new things that are introduced around ASP.NET Core. **ClientApp** is the first thing you will notice over here. This is the place where you will find all the client-side codes.

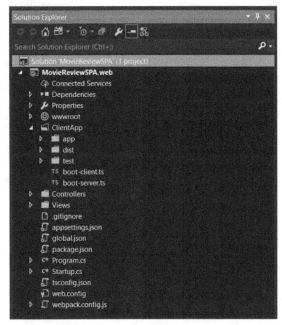

This is just like other Angular applications. We will delve further into these components in the upcoming section. We also have the Controllers and Views folder that belong to ASP.NET Core; just like the previous versions of MVC. We have a new folder **wwwroot**. This is where we place our public assets related to the site.

We have the **dist** folder here. Inside this **dist** folder, we have couple of JavaScript files like **main-client.js** which is a compilation of an Angular application into JavaScript. We also have vendor.js which is a compilation of all the third-party libraries in this Angular application. Similarly, we have **vendor.css** which is a compilation of all third-party css. Here, I also have another copy of css, which is custom to this project; basically, a different theme. We will take a look at that in the upcoming chapters. We also have **appsettings.json**.

In ASP.NET Core, we can store our application settings. In the previous versions of ASP.NET, we stored our application settings in **web.config**. You will also notice that here we have a hierarchy such as **Logging** → **LogLevel** → **Default**. In web.config, we didn't have any hierarchy instead we had name-value pairs under the **appsettings** section. However, in ASP.NET Core, this is inherently supported and it is very easy to access these settings. We also have **program.cs** and **startup.cs** which are responsible for booting our app. We will delve into these files in the upcoming section. We can also see/edit our **.csproj** file. as shown below.

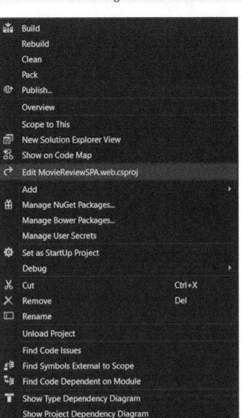

```xml
<Project ToolsVersion="15.0" Sdk="Microsoft.NET.Sdk.Web">
  <PropertyGroup>
    <TargetFramework>netcoreapp1.1</TargetFramework>
<TypeScriptCompileBlocked>true</TypeScriptCompileBlocked>
  <IsPackable>false</IsPackable>
  </PropertyGroup>
  <ItemGroup>
    <PackageReference Include="Microsoft.AspNetCore"
Version="1.1.0" />
    <PackageReference Include="Microsoft.AspNetCore.Mvc"
Version="1.1.1" />
    <PackageReference Include="Microsoft.AspNetCore.
SpaServices" Version="1.1.1" />
    <PackageReference Include="Microsoft.AspNetCore.
StaticFiles" Version="1.1.0" />
    <PackageReference Include="Microsoft.Extensions.
Logging.Debug" Version="1.1.0" />
```

```xml
    </ItemGroup>
    <ItemGroup>
      <!-- Files not to show in IDE -->
      <None Remove="yarn.lock" />

      <!-- Files not to publish (note that the 'dist'
subfolders are re-added below) -->
      <Content Remove="ClientApp\**" />
    </ItemGroup>
    <ItemGroup>
      <Content Include="wwwroot\dist\vendor.css">
      <CopyToPublishDirectory>PreserveNewest</
CopyToPublishDirectory>
      </Content>
      <Content Include="wwwroot\dist\vendor-2nd.css" />
    </ItemGroup>
    <Target Name="RunWebpack" AfterTargets="ComputeFilesToP
ublish">
      <!-- As part of publishing, ensure the JS resources
are freshly built in production mode -->
      <Exec Command="npm install" />
      <Exec Command="node node_modules/webpack/bin/webpack.
js --config webpack.config.vendor.js --env.prod" />
    <Exec Command="node node_modules/webpack/bin/webpack.js
--env.prod" />

      <!-- Include the newly-built files in the publish output -->
      <ItemGroup>
      <DistFiles Include="wwwroot\dist\**; ClientApp\dist\**" />
      <ResolvedFileToPublish Include="@(DistFiles-
>'%(FullPath)')" Exclude="@(ResolvedFileToPublish)">
      <RelativePath>%(DistFiles.Identity)</RelativePath>
<CopyToPublishDirectory>PreserveNewest</
CopyToPublishDirectory>
      </ResolvedFileToPublish>
    </ItemGroup>
  </Target>
</Project>
```

I have pasted the code snippet above for the same. This is the project file which Visual Studio recognizes. This file is very different from the earlier version of .the csproj file, as you won't see any guide here. Also, all nuget package dependencies are listed here. Next, we also have the web.config file here.

```xml
<?xmlversion="1.0"encoding="utf-8"?>
<configuration>
<!--
```

```
Configure your application settings in appsettings.
json. Learn more at https://go.microsoft.com/
fwlink/?LinkId=786380
-->

  <system.webServer>
    <handlers>
    <add name="aspNetCore" path="*" verb="*"
modules="AspNetCoreModule" resourceType="Unspecified"/>
    </handlers>
    <aspNetCore processPath="%LAUNCHER_PATH%"
arguments="%LAUNCHER_ARGS%" stdoutLogEnabled="false"
stdoutLogFile=".\logs\stdout" forwardWindowsAuthToken="false"/>
  </system.webServer>
</configuration>
```

The only thing that we have in this web.config is **<system.webServer>,** which is used for the configuration of IIS and nothing else. And finally, we have a couple of **webpack** configuration files. Therefore, if you have worked earlier with Angular CLI, you must be familiar with that. It's a bundler for client-side code. Therefore, it can compile and minify all the JavaScript and CSS files. The default structure of a webpack file is given below:

```
const path = require('path');
const webpack = require('webpack');
const merge = require('webpack-merge');
const CheckerPlugin = require('awesome-typescript-
loader').CheckerPlugin;

module.exports = (env) => {
  // Configuration in common to both client-side and
server-side bundles
  const isDevBuild = !(env && env.prod);
  const sharedConfig = {
    stats: { modules: false },
    context: __dirname,
    resolve: { extensions: [ '.js', '.ts' ] },
    output: {
      filename: '[name].js',
      publicPath: '/dist/' // Webpack dev middleware, if
enabled, handles requests for this URL prefix
    },
    module: {
      rules: [
        { test: /\.ts$/, include: /ClientApp/, use: ['awesome-
typescript-loader?silent=true', 'angular2-template-loader'] },
        { test: /\.html$/, use: 'html-loader?minimize=false' },
```

```
        { test: /\.css$/, use: [ 'to-string-loader',
isDevBuild ? 'css-loader' : 'css-loader?minimize' ] },
        { test: /\.(png|jpg|jpeg|gif|svg)$/, use: 'url-
loader?limit=25000' }
      ]
    },
    plugins: [new CheckerPlugin()]
  };


  // Configuration for client-side bundle suitable for
running in browsers
  const clientBundleOutputDir = './wwwroot/dist';
  const clientBundleConfig = merge(sharedConfig, {
    entry: { 'main-client': './ClientApp/boot-client.ts' },
    output: { path: path.join(__dirname,
clientBundleOutputDir) },
    plugins: [
      new webpack.DllReferencePlugin({
        context: __dirname,
        manifest: require('./wwwroot/dist/vendor-manifest.json')
      })
    ].concat(isDevBuild ? [
      // Plugins that apply in development builds only
      new webpack.SourceMapDevToolPlugin({
        filename: '[file].map', // Remove this line if you
prefer inline source maps
        moduleFilenameTemplate: path.
relative(clientBundleOutputDir, '[resourcePath]') // Point
sourcemap entries to the original file locations on disk
      })
    ] : [
      // Plugins that apply in production builds only
      new webpack.optimize.UglifyJsPlugin()
    ])
  });


  // Configuration for server-side (prerendering) bundle
suitable for running in Node
  const serverBundleConfig = merge(sharedConfig, {
    resolve: { mainFields: ['main'] },
    entry: { 'main-server': './ClientApp/boot-server.ts' },
    plugins: [
      new webpack.DllReferencePlugin({
        context: __dirname,
```

```
        manifest: require('./ClientApp/dist/vendor-
manifest.json'),
          sourceType: 'commonjs2',
          name: './vendor'
        })
      ],
      output: {
        libraryTarget: 'commonjs',
        path: path.join(__dirname, './ClientApp/dist')
      },
    target: 'node',
    devtool: 'inline-source-map'
  });


  return [clientBundleConfig, serverBundleConfig];
};
```

In this code, we are showing where our source codes are, how these should be processed, and where they should be stored. We will look into these settings as we progress further with our app. We also have one more webpack file which is **webpack.config.vendor.js**. In this file, we have the configuration to compile all the third-party libraries. The sample snippet is given below:

```
const path = require('path');
const webpack = require('webpack');
const ExtractTextPlugin = require('extract-text-webpack-
plugin');
const merge = require('webpack-merge');


module.exports = (env) => {
    const extractCSS = new ExtractTextPlugin('vendor.css');
    const isDevBuild = !(env && env.prod);
    const sharedConfig = {
        stats: { modules: false },
        resolve: { extensions: [ '.js' ] },
        module: {
            rules: [
                { test: /\.(png|woff|woff2|eot|ttf|svg)
(\?|$)/, use: 'url-loader?limit=100000' }
            ]
        },
        entry: {
            vendor: [
                '@angular/animations',
                '@angular/common',
                '@angular/compiler',
```

```
                '@angular/core',
                '@angular/forms',
                '@angular/http',
                '@angular/platform-browser',
                '@angular/platform-browser-dynamic',
                '@angular/router',
                'bootstrap',
                'bootstrap/dist/css/bootstrap.css',
                'es6-shim',
                'es6-promise',
                'event-source-polyfill',
                'jquery',
                'zone.js',
            ]
        },
        output: {
            publicPath: '/dist/',
            filename: '[name].js',
            library: '[name]_[hash]'
        },
        plugins: [
            new webpack.ProvidePlugin({ $: 'jquery', jQuery:
'jquery' }), // Maps these identifiers to the jQuery package
(because Bootstrap expects it to be a global variable)
            new webpack.ContextReplacementPlugin(/\@
angular\b.*\b(bundles|linker)/, path.join(__dirname,
'./ClientApp')), // Workaround for https://github.com/
angular/angular/issues/11580
            new webpack.ContextReplacementPlugin(/
angular(\\|\/)core(\\|\/)@angular/, path.join(__dirname,
'./ClientApp')), // Workaround for https://github.com/
angular/angular/issues/14898
            new webpack.IgnorePlugin(/^vertx$/) // Workaround
for https://github.com/stefanpenner/es6-promise/issues/100
        ]
    };


    const clientBundleConfig = merge(sharedConfig, {
        output: { path: path.join(__dirname, 'wwwroot', 'dist') },
        module: {
            rules: [
                { test: /\.css(\?|$)/, use: extractCSS.
extract({ use: isDevBuild ? 'css-loader' : 'css-
loader?minimize' }) }
            ]
        },
```

```
    plugins: [
        extractCSS,
        new webpack.DllPlugin({
            path: path.join(__dirname, 'wwwroot',
'dist', '[name]-manifest.json'),
            name: '[name]_[hash]'
        })
    ].concat(isDevBuild ? [] : [
        new webpack.optimize.UglifyJsPlugin()
    ])
});


const serverBundleConfig = merge(sharedConfig, {
    target: 'node',
    resolve: { mainFields: ['main'] },
    output: {
        path: path.join(__dirname, 'ClientApp', 'dist'),
        libraryTarget: 'commonjs2',
    },
    module: {
        rules: [ { test: /\.css(\?|$)/, use: ['to-
string-loader', isDevBuild ? 'css-loader' : 'css-
loader?minimize' ] } ]
    },
    entry: { vendor: ['aspnet-prerendering'] },
    plugins: [
        new webpack.DllPlugin({
            path: path.join(__dirname, 'ClientApp',
'dist', '[name]-manifest.json'),
            name: '[name]_[hash]'
        })
    ]
});


return [clientBundleConfig, serverBundleConfig];
```

Application Startup

Let's take a look at the **Program.cs** file. Here is a sample snippet.

```
using System;
using System.Collections.Generic;
using System.IO;
using System.Linq;
using System.Threading.Tasks;
using Microsoft.AspNetCore.Hosting;
```

```
namespace MovieReview
{
publicclassProgram
    {
publicstaticvoid Main(string[] args)
        {
var host = newWebHostBuilder()
              .UseKestrel()

.UseContentRoot(Directory.GetCurrentDirectory())
              .UseIISIntegration()
              .UseStartup<Startup>()
              .Build();
          host.Run();
        }
    }
}
```

One point to remember here is that every web application in ASP.NET Core is basically a console application. Here, in the main method, we are configuring and running a web-server to host our application. ASP.NET Core comes with two in-process HTTP servers: Kestrel and WebListener.

Kestrel is a cross-platform HTTP server and **WebListener** is a Windows-only HTTP server. Here, we will be working with Kestrel. Kestrel is a new web server. It doesn't have all the features of IIS or APACHE which means it's not very secure. However, it's good enough to be used in internal network. Therefore, for public websites, Kestrel should be used behind IIS or APACHE or NGINX. In the main method, we are doing method chaining here and using Kestrel. Then we are specifying the root of our application, using IIS Integration and lastly we are specifying the startup class.

Finally, when we are building the host and running it. And at this point, Kestrel will start listening on port 5000 if we are running it from Visual Studio Code else it will start listening on the development port that Visual Studio has allotted it. Now, let's take a look at the **Startup.cs** class. Here is the sample snippet.

```
using System;
using System.Collections.Generic;
using System.Linq;
using System.Threading.Tasks;
using Microsoft.AspNetCore.Builder;
using Microsoft.AspNetCore.Hosting;
using Microsoft.AspNetCore.SpaServices.Webpack;
using Microsoft.Extensions.Configuration;
using Microsoft.Extensions.DependencyInjection;
using Microsoft.Extensions.Logging;

namespace MovieReview
```

```
{
publicclassStartup
    {
public Startup(IHostingEnvironment env)
        {
var builder = newConfigurationBuilder()
            .SetBasePath(env.ContentRootPath)
            .AddJsonFile("appsettings.json", optional:
true, reloadOnChange: true)

.AddJsonFile($"appsettings.{env.EnvironmentName}.json",
optional: true)
            .AddEnvironmentVariables();
            Configuration = builder.Build();
        }

publicIConfigurationRoot Configuration { get; }

// This method gets called by the runtime. Use this
method to add services to the container.
publicvoid ConfigureServices(IServiceCollection services)
      {
// Add framework services.
services.AddMvc();
      }

// This method gets called by the runtime. Use this
method to configure the HTTP request pipeline.
publicvoid Configure(IApplicationBuilder app,
IHostingEnvironment env, ILoggerFactory loggerFactory)
      {
loggerFactory.AddConsole(Configuration.
GetSection("Logging"));
        loggerFactory.AddDebug();
if (env.IsDevelopment())
          {
            app.UseDeveloperExceptionPage();
app.UseWebpackDevMiddleware(newWebpackDevMiddlewareOptions {
            HotModuleReplacement = true
          });
          }
else
          {
            app.UseExceptionHandler("/Home/Error");
          }
        app.UseStaticFiles();

        app.UseMvc(routes =>
          {
```

```
        routes.MapRoute(
          name: "default",
          template:
"{controller=Home}/{action=Index}/{id?}");
          routes.MapSpaFallbackRoute(
            name: "spa-fallback",
            defaults: new { controller = "Home", action
= "Index" });
        });
      }
    }
}
```

Here, we have two methods that are automatically called at runtime. The first one is **ConfigureServices** and the second one is **Configure**. ConfigureServices is used for Dependency Injection. Dependency Injection is a first-class citizen here in ASP.NET Core. Therefore, anything out of the box required in the application needs to be registered over here first. We will delve further into this method as we start building our app.

The next method is **Configure**. In the first two lines of this method, we configure the logging of our application. Therefore, we add the console as a log. Therefore, if we write anything to the log, it will appear on the console. This is good development scenario. However, in case of production, this can be substituted with some persistent log.

Then, in the rest of the code, it will configure middleware in the pipeline. When a request comes to the server, it goes through the pipeline. In this pipeline, there are multiple components which are called middleware. Each middleware is like a function that looks at the incoming request, and if it satisfies the request, then it will process the request else it just skips.

In the previous versions of ASP.NET Core, our request processing pipeline was fairly heavy-weight which means we didn't have any control over configuring these middleware. In ASP.NET Core, we can customize this request pipeline and add only those middleware that we need. We can improve the performance of our application in this manner.

We are saying that if we are in the development environment, then we are adding a couple of Middlewares. The first one uses the Developer Exception Page which renders an exception with the complete stack trace. And the other one is Webpack Dev Middleware. Therefore, if we change our client-side code like CSS, JavaScript file, webpack will automatically detect the changes and compile them and then push the changes in the browser. Hence, we don't even need to reload the page.

This process is called **Hot Module Replacement**. And these two middlewares are only used during development. Another middleware comes into picture which is used for static files. With this, we will be able to serve the static files like images, CSS, icons, etc. Finally, the last middleware is MVC. When the request comes in, this middleware looks for the request and based on the routes, it will forward the same to the respective action and controller.

DotNet Watch Tool

The Dotnet watch tool is just like a webpack. The only difference is that it is used for server-side. This means if we need to change anything on the server-side code, it will automatically compile. For this, we need to install the following. We just need to navigate to **http://bit.ly/dotnet-watch** and then follow the steps as mentioned here. I have directly copied the following line in my .csproj file and it has restored the required tool in the project.

```
<ItemGroup>
<DotNetCliToolReference
Include="Microsoft.DotNet.Watcher.Tools"
Version="1.0.0" />
</ItemGroup>
```

Then, I need to run **dotnet watch run**.

It started at port 5000. Therefore, if I navigate to **http://localhost:5000**, it will produce the same result.

However, when I see the console this time, I can see that some information has been written over there.

Now, let me change something at the server-side say throwing an exception.

```
HomeController.cs ⊕ ×
MovieReviewSPA.web                                        ▼  MovieReviewSPA.web.Controllers.HomeController           ▼
   1   using Microsoft.AspNetCore.Mvc;
   2
   3 ⊟namespace MovieReviewSPA.web.Controllers
   4   {
            0 references
   5 ⊟      public class HomeController : Controller
   6        {
                0 references
   7 ⊟          public IActionResult Index()
   8            {
   9                return View();
  10            }
  11
                0 references
  12 ⊟          public IActionResult Error()
  13            {
  14                return View();
  15            }
  16        }
  17  }
```

At this stage, when I see the console, I can see that it has been already compiled and an error has been logged.

```
C:\Dell\Books\ASPNETCorePlusAngular4\MovieReview>dotnet watch run
[90mwatch : [39mStarted
Hosting environment: Production
Content root path: C:\Dell\Books\ASPNETCorePlusAngular4\MovieReview
Now listening on: http://localhost:5000
Application started. Press Ctrl+C to shut down.
[90mwatch : [39m[91mExited with error code 1[39m
[90mwatch : [39mFile changed: C:\Dell\Books\ASPNETCorePlusAngular4\MovieReview\Controllers\HomeController.cs
[90mwatch : [39mStarted
Controllers\HomeController.cs(14,13): warning CS0162: Unreachable code detected [C:\Dell\Books\ASPNETCorePlusAngular4\Mo
vieReview\MovieReview.csproj]
Hosting environment: Production
Content root path: C:\Dell\Books\ASPNETCorePlusAngular4\MovieReview
Now listening on: http://localhost:5000
Application started. Press Ctrl+C to shut down.
```

Now, when I refresh the page, the following screenshot will appear on the screen:

Error.

An error occurred while processing your request.

Since Dotnet watch runs by default in the production mode, the user-friendly message appears on the screen. However, we can override these environment settings. We shall see this in upcoming chapters.

Adding Class Libraries

I will add a couple of other projects to separate my Data, Data-Contracts, Model, etc.

Once all the projects are created, the screen will look like this.

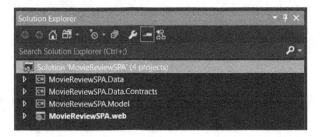

Adding Project References

I need to refer to all the class libraries in my web project, as shown below.

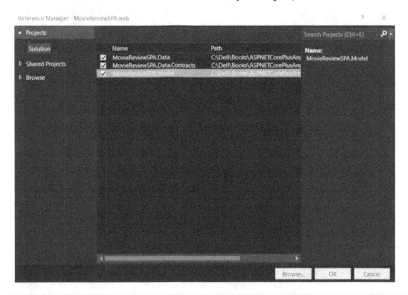

Once all these packages get added, the screen will look like this.

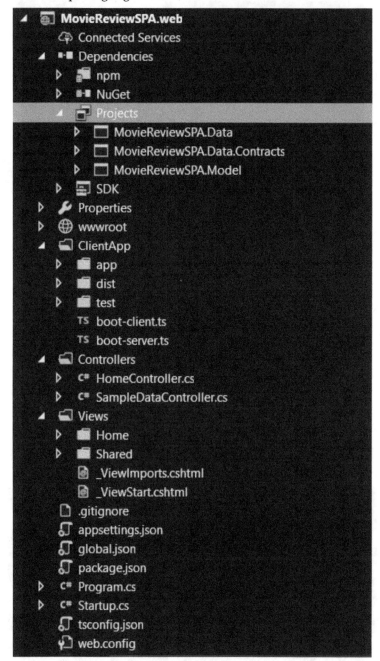

Adding Entity Framework

In this section, we will add required packages. Currently, we don't have anything like Entity Framework.

- ◢ 🌐 **MovieReviewSPA.web**
  - ☁ Connected Services
  - ◢ ▪▪ Dependencies
    - ▷ 🔳 npm
    - ▷ ▪▪ NuGet
    - ◢ 🗗 Projects
      - ▷ ☐ MovieReviewSPA.Data
      - ▷ ☐ MovieReviewSPA.Data.Contracts
      - ▷ ☐ MovieReviewSPA.Model
    - ▷ 🖥 SDK
  - ▷ 🔧 Properties
  - ▷ 🌐 wwwroot
  - ◢ 📁 ClientApp
    - ▷ 📁 app
    - ▷ 📁 dist
    - ▷ 📁 test
    - TS boot-client.ts
    - TS boot-server.ts
  - ◢ 📁 Controllers
    - ▷ C# HomeController.cs
    - ▷ C# SampleDataController.cs
  - ◢ 📁 Views
    - ▷ 📁 Home
    - ▷ 📁 Shared
    - 📄 _ViewImports.cshtml
    - 📄 _ViewStart.cshtml
  - 📄 .gitignore
  - 🎵 appsettings.json
  - 🎵 global.json
  - 🎵 package.json
  - ▷ C# Program.cs
  - ▷ C# Startup.cs
  - 🎵 tsconfig.json
  - 🔌 web.config

We can go ahead and add the same using NuGet, as shown below.

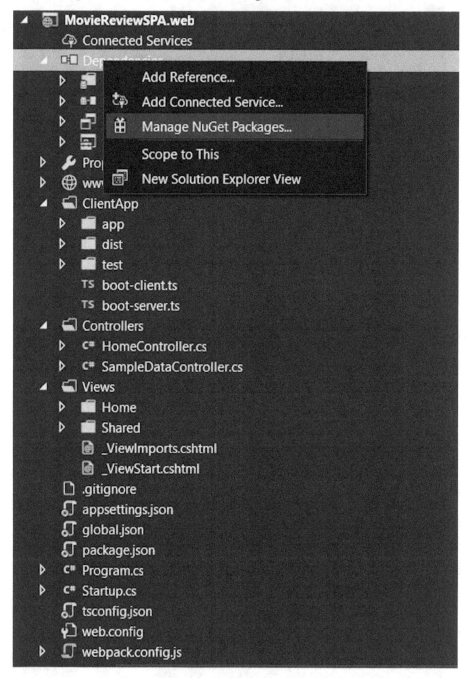

But as far as my class libraries are concerned, I need to add a few other references like Entity Framework to the Data project, as shown below. We can also search with the name "**Microsoft.EntityFrameWorkCore**".

Once it is installed, it will appear in the Installed section, as shown below. Here, I have installed v1.1.2 as the latest pre-release, which is having problem.

I need to repeat the same step in my data project as well. You can also verify this in NuGet dependencies.

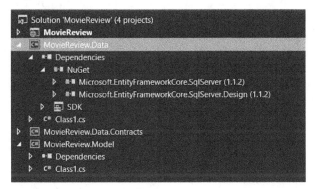

However, we will add many more packages as we progress with the app. I also need to add the following packages to both the projects.

Important Tools

Here are my tools of choice which I usually use to build any application. However, it's entirely your choice. Choose whichever one you want to use.

- Visual Studio 2017 - IDE
- ReSharper – Gives much better out-of-the-box Intellisense on the top of Visual Studio
- Visual Studio Code or Sublime for any outside editing

- ✪ http://www.responsinator.com/
- ✪ http://www.electricplum.com/
- ✪ http://www.opera.com/developer/mobile-emulator
- ✪ Chrome Mobile Emulator

Data Technologies

- ✪ **Data Storage:** In this context, we are going to set up our database. Here, I will be using **SQL Server** for persisting the data. However, there is no such restriction of using only SQL Server, you can choose any other database of your choice like Oracle, etc.
- ✪ **Object Relational Mapper:** In order to pull the records from the database and persist the same back to the database; I used **Entity Framework** as my **ORM**. Here, data is stored or fetched via its own **DBContext**.
- ✪ **Repository Pattern:** Repositories basically expose the ORM's data to save and retrieve the data to the context and then it is taken by our database.
- ✪ **Unit of Work Pattern: UOW** is one of the most important patterns which takes our changes and then issues the save/cancel request to the context. Basically, it aggregates the repositories so that we can commit or cancel multiple changes to the repositories.

Here is the data layer flow diagram.

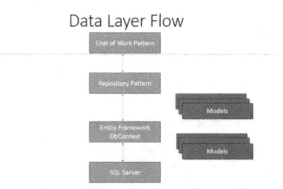

Data Layer Flow

This is going to be my basic architecture to show how the data layer is going to interact with my user interface. Here, we will interact with our SQL Server using Entity Framework DbContext via Models. Therefore EF will map; let's say **Movie** Plain Old Class Object (POCO) with **Movie** table in the database. Now, we can pass these models with the Repository Pattern. This extra layer of abstraction **Repository Pattern** allows you to simplify the call to the database. Therefore, all my calls to the database follow a very specific syntax.

Next comes the **Unit of Work Pattern**. The job of the **UOW** is to take the data from multiple places and put it in one place. Let's suppose a scenario where in I have to fetch a movie which has received the highest number of reviews. In order to resolve this kind of scenario, UOW will come into picture. UOW will get the data from different repositories and pass them down the layer. The other job of the UOW is to commit to the database which we will see in a moment.

Questions

1. How application gets bootstrapped?
2. How to use DotNet Watch Tool?
3. How to integrate Entity Framework Core?
4. What is Repository Pattern?
5. What is Unit of Work Pattern?

Summary

In this section, we started from scratch. Here, we laid down the complete architecture of the overall application. We created a couple of individual projects meant for individual responsibilities. Then we added different project references to each other. During the course, we also explored Entity Framework Code First Approach.

Creating Data Context

Introduction

In this module, we will begin from the last section. Here, we will focus on building data models right from the beginning and then we will continue by implementing Entity Framework. Here, we will use Code First Approach. Next, we will create DbContext class and utilize it while communicating models from API level to Angular. During the course, we will also implement different design patterns like Repository and Unit of Work Pattern for data consistency.

Creating Models

Models are basically data containers that carry data. Models are also properties that define our data. Models are often termed as entities. These models are like carriers for our data and EF will fill these models.

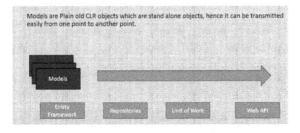

Now, I will create two model classes: **Movie** and **MovieReview,** as shown below in the snippet.

```
using System.Collections.Generic;

namespace MovieReviewSPA.Model
{
    public class Movie
    {
        public int Id { get; set; }
        public string MovieName { get; set; }
        public string DirectorName { get; set; }
        public string ReleaseYear { get; set; }
        public virtual ICollection<MovieReview> Reviews {
get; set; }
    }
}

namespace MovieReviewSPA.Model
{
    public class MovieReview
    {
        public int Id { get; set; }
        public string ReviewerName { get; set; }
        public string ReviewerComments { get; set; }
        public int ReviewerRating { get; set; }
        public int MovieId { get; set; }
    }
}
```

With the above changes in place, my Model project will look like this.

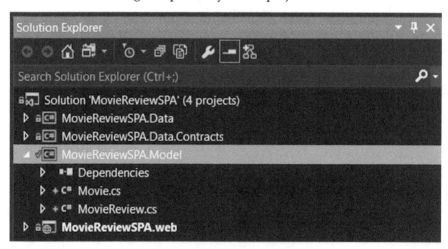

Creating Entity Framework

In this section, we will create our DbContext class. Now, the role of DbContext class is to create relations between Models and Database. The benefit of using DbContext is that it stores objects and changes in its memory. Therefore, here I will use Entity Framework to do all CRUD operations. In order to dive deep into Entity Framework with all different varieties of styles; you can check my blog at **http://myview.rahulnivi.net** and then check the Entity Framework thread. But, let me just give you a brief snapshot about the different approaches.

Schema First Approach: In this approach, we open a graphical designer in Visual Studio. Here, we are pointing the EF to an existing database so that we can import the database schema. Now, this will import the entire schema and generate the classes which we need to query and update the database.

Model First Approach: In this approach, we use the same graphical designer inside the Visual Studio to draw an overall model of our application. And then EF will generate both our class definitions and database schema.

Code First Approach: Last but not the least is **Code First Approach**. This one is my personal favorite. In this case, I just write C# classes and then EF uses the class definitions to create the database for me. And for doing the same, EF follows certain conventions like Naming Conventions. We can also provide explicit mappings wherein we can change the mappings if we don't like the default one. So in this book, I will use Code First Approach to begin with my database development.

Creating Entity Framework DbContext Class

Let's go ahead and create our DbContext class. Here is the snippet of DbContext class in the data project.

```
using Microsoft.EntityFrameworkCore;
using MovieReviewSPA.Model;

namespace MovieReviewSPA.Data
{
    public class MovieReviewDbContext :DbContext
    {
        public DbSet<Movie> Movies { get; set; }
        public DbSet<MovieReview> MovieReviews { get; set; }
    }
}
```

Here, I have set up the DBSet for the POCO classes which I have created earlier. However, I have to configure the services in the startup.cs file. Here is the snippet.

```
    public void ConfigureServices(IServiceCollection services)
    {
        services.AddEntityFramework()
          .AddDbContext<MovieReviewDbContext>(options =>
options.UseSqlServer(Configuration["Data:MovieReviewSPA:Co
nnectionString"]));
        // Add framework services.
```

```
services.AddMvc();
}
```

I have set up Entity Framework along with other dependencies like SQL Server and DbContext. It reads the connection string from the appsettings.json file, as shown below.

```
{
    "Data": {
        "MovieReviewSPA": {
        "ConnectionString":
"Server=(localdb)\\mssqllocaldb;Database=MovieReviewSPA;T
rusted_Connection=True;MultipleActiveResultSets=true"
    }
  },
  "Logging": {
    "IncludeScopes": false,
    "LogLevel": {
        "Default": "Verbose",
        "System": "Information",
        "Microsoft": "Information"
    }
  }
}
```

Here, you can see that there is only one connection string for Movies database. Later on, as the application grows, you may choose to extend the database as well. After this, I have provided another level of connection string with the name **MovieReviewSPA**.

Using DbContext Class

In this section, we will use DBContext, which we have created previously. In order to do so, I will use my home controller and inject the required dependency as shown below.

```
using Microsoft.AspNetCore.Mvc;
using MovieReviewSPA.Data;

namespace MovieReviewSPA.web.Controllers
{
    public class HomeController : Controller
    {
        private MovieReviewDbContext _dbContext;

        public HomeController(MovieReviewDbContext dbContext)
        {
            _dbContext = dbContext;
        }
        public IActionResult Index()
        {
            return View();
```

```
        }

        public IActionResult Error()
        {
            return View();
        }
    }
}
```

With the above setup in place, we can go ahead and query the database using dbContext as shown below.

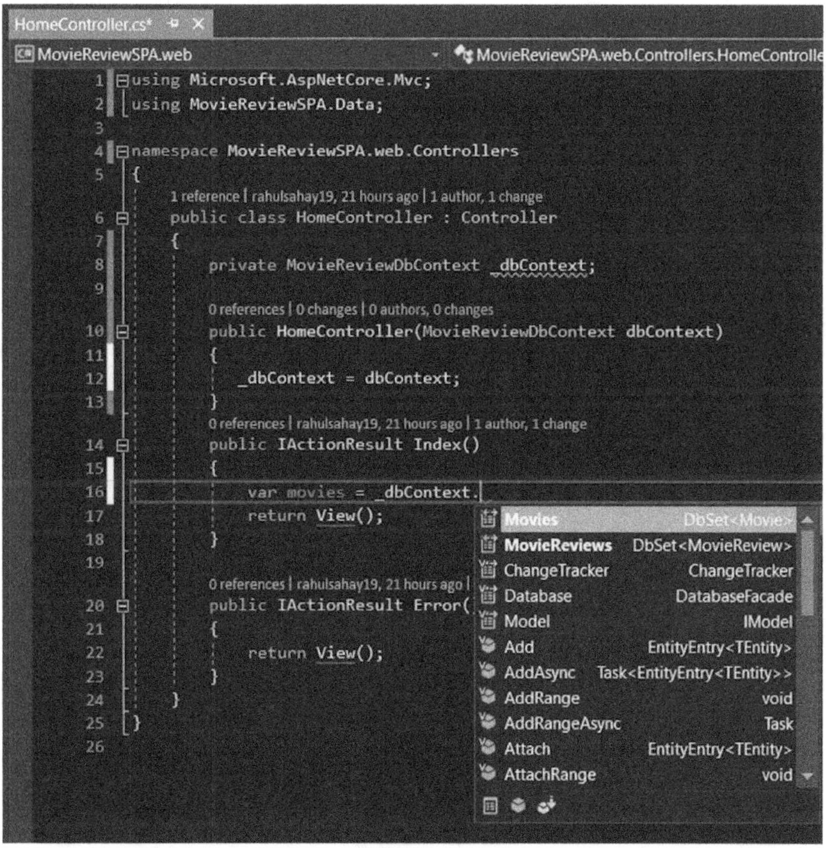

With the completed query, the action method will look like this.

```
public IActionResult Index()
    {
        var movies = _dbContext.Movies.ToList();
        return View(movies);
    }
```

Now, when I go ahead and run the app, it will show the following error:

An unhandled exception occurred while processing the request.

InvalidOperationException: No database provider has been configured for this DbContext. A provider can be configured by overriding DbContext.OnConfiguring method or by using AddDbContext on the application service provider. If AddDbContext is used, then also that your DbContext type accepts a DbContextOptions<TContext> object in its constructor and passes it to the base constructor for DbContext.

Microsoft.EntityFrameworkCore.Internal.DatabaseProviderSelector.SelectServices()

Basically, it says no provider has been configured. In order to set up the provider, we need to go to the **MovieReviewDbContext** class and provide the following settings:

```
using Microsoft.EntityFrameworkCore;
using MovieReviewSPA.Model;

namespace MovieReviewSPA.Data
{
    public class MovieReviewDbContext :DbContext
    {
        public DbSet<Movie> Movies { get; set; }
        public DbSet<MovieReview> MovieReviews { get; set; }

        public
MovieReviewDbContext(DbContextOptions<MovieReviewDbConte
xt> options) : base(options)
        {
        //It will look for connection string from appsettings
        }
    }
}
```

With the above changes in place, it will look for the connection string. Now, when I build and run the app, it will show the following screenshot:

An unhandled exception occurred while processing the request.

SqlException: Cannot open database "MovieReviewSPA" requested by the login. The login failed.
Login failed for user 'DESKTOP-M8COS0C\hp'.

System.Data.SqlClient.SqlInternalConnectionTds..ctor(DbConnectionPoolIdentity identity, SqlConnectionString connectionOptions, object providerInfo, bool redirectedUserInstance, SqlConnectionString userConnectionOptions, SessionData reconnectSessionData, bool applyTransientFaultHandling)

Here, it says that the database is not getting created. We can ensure this from the DbContext constructor and use DB-Migrations.

Installing Dotnet Cli for EF

In this section, we will use Migrations to build our database. Migrations are ways to use tooling in Entity Framework to look at the database and requirements of the application and build a set of code to toggle the database from one version to another. When we run migrations or use migrations for the first time, it will build the database. This will become version one of the database.

And as the development progresses, we can add new versions to the project. Here, in order to do the migrations, we will use the command line tool. But, in order to use this tool, we need to add Command Line Interface (CLI) support. Now, the easy way to do this is to add the following command to the .csproj file and then restore the same.

```
<ItemGroup>
    <DotNetCliToolReference
Include="Microsoft.EntityFrameworkCore.Tools.DotNet"
Version="1.0.0" />
    </ItemGroup>
```

Here is a glimpse of the finished one.

```
1  ⊟<Project ToolsVersion="15.0" Sdk="Microsoft.NET.Sdk.Web">
2  ⊟  <PropertyGroup>
3        <TargetFramework>netcoreapp1.1</TargetFramework>
4        <TypeScriptCompileBlocked>true</TypeScriptCompileBlocked>
5        <IsPackable>false</IsPackable>
6      </PropertyGroup>
7  ⊟  <ItemGroup>
8        <PackageReference Include="Microsoft.AspNetCore" Version="1.1.0" />
9        <PackageReference Include="Microsoft.AspNetCore.Mvc" Version="1.1.1" />
10       <PackageReference Include="Microsoft.AspNetCore.SpaServices" Version="1.1.1" />
11       <PackageReference Include="Microsoft.AspNetCore.StaticFiles" Version="1.1.0" />
12       <PackageReference Include="Microsoft.EntityFrameworkCore" Version="1.1.2" />
13       <PackageReference Include="Microsoft.EntityFrameworkCore.SqlServer" Version="1.1.2" />
14       <PackageReference Include="Microsoft.EntityFrameworkCore.SqlServer.Design" Version="1.1.2" />
15       <PackageReference Include="Microsoft.Extensions.Logging.Debug" Version="1.1.0" />
16     </ItemGroup>
17 ⊟   <ItemGroup>
18       <DotNetCliToolReference Include="Microsoft.EntityFrameworkCore.Tools.DotNet" Version="1.0.0" />
19     </ItemGroup>
20 ⊟   <ItemGroup>
21       <!-- Files not to show in IDE -->
22       <None Remove="yarn.lock" />
23
```

Once it gets installed in the project, we can go ahead and execute **dotnet ef**.

```
C:\Dell\Books\ASPNETCorePlusAngular4\MovieReviewSPA\MovieReviewSPA.web (Another) (MovieReviewSPA_web@0.0.0)
λ dotnet ef

                     ---==/      \\
                   |.         \\\
             _/\__       /   |   \\\
         ---==/    \\     |   | .| \\\
        _/ .    \\     | ) | )||
       ( )  )   ) ) //|\\
                     /     \\\/\\

Entity Framework Core .NET Command Line Tools 1.0.0-rtm-10308

Usage: dotnet ef [options] [command]

Options:
  --version          Show version information
  -h|--help          Show help information
  -v|--verbose       Show verbose output.
  --no-color         Don't colorize output.
  --prefix-output    Prefix output with level.

Commands:
  database       Commands to manage the database.
  dbcontext      Commands to manage DbContext types.
  migrations     Commands to manage migrations.

Use "dotnet ef [command] --help" for more information about a command.

C:\Dell\Books\ASPNETCorePlusAngular4\MovieReviewSPA\MovieReviewSPA.web (Another) (MovieReviewSPA_web@0.0.0)
λ
```

Here it shows the different Entity Framework commands options.

Creating The Database

In order to create the database, we will do migrations. In order to use migrations, we need to execute **dotnet ef migrations add InitialDb**. As soon as I execute this file, it will show the following error:

It clearly says that I forgot to add the following package. I can add the package from NuGet itself. However, this time; I will add it via the command line

"**dotnet add package Microsoft.EntityFrameworkCore. Design**" as shown below.

After this, I will use the command **dotnet restore**. Once the restore is completed, I will again execute the migration command **dotnet ef migrations add InitialDb**. It will show the following error:

Here, it's basically saying that you need to change the migration assembly to **MovieReviewSPA.web** via **DBContextOptionsBuilder**. Here is the snippet for the same.

```
public void ConfigureServices(IServiceCollection services)
    {
        services.AddEntityFramework()
            .AddDbContext<MovieReviewDbContext>(options =>
options.UseSqlServer(Configuration["Data:MovieReviewSPA:Co
nnectionString"],
                b =>
b.MigrationsAssembly("MovieReviewSPA.web")));
        // Add framework services.
        services.AddMvc();
    }
```

Here, I have said consider the web project for migration. Keeping this change in place, let me go ahead and run the migration command again.

Now, it has successfully applied the migration and created a new **Migrations** folder in the Solution Explorer.

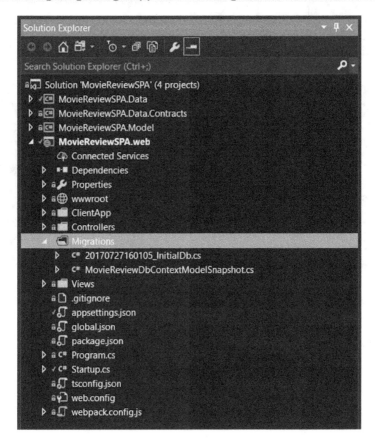

Here is the auto-generated snippet.

```
using System;
using System.Collections.Generic;
using Microsoft.EntityFrameworkCore.Migrations;
using Microsoft.EntityFrameworkCore.Metadata;

namespace MovieReviewSPA.web.Migrations
{
    public partial class InitialDb : Migration
    {
        protected override void Up(MigrationBuilder
migrationBuilder)
        {
            migrationBuilder.CreateTable(
                name: "Movies",
                columns: table => new
                {
                    Id = table.Column<int>(nullable: false)
                        .Annotation("SqlServer:ValueG
```

```
enerationStrategy", SqlServerValueGenerationStrategy.
IdentityColumn),
                    DirectorName = table.
Column<string>(nullable: true),
                    MovieName = table.
Column<string>(nullable: true),
                    ReleaseYear = table.
Column<string>(nullable: true)
                },
                constraints: table =>
                {
                    table.PrimaryKey("PK_Movies", x => x.Id);
                });

        migrationBuilder.CreateTable(
            name: "MovieReviews",
            columns: table => new
            {
                Id = table.Column<int>(nullable: false)
                    .Annotation("SqlServer:ValueG
enerationStrategy", SqlServerValueGenerationStrategy.
IdentityColumn),
                MovieId = table.Column<int>(nullable: false),
                ReviewerComments = table.
Column<string>(nullable: true),
                ReviewerName = table.
Column<string>(nullable: true),
                ReviewerRating = table.
Column<int>(nullable: false)
                },
                constraints: table =>
                {
                 table.PrimaryKey("PK_MovieReviews", x => x.Id);
                    table.ForeignKey(
                       name: "FK_MovieReviews_Movies_MovieId",
                        column: x => x.MovieId,
                        principalTable: "Movies",
                        principalColumn: "Id",
                        onDelete: ReferentialAction.Cascade);
                });

        migrationBuilder.CreateIndex(
            name: "IX_MovieReviews_MovieId",
            table: "MovieReviews",
            column: "MovieId");
```

```
        }
        protected override void Down(MigrationBuilder
migrationBuilder)
        {
            migrationBuilder.DropTable(
                name: "MovieReviews");
            migrationBuilder.DropTable(
                name: "Movies");
        }
    }
}
```

And,

```
using System;
using Microsoft.EntityFrameworkCore;
using Microsoft.EntityFrameworkCore.Infrastructure;
using Microsoft.EntityFrameworkCore.Metadata;
using Microsoft.EntityFrameworkCore.Migrations;
using MovieReviewSPA.Data;

namespace MovieReviewSPA.web.Migrations
{
    [DbContext(typeof(MovieReviewDbContext))]
    partial class MovieReviewDbContextModelSnapshot :
ModelSnapshot
    {
        protected override void BuildModel(ModelBuilder
modelBuilder)
        {
            modelBuilder
                .HasAnnotation("ProductVersion", "1.1.2")
                .HasAnnotation("SqlServer:ValueGenerationStrate
gy", SqlServerValueGenerationStrategy.IdentityColumn);

            modelBuilder.Entity("MovieReviewSPA.Model.Movie", b =>
                {
                    b.Property<int>("Id")
                        .ValueGeneratedOnAdd();
                    b.Property<string>("DirectorName");
                    b.Property<string>("MovieName");
                    b.Property<string>("ReleaseYear");
                    b.HasKey("Id");
                      b.ToTable("Movies");
                });
            modelBuilder.Entity("MovieReviewSPA.Model.
```

```
MovieReview", b =>
                {
                    b.Property<int>("Id")
                        .ValueGeneratedOnAdd();
                    b.Property<int>("MovieId");
                    b.Property<string>("ReviewerComments");
                    b.Property<string>("ReviewerName");
                    b.Property<int>("ReviewerRating");
                    b.HasKey("Id");
                    b.HasIndex("MovieId");
                    b.ToTable("MovieReviews");
                });

            modelBuilder.Entity("MovieReviewSPA.Model.
MovieReview", b =>
                {
                    b.HasOne("MovieReviewSPA.Model.Movie")
                        .WithMany("Reviews")
                        .HasForeignKey("MovieId")
                        .OnDelete(DeleteBehavior.Cascade);
                });
        }
    }
}
```

Now, I need to apply this migration to the database with the **dotnet ef database update** command.

With the above change in place, I can now see my Tables in the database.

Seeding The Database

Seeding the database means providing the initial data to work with the app. Entity Framework provides a very easy way to do it. Here, I have created a new folder in the Data project with one class file to seed the data.

```csharp
using System;
using System.Collections.Generic;
using System.Linq;
using System.Text;
using MovieReviewSPA.Model;

namespace MovieReviewSPA.Data.SampleData
{
    public class InitialData
    {
        private MovieReviewDbContext _dbContext;

        public InitialData(MovieReviewDbContext dbContext)
        {
            _dbContext = dbContext;
        }

        public void SeedData()
        {
            //Making sure that database has nothing
before seeding
            if (!_dbContext.Movies.Any())
```

```
{
    //Add New Data
    var movie = new Movie
    {
        MovieName = "Avatar",
        DirectorName = "James Cameron",
        ReleaseYear = "2009"
    };
    _dbContext.Movies.Add(movie);

    var secondMovie = new Movie()
    {
        MovieName = "Titanic",
        DirectorName = "James Cameron",
        ReleaseYear = "1997"
    };
    _dbContext.Movies.Add(secondMovie);

    var thirdMovie = new Movie()
    {
        MovieName = "Die Another Day",
        DirectorName = "Lee Tamahori",
        ReleaseYear = "2002"
    };
    _dbContext.Movies.Add(thirdMovie);

    var anotherMovieWithReview = new Movie()
    {
        MovieName = "Godzilla",
        DirectorName = "Gareth Edwards",
        ReleaseYear = "2014",
        Reviews = new List<MovieReview>
        {
            new MovieReview
            {
                ReviewerRating = 5,
                ReviewerComments = "Excellent",
                ReviewerName = "Rahul Sahay"
            },new MovieReview
            {
                ReviewerRating = 5,
                ReviewerComments = "Awesome",
                ReviewerName = "John"
            },new MovieReview
```

```
                    {
                        ReviewerRating = 5,
                        ReviewerComments = "Mind Blowing",
                        ReviewerName = "Black Dave"
                    }
                }
            };
            _dbContext.Movies.
Add(anotherMovieWithReview);
            _dbContext.MovieReviews.
AddRange(anotherMovieWithReview.Reviews);
            _dbContext.SaveChanges();
        }
      }
   }
}
```

The above snippet is very simple. Here, it first checks whether any movies are there in the database. If not, then it pushes the above collection. Now, this seed data needs to be initiated from somewhere. The best place from where you can do it is from the startup file, as shown below.

```
public void ConfigureServices(IServiceCollection services)
    {
        services.AddEntityFramework()
            .AddDbContext<MovieReviewDbContext>(options =>
options.UseSqlServer(Configuration["Data:MovieReviewSPA:Co
nnectionString"],
                b => b.MigrationsAssembly("MovieRevie
wSPA.web")));
        // Add framework services.
        services.AddMvc();
        //Initiating Seed Data
        services.AddTransient<InitialData>();
    }
```

Here in the **ConfigureServices**, I have added the Transient for **InitialData**. This always guarantees that we get fresh data. In our case, this is the most suitable option for seeding the database. Now, in order to use it, I need to supply it in the Configure section, as shown in the following snippet:

```
// This method gets called by the runtime. Use this
method to configure the HTTP request pipeline.
        public void Configure(IApplicationBuilder app,
IHostingEnvironment env, ILoggerFactory loggerFactory,
InitialData seedDbContext)
        {
            loggerFactory.AddConsole(Configuration.
GetSection("Logging"));
```

```
        loggerFactory.AddDebug();

        if (env.IsDevelopment())
        {
            app.UseDeveloperExceptionPage();
            app.UseWebpackDevMiddleware(new
WebpackDevMiddlewareOptions {
                HotModuleReplacement = true
            });
        }
        else
        {
            app.UseExceptionHandler("/Home/Error");
        }
        app.UseStaticFiles();
        app.UseMvc(routes =>
        {
            routes.MapRoute(
                name: "default",
                template: "{controller=Home}/
{action=Index}/{id?}");

            routes.MapSpaFallbackRoute(
                name: "spa-fallback",
                defaults: new { controller = "Home",
action = "Index" });
        });
        //Initiating from here
        seedDbContext.SeedData();
    }
```

With the above change in place, when I go ahead and run it, it will show me the desired following result.

Similarly, if I take a look at the database, it will show the results as well.

▦ Results ▤ Messages

	Id	DirectorName	MovieName	ReleaseY...
1	1	James Cameron	Avatar	2009
2	2	James Cameron	Titanic	1997
3	3	Lee Tamahori	Die Another Day	2002
4	4	Gareth Edwards	Godzilla	2014

▦ Results ▤ Messages

	Id	MovieId	ReviewerComme...	ReviewerNa...	ReviewerRati...
1	1	4	Excellent	Rahul Sahay	5
2	2	4	Awesome	John	5
3	3	4	Mind Blowing	Black Dave	5

Implementing The Repository Pattern

Before we implement the repository pattern, let's understand why we need to use the repository pattern? That's a great question. To answer this, let me list the following points for you:

- ✪ Code Maintainability: It's very easy to use data access code to debug or to make any changes.
- ✪ Code Reuse: Let's suppose I am directly talking to my _dBContext via controllers and I have 20 odd controllers. Every time a change is made to any data access code, I need to make changes in 20 different places. Hence, rather than wasting time on this, I'll have one repository which will take care of the data access job. It also raises a couple of more points that need to be listed here.
- ✪ Focused on CRUD operations.
- ✪ Consistent APIs which can be unit tested as well.
- ✪ Focused on Single Repository Principle (SRP):It means every class or API will have an individual role.

With the above explanations, let's go ahead and create my Entity Framework repository which will serve as a base for all db interactions. I will create one in my data project.

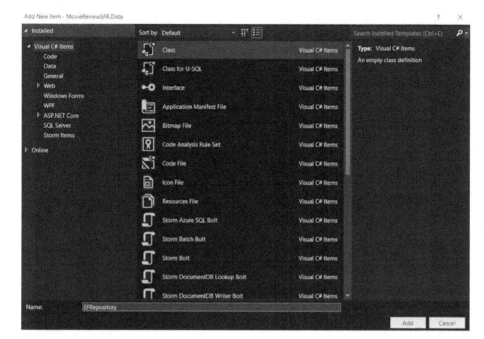

Here is the snippet.

```csharp
using System;
using System.Linq;
using Microsoft.EntityFrameworkCore;
using Microsoft.EntityFrameworkCore.ChangeTracking;

namespace MovieReviewSPA.Data
{
    public class EFRepository<T> : IRepository<T> where T
: class
    {
        public EFRepository(DbContext dbContext)
        {
            if (dbContext == null)
                throw new ArgumentNullException("dbContex
t");
            DbContext = dbContext;
            DbSet = DbContext.Set<T>();
        }

        protected DbContext DbContext { get; set; }
        protected DbSet<T> DbSet { get; set; }
        public virtual IQueryable<T> GetAll()
        {
```

```
            return DbSet;
        }

        public virtual T GetById(int id)
        {
            //EF Core Will be updated shortly with Find
Extension by Default
            //Here, I have written Extension method for
the same
            //Source:- http://stackoverflow.com/
questions/29030472/dbset-doesnt-have-a-find-method-in-
ef7/29082410#29082410
            return DbSet.Find(id);
        }

        public virtual void Add(T entity)
        {
            EntityEntry<T> dbEntityEntry = DbContext.
Entry(entity);
            if (dbEntityEntry.State != (EntityState)
EntityState.Detached)
            {
                dbEntityEntry.State = EntityState.Added;
            }
            else
            {
                DbSet.Add(entity);
            }
        }

        public virtual void Update(T entity)
        {
            EntityEntry<T> dbEntityEntry = DbContext.
Entry(entity);
            if (dbEntityEntry.State != (EntityState)
EntityState.Detached)
            {
                DbSet.Attach(entity);
            }
            dbEntityEntry.State = EntityState.Modified;
        }

        public void Delete(T entity)
        {
            EntityEntry<T> dbEntityEntry = DbContext.
```

```
Entry(entity);
            if (dbEntityEntry.State != (EntityState)
EntityState.Deleted)
            {
                dbEntityEntry.State = EntityState.Deleted;
            }
            else
            {
                DbSet.Attach(entity);
                DbSet.Remove(entity);
            }
        }

        public void Delete(int id)
        {
            var entity = GetById(id);
            if (entity == null) return;

            Delete(entity);
        }

    /*  public virtual object Include<TEntity,
TProperty>(Func<TEntity, TProperty> p) where TEntity : class
        {
            return DbSet;
        }*/
    }
}
```

As you can see in the above snippet that my **EFRepository** is dependent on **IRepository** which I'll create in a moment. But let's understand what it is doing here. It is just taking instructions from **UOW** (Unit of Work Pattern). Let's say I would like to create a new movie, and then in that case, it will consider **T** as **Movie.** Then it will first check whether _dbContext has been created or not.

If not, then it will go ahead and create the _dbContext and then implement the required CRUD operation based on the API call. Hence, a lot of code reuse makes sense right☺.Now, let's go ahead and create the **IRepository** interface. And I'll put this in the Contracts project, as shown below.

```
using System.Linq;

namespace MovieReviewSPA.Data.Contracts
{
    public interface IRepository<T> where T : class
    {
```

```
        //To query using LINQ
        IQueryable<T> GetAll();

        //Returning Movie or Review by id
        T GetById(int id);

        //Adding Movie or Review
        void Add(T entity);

        //Updating Movie or Review
        void Update(T entity);

        //Deleting Moovie or Review
        void Delete(T entity);

        //Deleting Movie or Review by id
        void Delete(int id);

    }
}
```

Let's suppose I would like to query Movie table, then **IRepository** of T will replace T with **Movie** and perform any of the invoked operations. In this way, you can build a very clean and maintainable piece of the **Data Access** layer. With this change in place, my reference will automatically get resolved, as seen in the following screenshot:

```
namespace MovieReviewSPA.Data
{
    1 reference | 0 changes | 0 authors, 0 changes
    public class EFRepository<T> : IRepository<T> where T : class
    {
        0 references | 0 changes | 0 authors, 0 changes
        public EFRepository(DbContext dbContext)
        {
            if (dbContext == null)
                throw new ArgumentNullException("dbContext");
            DbContext = dbContext;
            DbSet = DbContext.Set<T>();
        }

        5 references | 0 changes | 0 authors, 0 changes
        protected DbContext DbContext { get; set; }
        7 references | 0 changes | 0 authors, 0 changes
        protected DbSet<T> DbSet { get; set; }
        1 reference | 0 changes | 0 authors, 0 changes
        public virtual IQueryable<T> GetAll()
        {
            return DbSet;
        }
```

Appying Database Constraints

In this section, we will apply database constraints. If you take a look at the table, you won't find constraints over here which means it can accept null values as well.

```
⊟ ▦ dbo.Movies
  ⊟ ▭ Columns
      🔑 Id (PK, int, not null)
      ▤ DirectorName (nvarchar(max), null)
      ▤ MovieName (nvarchar(max), null)
      ▤ ReleaseYear (nvarchar(max), null)
```

Here is the snippet for the **Movie** and **MovieReview** classes.

```
using System;
using System.Collections.Generic;
using System.ComponentModel.DataAnnotations;

namespace MovieReviewSPA.Model
{
    public class Movie
    {
        public int Id { get; set; }
        [Required]
        [StringLength(255)]
        public string MovieName { get; set; }
        [Required]
        [StringLength(255)]
        public string DirectorName { get; set; }
        [Required]
        [StringLength(10)]
        public string ReleaseYear { get; set; }
        public virtual ICollection<MovieReview> Reviews {
get; set; }
    }
}

using System.ComponentModel.DataAnnotations;

namespace MovieReviewSPA.Model
{
    public class MovieReview
    {
        public int Id { get; set; }
        [Required]
        [StringLength(255)]
        public string ReviewerName { get; set; }
        [Required]
        [StringLength(500)]
        public string ReviewerComments { get; set; }
        [Required]
        public int ReviewerRating { get; set; }
```

```
    public int MovieId { get; set; }
  }
}
```

As you can see that I have applied the data-annotations to the required fields. They will take effect once we apply migrations. Hence, I will execute **dotnet ef migrations add applyconstraints**. On executing, it shows me the following error.

Here, it's expecting to have **MovieReviewSPA.Data** as the migration assembly. We have already seen how to get rid of this error. Therefore, in order to fix the error, we will change the assembly name, as shown in the following snippet:

```
public void ConfigureServices(IServiceCollection services)
    {
        services.AddEntityFramework()
            .AddDbContext<MovieReviewDbContext>(options
=>
options.UseSqlServer(Configuration["Data:MovieReviewSPA:Co
nnectionString"],
                b => b.MigrationsAssembly("MovieReviewS
PA.Data")));
        // Add framework services.
        services.AddMvc();
        //Initiating Seed Data
        services.AddTransient<InitialData>();
        //DI Setup
        services.AddScoped<RepositoryFactories,
RepositoryFactories>();
        services.AddScoped<IRepositoryProvider,
RepositoryProvider>();
        services.AddScoped<IMovieReviewUow,
MovieReviewUow>();
    }
```

With the above change in place, we will go ahead and run the same.

Creating the Unit Of Work Pattern (UOW)

In the previous sections, we looked at how to create the repository pattern to talk to the Entity Framework DbContext. In this section, we will focus on **Unit of Work Pattern.** Here we will see how to interact with repositories and DbContext to expose our models to Web API controllers. UOW aggregates all the data for our repository pattern. Now, the question arises why is this additional piece of layer required? To answer this question, I will again list a few basic points here.

- ✪ Fits all tiny pieces together: Decouples Web API controllers from the Repositories and DBContext.
- ✪ Aggregates all calls to Repositories.
- ✪ Simple Interface basically implementing IRepository<T> and commit action.

Now, with the above explanations, let me go ahead and first create my UOW pattern interface in my Data Contract project. Here is the code snippet.

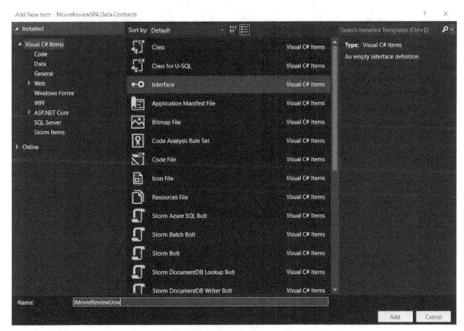

```csharp
using MovieReviewSPA.Model;

namespace MovieReviewSPA.Data.Contracts
{
    public interface IMovieReviewUow
    {
        void Commit();
        IRepository<Movie> Movies { get; }
        IRepository<MovieReview> MovieReviews { get; }
    }
}
```

As you can see in the above code snippet, the code is pretty simple and straight forward. It basically aggregates all entities; in this case, I have only two. Here, I have also added my Model project as the project dependency. Currently, my solution looks like this.

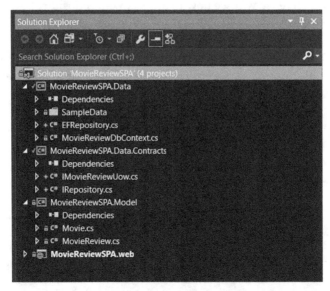

Now, to implement this, I need to create a class in my data project, as shown below.

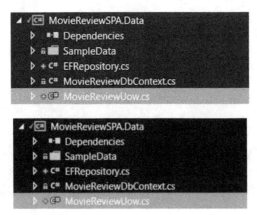

Here is the code snippet.

```
using System;
using MovieReviewSPA.Data.Contracts;
using MovieReviewSPA.Model;

namespace MovieReviewSPA.Data
{
    public class MovieReviewUow : IMovieReviewUow, IDisposable
    {
```

```
    public MovieReviewUow(IRepositoryProvider
repositoryProvider)
    {
        CreateDbContext();
        repositoryProvider.DbContext = DbContext;
        RepositoryProvider = repositoryProvider;
    }

    public IRepository<Movie> Movies { get { return
GetStandardRepo<Movie>(); } }
    public IRepository<MovieReview> MovieReviews { get {
return GetStandardRepo<MovieReview>(); } }

    public void Commit()
    {
        DbContext.SaveChanges();
    }
    protected void CreateDbContext()
    {
        DbContext = new MovieReviewDbContext();
    }

    protected IRepositoryProvider RepositoryProvider { get; set; }

    private IRepository<T> GetStandardRepo<T>() where T :
class
    {
        return RepositoryProvider.GetRepositoryForEntityT
ype<T>();
    }
    private T GetRepo<T>() where T : class
    {
        return RepositoryProvider.GetRepository<T>();
    }
    private MovieReviewDbContext DbContext { get; set; }

    public void Dispose()
    {
        Dispose(true);
        GC.SuppressFinalize(this);
    }
    protected virtual void Dispose(bool disposing)
    {
        if (disposing)
        {
            if (DbContext != null)
            {
                DbContext.Dispose();
```

```
            }
        }
    }
}
}
```

Let me first explain the code. **MovieReviewUOW** first creates DbContext. I have mentioned how I want my DbContext to look and behave. Since we have our DbContext in place, we can go ahead and implement our repositories easily. Let's take a look at how our repositories are created. **IRepository<Movie>** calls the **GetStandardRepo<Movie>** method which in return calls the Repository Provider. Now, the Repository Provider calls **GetRepositoryForEntityType<T>**. Here, T will get replaced by **Movie**.

GetRepositoryForEntityType<T> is a method which is in the **RepositoryProvider** file under the Helper folder in the Data project. Now, this method helps in creating the repository for a given entity type. It can either be Movie or MovieReview or anything. This method first checks whether the instance has been created or not. If not, then it creates one and returns the same. This piece of code basically follows **Factory Pattern** which does nothing but creates a repository whenever invoked. The best thing we can do is easily go ahead and add more repositories here if we want. In this way, the code is really scalable and maintainable. You can refer to the Helper folder code and all other pieces in the downloaded project.

The next thing is the commit method. The **Commit** method is used to save changes back to the database. Until **SaveChanges()** is called, it will not commit the changes back to the database; it will remain in the memory itself.

Questions

1. How to create models?
2. Why do we need Models?
3. What is DbContext Class? Why it is needed?
4. What is Generic Repository Pattern?
5. How to implement Generic Repository Pattern?
6. How to implement Unit of Work Pattern?
7. How to write seeding mechanism for database?
8. How to Apply Database Constraints?

Summary

In this module, we continued from the last section. Here, we started with data models for the database. Then, we implemented Entity Framework Code First Approach. During the course, we also used DbContext to communicate to and fro with models. We also saw how to get started with the Repository Pattern and how to use the Unit of Work Pattern to aggregate different repositories. We also took a look at the generic methodologies using the Factory Pattern and how to use it. In the next module, we will go one step ahead and implement a Web API Project.

CHAPTER 4

Implementing Web API

What do you find in this Chapter?

- ✪ Introduction
- ✪ Creating the First Web API Controller
- ✪ Implementing HTTP Put Request
- ✪ Implementing HTTP Post Request
- ✪ Implementing HTTP Delete Request
- ✪ Improvising Web APIs
- ✪ Adding More Controllers
- ✪ Questions
- ✪ Summary

Introduction

While building any application, passing the data to and fro from the client and saving the data back to the server is really important. Here Web API is going to be the glue between our client and data layer. In this section, our main focus will be on the top two components, as shown in the following diagram. Here, first we will design our Web APIs to talk to our repositories via the UOW Pattern. Once this is designed, we'll see how to invoke our APIs. In this case, it will be via AJAX. Therefore, without wasting time, let's get started with our API Design.

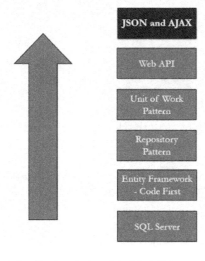

Creating The First Web API Controller

In this section, I have first created the API folder under the Controllers folder which you can see in the following screenshot. Now, this will be the repository for serving all API related queries.

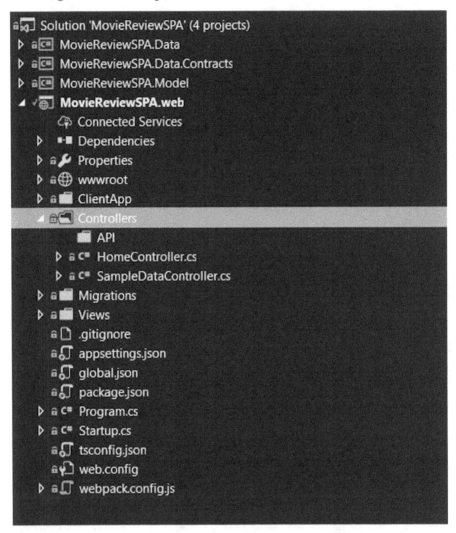

Let me go ahead and add the first controller here. One thing to note here is that in ASP.NET Core, everything is derived from the Controller class. It doesn't matter whether the request is to serve Pure MVC controller like home controller or Pure Web API Data as shown below; everything is now merged under the same stack. The only difference is that I have annotated the same with **HttpGet** along with the **Route**. Here is the code snippet.

```
using System.Collections.Generic;
using System.Linq;
```

```
using Microsoft.AspNetCore.Mvc;
using MovieReviewSPA.Data.Contracts;
using MovieReviewSPA.Model;

namespace MovieReviewSPA.web.Controllers.API
{
public class MoviesController : Controller
{
    private IMovieReviewUow UOW;

    public MoviesController(IMovieReviewUow uow)
    {
        UOW = uow;
    }

    // GET api/movies
    [HttpGet("api/movies")]
    public IEnumerable<Movie> Get()
    {
        return UOW.Movies.GetAll().OrderBy(s =>
s.MovieName);
    }
  }
}
```

With the above change in place, when I run the app, it shows the following error for http://localhost:35334/api/movies:

An unhandled exception occurred while processing the request.

InvalidOperationException: Unable to resolve service for type 'MovieReviewSPA.Data.Contracts.IMovieReviewUow' while attempting to activate 'MovieReviewSPA.web.Controllers.API.MoviesController'.

Microsoft.Extensions.Internal.ActivatorUtilities.GetService(IServiceProvider sp, Type type, Type requiredBy, bool isDefaultParameterRequired)

 Query   Cookies   Headers

Here, it basically says that Dependency Injection for the above API has not been set up. Therefore, it displays the above error. Now, in order to fix the issue, let's first set up the DI (Dependency Injection). I have copied the required dependency which needs to be included in the **startup.cs** file.

```
//DI Setup
    services.AddScoped<RepositoryFactories,
RepositoryFactories>();
    services.AddScoped<IRepositoryProvider,
RepositoryProvider>();
    services.AddScoped<IMovieReviewUow, MovieReviewUow>();
```

This will resolve all the required components needed at runtime from the API. At this stage, when I go ahead and run the app, it will display the following error.

An unhandled exception occurred while processing the request.

InvalidOperationException: No database provider has been configured for this DbContext. A provider can be configured by overriding DbContext.OnConfiguring method or by using AddDbContext on the application service provider. If AddDbContext is used, then also that your DbContext type accepts a DbContextOptions<TContext> object in its constructor and passes it to the base constructor for DbContext.

In order to fix this, I need to make one more change and that is to supply the connection string while it gets invoked from the API.

```
using Microsoft.EntityFrameworkCore;
using MovieReviewSPA.Model;

namespace MovieReviewSPA.Data
{
    public class MovieReviewDbContext :DbContext
    {
        public MovieReviewDbContext()
        {
            Database.EnsureCreated();
        }
        public DbSet<Movie> Movies { get; set; }
        public DbSet<MovieReview> MovieReviews { get; set; }

        protected override void OnConfiguring(DbContextOpt
ionsBuilder optionsBuilder)
        {
            if (!optionsBuilder.IsConfigured)
            {
                //While deploying to azure, make sure to
change the connection string based on azure settings
optionsBuilder.UseSqlServer(@"Server=(localdb)\
mssqllocaldb;
Database=MovieReviewSPA;Trusted_Connection=True;MultipleA
ctiveResultSets=true;");
            }
        }
        public MovieReviewDbContext(DbContextOptions<Movi
eReviewDbContext> options) : base(options)
        {
            //It will look for connection string from appsettings
        }
    }
}
```

Here, with the help of **optionsBuilder**, I have set up the Connection String, if it gets invoked from the API section. With the above change in place, when I once again run the app, it will show me the following result.

```
[
    - {
        id: 1,
        movieName: "Avatar",
        directorName: "James Cameron",
        releaseYear: "2009",
        reviews: null
    },
    - {
        id: 3,
        movieName: "Die Another Day",
        directorName: "Lee Tamahori",
        releaseYear: "2002",
        reviews: null
    },
    - {
        id: 4,
        movieName: "Godzilla",
        directorName: "Gareth Edwards",
        releaseYear: "2014",
        reviews: null
    },
    - {
        id: 2,
        movieName: "Titanic",
        directorName: "James Cameron",
        releaseYear: "1997",
        reviews: null
    }
]
```

Implementing An HTTP PUT Request

In the previous section, we saw how to create an HTTP GET Request. Now, in this section, we will see how to create the PUT request and test it with Postman. Here, you will notice that I have used the **[FromBody]** attribute. FromBody means it will force the WEB API to read a simple type from the request body. We generally use **FromBody** to override the default behavior of WEB-API parameter binding. Here is a sample snippet to update the existing movie.

```
// Update an existing movie
        // PUT /api/movie/
        [HttpPut("api/movies")]
        public HttpResponseMessage Put([FromBody]Movie movie)
        {
            UOW.Movies.Update(movie);
            UOW.Commit();
            return new HttpResponseMessage(HttpStatusCo
de.NoContent);
        }
```

Before I run the code, let me explain the Postman tool. Postman is similar to fiddler. I usually use Postman for any of my API testing activities. You can get Postman from **https://www.getpostman.com/**. This is a Chrome browser extension. It can be launched from the Chrome App Launcher, as shown below.

On clicking the above icon, the following window will be launched. Here, I have first tested my get request as shown below.

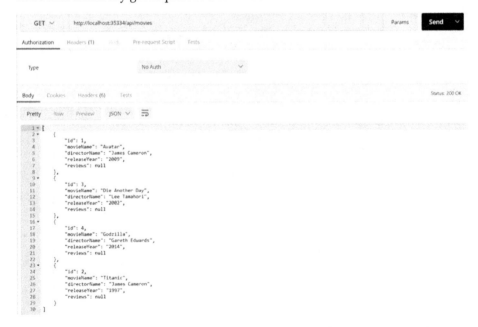

In order to test the PUT method, I have changed GET to PUT, as shown below and simply copied and pasted one of GET's responses into the body and just changed the release year to 2017.

Now, when I click on the Send button, it will hit the break point shown below.

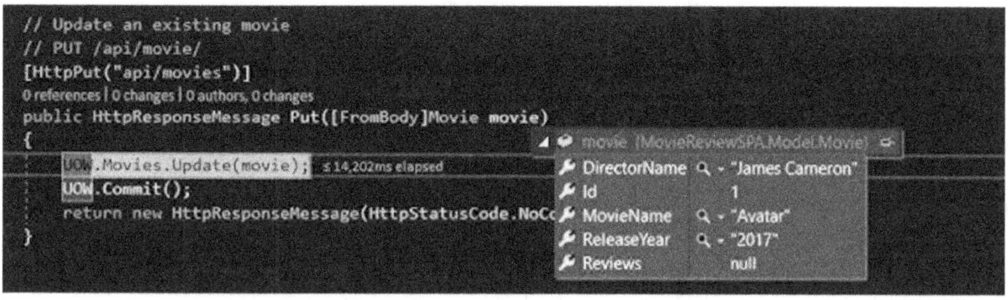

On successful completion, it returns no content with 204 Status code, as shown below.

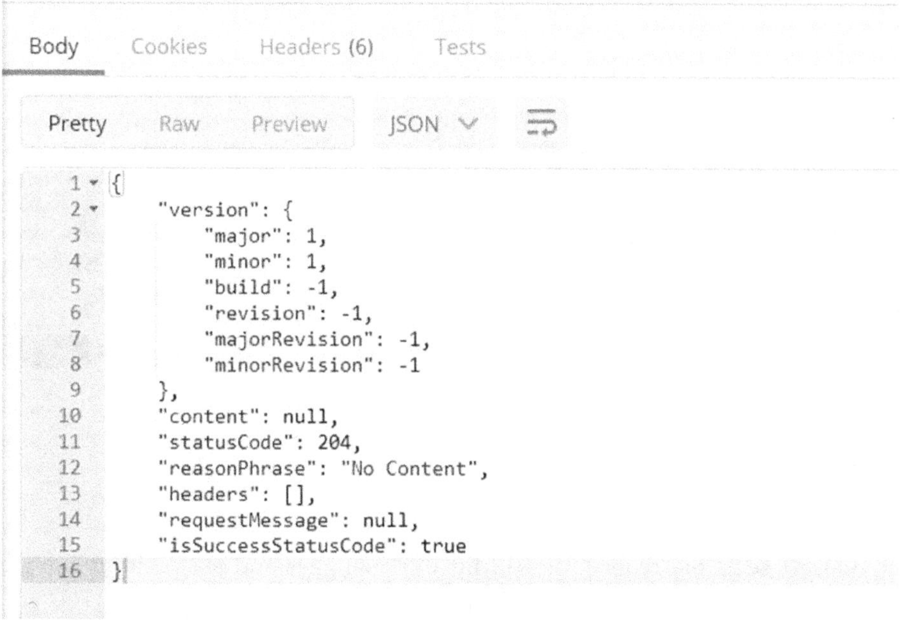

Now, I might get the same request as shown below.

Implementing HTTP Post Request

Similarly, in this section, we will implement the HTTP Post Request. Here is the snippet.

```
// Create a new movie
    // POST /api/movies
    [HttpPost("api/movies")]
    public int Post([FromBody]Movie movie)
    {
        UOW.Movies.Add(movie);
        UOW.Commit();
        return Response.StatusCode = (int)
HttpStatusCode.Created;
    }
```

And from the postman, this will be the request body.

Once I send the request, it will hit the debugger and show the following results.

```
// Create a new movie
// POST /api/movies
[HttpPost("api/movies")]
0 references | 0 changes | 0 authors, 0 changes
public int Post([FromBody]Movie movie)
{
    UOW.Movies.Add(movie);  ≤ 189.975ms elap    movie [MovieReviewSPA.Model.Movie]
    UOW.Commit();                                DirectorName   ▪ "Zack Snyder"
    return Response.StatusCode = (int)           Id             0
}                                                MovieName      ▪ "Batman Vs Superman"
                                                 ReleaseYear    ▪ "2016"
                                                 Reviews        null
```

After the successful creation of the record, it just returns the created status.

Now, when I check the get result, it gives me a newly inserted record as well.

```
[
    {
        "id": 1,
        "movieName": "Avatar",
        "directorName": "James Cameron",
        "releaseYear": "2017",
        "reviews": null
    },
    {
        "id": 5,
        "movieName": "Batman Vs Superman",
        "directorName": "Zack Snyder",
        "releaseYear": "2016",
        "reviews": null
    },
    {
        "id": 3,
        "movieName": "Die Another Day",
        "directorName": "Lee Tamahori",
        "releaseYear": "2002",
        "reviews": null
    },
    {
        "id": 4,
        "movieName": "Godzilla",
        "directorName": "Gareth Edwards",
        "releaseYear": "2014",
        "reviews": null
    }
```

Since the ID is the identity column, it automatically gets incremented based on the latest value in the database.

Implementing The HTTP Delete Request

In this section, we'll follow the same pattern but we will see how HTTP Delete works.

```
// DELETE api/movies/5
[HttpDelete("api/movies/{id}")]
    public HttpResponseMessage Delete(int id)
    {
    UOW.Movies.Delete(id);
    UOW.Commit();
return new HttpResponseMessage(HttpStatusCode.NoContent);
    }
```

Once done, I can now send the request with the following details.

It again hits my breakpoint with the given id.

```
47        // DELETE api/movies/5
48        [HttpDelete("api/movies/{id}")]
          0 references | 0 changes | 0 authors, 0 changes
49 ▷      public HttpResponseMessage Delete(int id)
50          ≤ 64,394ms elapsed                    ● id 5 ⤶
51            UOW.Movies.Delete(id);
52            UOW.Commit();
53            return new HttpResponseMessage(HttpStatusCode.NoContent);
54          }
55
56        }
57 }
58
```

Finally, it shows the following result:

```
Pretty    Raw    Preview    JSON ∨    ⇆

 1 ▾ {
 2 ▾     "version": {
 3             "major": 1,
 4             "minor": 1,
 5             "build": -1,
 6             "revision": -1,
 7             "majorRevision": -1,
 8             "minorRevision": -1
 9         },
10         "content": null,
11         "statusCode": 204,
12         "reasonPhrase": "No Content",
13         "headers": [],
14         "requestMessage": null,
15         "isSuccessStatusCode": true
16   }
```

Now, when I make a GET request, it will show the original set.

```
[
  {
    "Id": 1,
    "MovieName": "Avatar",
    "DirectorName": "James Cameron",
    "ReleaseYear": "2016",
    "Reviews": null
  },
  {
    "Id": 3,
    "MovieName": "Die Another Day",
    "DirectorName": "Lee Tamahori",
    "ReleaseYear": "2002",
    "Reviews": null
  },
  {
    "Id": 4,
    "MovieName": "Godzilla",
    "DirectorName": "Gareth Edwards",
    "ReleaseYear": "2014",
    "Reviews": null
  },
  {
    "Id": 2,
    "MovieName": "Titanic",
    "DirectorName": "James Cameron",
    "ReleaseYear": "1997",
    "Reviews": null
  }
]
```

However, this was the basic understanding of how APIs are going to work throughout this project. But, let me modify them to give them a final shape.

Improvising Web APIS

Until now, we have not seen any reviews in the GET call; however, we do have one review associated with one movie if you remember from Seed data. In order to show it, I am going to construct a **ViewModel** and I am going to query against it. I will create this ViewModel in my **ViewModels** folder, as shown in the following screenshot:

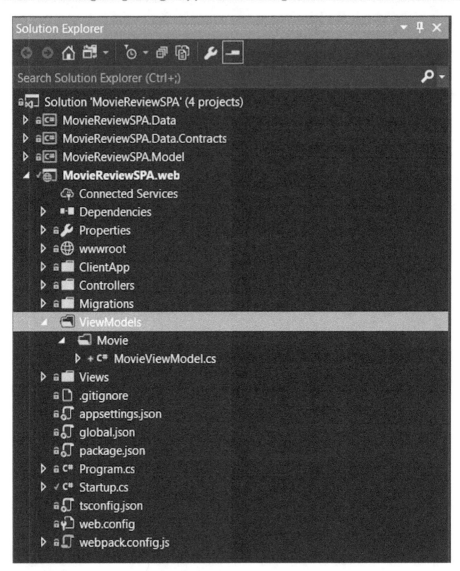

Here is the snippet for the same.

```
namespace MovieReviewSPA.web.ViewModels.Movie
{
    public class MovieViewModel
    {
        public int Id { get; set; }
        public string MovieName { get; set; }
        public string DirectorName { get; set; }
        public string ReleaseYear { get; set; }
        public int NoOfReviews { get; set; }
    }
}
```

Here, I need to improvise my **GET** call a bit. Here is the modified Get Call that lists my Reviews as well.

```
        // GET api/movies
    // GET api/movies
            [HttpGet("api/movies")]
            public IQueryable Get()
            {
                var model = UOW.Movies.GetAll().
OrderByDescending(m => m.Reviews.Count())
                    .Select(m => new MovieViewModel
                    {
                        Id = m.Id,
                        MovieName = m.MovieName,
                        DirectorName = m.DirectorName,
                        ReleaseYear = m.ReleaseYear,
                        NoOfReviews = m.Reviews.Count()
                    });
            return model;
        }
```

With the above change in place, it will show the following result.

```
 1 ▼ [
 2 ▼     {
 3           "id": 4,
 4           "movieName": "Godzilla",
 5           "directorName": "Gareth Edwards",
 6           "releaseYear": "2014",
 7           "noOfReviews": 3
 8       },
 9 ▼     {
10           "id": 1,
11           "movieName": "Avatar",
12           "directorName": "James Cameron",
13           "releaseYear": "2017",
14           "noOfReviews": 0
15       },
16 ▼     {
17           "id": 2,
18           "movieName": "Titanic",
19           "directorName": "James Cameron",
20           "releaseYear": "1997",
21           "noOfReviews": 0
22       },
23 ▼     {
24           "id": 3,
25           "movieName": "Die Another Day",
26           "directorName": "Lee Tamahori",
27           "releaseYear": "2002",
28           "noOfReviews": 0
29       }
30   ]
```

We can also improvise the controller a little more as shown below.

```
using System;
using System.Collections.Generic;
using System.Linq;
using System.Net;
using System.Net.Http;
using Microsoft.AspNetCore.Mvc;
using MovieReviewSPA.Data.Contracts;
using MovieReviewSPA.Model;
using MovieReviewSPA.web.ViewModels.Movie;

namespace MovieReviewSPA.web.Controllers.API
{
    [Route("api/[controller]")]
    public class MoviesController : Controller
    {
        private IMovieReviewUow UOW;

        public MoviesController(IMovieReviewUow uow)
        {
            UOW = uow;
        }

        // GET api/movies
        [HttpGet("")]
        public IQueryable Get()
        {
            var model = UOW.Movies.GetAll().
OrderByDescending(m => m.Reviews.Count())
                .Select(m => new MovieViewModel
                {
                    Id = m.Id,
                    MovieName = m.MovieName,
                    DirectorName = m.DirectorName,
                    ReleaseYear = m.ReleaseYear,
                    NoOfReviews = m.Reviews.Count()
                });
            return model;

        }

        // GET api/movies/1
        [HttpGet("{id}")]
        public Movie Get(int id)
```

```
        {
            var movie = UOW.Movies.GetById(id);
            if (movie != null) return movie;
            throw new Exception(new HttpResponseMessage(H
ttpStatusCode.NotFound).ToString());
        }


        // Update an existing movie
        // PUT /api/movie/
        [HttpPut("")]
        public HttpResponseMessage Put([FromBody]Movie movie)
        {
            UOW.Movies.Update(movie);
            UOW.Commit();
            return new HttpResponseMessage(HttpStatusCo
de.NoContent);
        }


        // Create a new movie
        // POST /api/movies
        [HttpPost("")]
        public int Post([FromBody]Movie movie)
        {
            UOW.Movies.Add(movie);
            UOW.Commit();
            return Response.StatusCode = (int)
HttpStatusCode.Created;
        }


        // DELETE api/movies/5
        [HttpDelete("{id}")]
        public HttpResponseMessage Delete(int id)
        {
            UOW.Movies.Delete(id);
            UOW.Commit();
            return new HttpResponseMessage(HttpStatusCo
de.NoContent);
        }


    }
}
```

As you can see in the above snippet, I have taken the route at controller level rather than repeating it at every action, and just provided the HTTP-VERB with an empty set if nothing is required. In case of Delete and GET by Id, I have specified only id as a parameter.

Adding More Controllers

In this section, I will add a couple of more controllers to make it more reasonable and CRUD oriented. I have already added new controllers to my solution, as shown in the following screenshot.

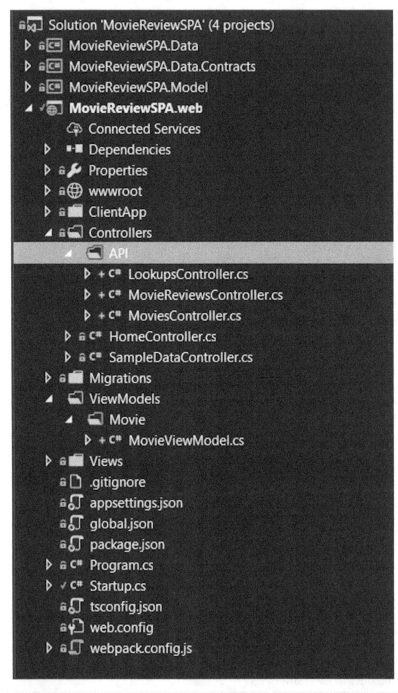

Now, let me paste the finished code for the same.

```
using System;
using System.Collections.Generic;
using System.Linq;
using System.Net;
using System.Net.Http;
using Microsoft.AspNetCore.Authorization;
using Microsoft.AspNetCore.Mvc;
using MovieReviewSPA.Data.Contracts;
using MovieReviewSPA.Model;

namespace MovieReviewSPA.Web.Controllers.API
{
    [Route("api/[controller]")]
    public class MovieReviewsController : Controller
    {
        private readonly IMovieReviewUow UOW;

        public MovieReviewsController(IMovieReviewUow uow)
        {
            UOW = uow;
        }
        [HttpGet("")]
        public IEnumerable<MovieReview> Get()
        {
            return UOW.MovieReviews.GetAll().OrderBy(m =>
m.MovieId);
        }

        [HttpGet("{id}")]
        public IEnumerable<MovieReview> Get(int Id)
        {
            return UOW.MovieReviews.GetAll().Where(m =>
m.MovieId == Id);
        }

        // /api/MovieReviews/getbyreviewername?value=rahul
        [HttpGet("[action]")]
        public MovieReview GetByReviewerName(string value)
        {
            var review = UOW.MovieReviews.GetAll().
FirstOrDefault(m => m.ReviewerName.StartsWith(value));

            if (review != null) return review;
```

```
                throw new Exception(new HttpResponseMessage(H
ttpStatusCode.NotFound).ToString());
        }

        // Update an existing review
        // PUT /api/MovieReviews/
        [HttpPut("")]
        public HttpResponseMessage Put([FromBody]
MovieReview review)
        {
            //review.Id = Id;
            UOW.MovieReviews.Update(review);
            UOW.Commit();
            return new HttpResponseMessage(HttpStatusCo
de.NoContent);
        }


        // Create a new review
        // POST /api/MovieReviews
        [HttpPost("{id}")]
        public int Post(int Id, [FromBody]MovieReview review)
        {
            review.MovieId = Id;
            UOW.MovieReviews.Add(review);
            UOW.Commit();

            return Response.StatusCode = (int)
HttpStatusCode.Created;
        }


        //Delete a review
        //Delete /api/MovieReviews/5
        [HttpDelete("{id}")]
        public HttpResponseMessage Delete(int id)
        {
            UOW.MovieReviews.Delete(id);
            UOW.Commit();
            return new HttpResponseMessage(HttpStatusCo
de.NoContent);
        }
    }
}
```

This is also very straightforward and simple to understand. However, let me explain a couple of actions shown in the above code snippet. Here, while running, when I refer to the GET URL, it will show me the following results:

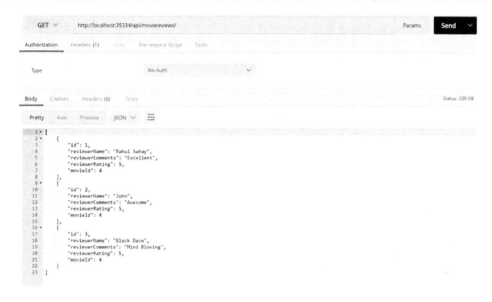

I can refer to the movie review by the movie id as shown below. It produces the same result as all the reviews are associated with one movie itself.

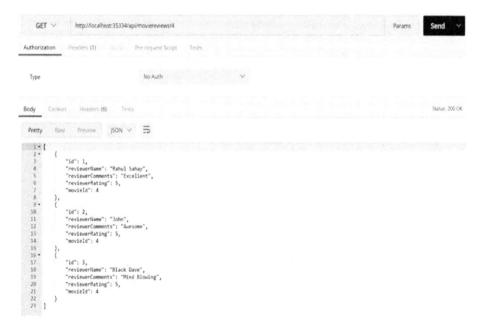

Likewise, I can also refer to the review by its reviewer name as shown below. Here, in this case, I have annotated the method with the **[action]** attribute.

Similarly, I have written another controller for future reference. Here is the snippet for the same.

```csharp
using System.Collections.Generic;
using System.Linq;
using Microsoft.AspNetCore.Mvc;
using MovieReviewSPA.Data.Contracts;
using MovieReviewSPA.Model;

namespace MovieReviewSPA.web.Controllers.API
{
    [Route("api/[controller]")]
    public class LookupsController : Controller
    {
        private readonly IMovieReviewUow UOW;
        public LookupsController(IMovieReviewUow uow)
        {
            UOW = uow;
        }
        // GET: api/lookups/movies
        [HttpGet("movies")]
        public IEnumerable<Movie> GetMovies()
        {
            return UOW.Movies.GetAll().OrderBy(m => m.Id);
        }

        // /api/Lookups/getbyreviewerid?id=1
        [HttpGet("getbyreviewerid")]
        public MovieReview GetByReviewerId(int id)
        {
            return UOW.MovieReviews.GetById(id);
        }

        #region OData Future: IQueryable<T>
        //[Queryable]
        // public IQueryable<Movie> Get()
        // public IQueryable<MovieReview> Get()
```

```
    #endregion

    }
}
```

Here, you can see that I have used routing in a number of different ways. I have pasted the results below.

Questions

1. What is Web API and why it is needed?
2. How to create a new Web API controller?
3. What is the difference between HTTP-GET and HTTP-POST?
4. How to specify Routes for Web API?
5. Can we define Routes at controller Level?

6. Can we define Route at action level?
7. How to define custom routes at action level?

Summary

In this section, we started with the design of our API controllers. While getting started with the basics; we wrote some simple queries just to demonstrate the functioning of API. After that, we wrote more complex queries to achieve the meaningful results. We also saw how to wire up Entity Framework with Dependency Injection. Later, we wrote a few more controllers with extra APIs to make the app more robust. In the next section, we will get started with Angular Implementation.

CHAPTER 5

Getting Started with Angular

Introduction

In this section, we'll start with the basics. This is not an Angular guide, but I expect you to have working knowledge of Angular 2 or 4. We have already scaffolded our project using the dotnet command, which means we already have the initial setup in place. Therefore, in this section; we will be utilizing and extending the same.

Creating a New Angular Component

In this section, we will create a new component for our Angular app. One way is to create the component manually by creating a new folder and then creating the component and other related files like HTML and CSS if required. Another way is via Angular CLI. You can refer to the complete step by step document at **https://cli.angular.io/**. First of all, we need to install the Angular CLI in the project via the **npm install --save-dev @angular/cli@latest** command. This will install Angular CLI as dev dependency in the project. Once it's installed, we can go ahead and create components via the command line like **ng g c Movies**. Once I do so, it will show me the following error:

```
C:\Dell\Books\ASPNETCorePlusAngular4\MovieReviewSPA\MovieReviewSPA.web (Another) (MovieReviewSPA_web@0.0.0)
λ ng g c movies
installing component
Error locating module for declaration
      SilentError: No module files found
```

I have already discussed this error in detail in my blog. You can refer to the same at thread **http://bit.ly/No-Modules**. The basic reason is that a new structure is not in lines with Angular CLI where in it expects to have the **app.module.ts** file. In order to fix this error quickly, we can rename **app.module.client.ts** to **app. module.ts.** Now, open the **app.module.ts** file and make changes as shown below.

```
import { NgModule } from' @angular/core';
```

```
import { BrowserModule } from' @angular/platform-browser';
import { FormsModule } from' @angular/forms';
import { HttpModule } from' @angular/http';
import { sharedConfig } from' ./app.module.shared';

@NgModule({
    bootstrap: sharedConfig.bootstrap,
    declarations: [...sharedConfig.declarations],
    imports: [
        BrowserModule,
        FormsModule,
        HttpModule,
        ...sharedConfig.imports
    ],
    providers: [
        { provide: 'ORIGIN_URL', useValue: location.
origin }
    ]
})
Export class AppModule {
}
```

Now, we need to fix the reference in the **boot-client.ts** file as shown below.

```
import' reflect-metadata';
import' zone.js';
import { enableProdMode } from' @angular/core';
import { platformBrowserDynamic } from' @angular/platform-
browser-dynamic';
import { AppModule } from' ./app/app.module';

if (module['hot']) {
    module['hot'].accept();
    module['hot'].dispose(() => {
// Before restarting the app, we create a new root
element and dispose the old one
const oldRootElem = document.querySelector('app');
const newRootElem = document.createElement('app');
        oldRootElem.parentNode.insertBefore(newRootElem,
oldRootElem);
        modulePromise.then(appModule => appModule.destroy());
    });
} else {
    enableProdMode();
}

// Note: @ng-tools/webpack looks for the following
expression when performing production
```

```
// builds. Don't change how this line looks, otherwise
you may break tree-shaking.
const modulePromise = platformBrowserDynamic().
bootstrapModule(AppModule);
```

Once done, we can go ahead and create our new component as shown below.

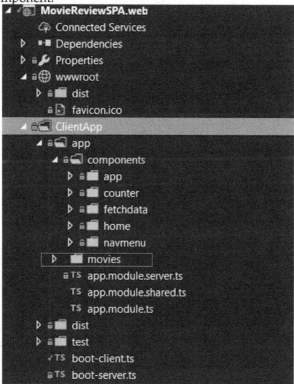

As you can see in the above screenshot, it has created all the files required for the component and has also registered the newly created component in the app. module.ts file. In the following screenshot, you can see that it has successfully created the component.

But it has been created at the app level rather than at the components level. One way to fix this is to manually drag and drop the folder inside components and update the references in the app.module.ts file. However, I would rather prefer the other way which is via CLI as shown below.

First of all let me delete this movies folder and get rid of movies reference from the module file. After that, I execute ng g c components/movies. Here, I have specified the exact location.

```
C:\Dell\Books\ASPNETCorePlusAngular4\MovieReviewSPA\MovieReviewSPA.web (Another) (MovieReviewSPA_web@0.0.0)
λ ng g c components/movies
installing component
  create ClientApp\app\components\movies\movies.component.css
  create ClientApp\app\components\movies\movies.component.html
  create ClientApp\app\components\movies\movies.component.spec.ts
  create ClientApp\app\components\movies\movies.component.ts
  update ClientApp\app\app.module.ts
```

With the above change in place, my solution looks like this.

Here is a glimpse of the component.

Here, I need to delete this spec file as I am not writing a test case for this at the moment. Hence, in order to avoid any runtime error, we can get rid of this file. When I create this component from CLI, it also gets registered with my module as shown below.

```typescript
import { NgModule } from '@angular/core';
import { BrowserModule } from '@angular/platform-browser';
import { FormsModule } from '@angular/forms';
import { HttpModule } from '@angular/http';
import { sharedConfig } from './app.module.shared';
import { MoviesComponent } from './components/movies/movies.component';

@NgModule({
    bootstrap: sharedConfig.bootstrap,
    declarations: [...sharedConfig.declarations, MoviesComponent],
    imports: [
        BrowserModule,
        FormsModule,
        HttpModule,
        ...sharedConfig.imports
    ],
    providers: [
        { provide: 'ORIGIN_URL', useValue: location.origin }
    ]
})
export class AppModule {
}
```

Creating a New Route

In the last section, we created our first component. Now we need to register our new route for this new page. In order to do so, first I need to go to the **app. module.shared.ts** file and register my new route as shown below.

```
import { NgModule } from' @angular/core';
import { RouterModule } from' @angular/router';

import { AppComponent } from'./components/app/app.component'
import { NavMenuComponent } from'./components/navmenu/
navmenu.component';
import { HomeComponent } from'./components/home/home.
component';
import { FetchDataComponent } from'./components/
fetchdata/fetchdata.component';
import { CounterComponent } from'./components/counter/
counter.component';
import { MoviesComponent } from'./components/movies/
movies.component';
export const sharedConfig: NgModule = {
        bootstrap: [ AppComponent ],
        declarations: [
        AppComponent,
        NavMenuComponent,
        CounterComponent,
        FetchDataComponent,
        HomeComponent,
        MoviesComponent
    ],
    imports: [
        RouterModule.forRoot([
            { path: '', redirectTo: 'home', pathMatch:
'full' },
                { path: 'movies', component:MoviesComponent },
                { path: 'home', component: HomeComponent },
                { path: 'counter', component: CounterComponent },
                { path: 'fetch-data', component:
FetchDataComponent },
                { path: '**', redirectTo: 'home' }
        ])
    ]
};
```

Here, I am utilizing the shared module file just to maintain the Visual Studio solution structure. However, if you would like to merge the whole thing in the app.module.ts file, then you can do so. It's your personal choice. Once done, I also need to add the new link to the navmenu.component.html page. Here is the code snippet. Basically, I have added one more li element.

```html
<div class='main-nav'>
    <div class='navbar navbar-inverse'>
        <div class='navbar-header'>
            <button type='button' class='navbar-toggle'
data-toggle='collapse' data-target='.navbar-collapse'>
                <span class='sr-only'>Toggle navigation</
span>
                <span class='icon-bar'></span>
                <span class='icon-bar'></span>
                <span class='icon-bar'></span>
            </button>
            <a class='navbar-brand' [routerLink]="['/
home']">MovieReviewSPA_web</a>
        </div>
        <div class='clearfix'></div>
        <div class='navbar-collapse collapse'>
            <ul class='nav navbar-nav'>
                <li [routerLinkActive]="['link-active']">
                    <a [routerLink]="['/home']">
                        <span class='glyphicon glyphicon-
home'></span> Home
                    </a>
                </li>
                <li [routerLinkActive]="['link-active']">
                    <a [routerLink]="['/movies']">
                        <span class='glyphicon glyphicon-
film'></span> Movies
                    </a>
                </li>
                <li [routerLinkActive]="['link-active']">
                    <a [routerLink]="['/counter']">
                        <span class='glyphicon glyphicon-
education'></span> Counter
                    </a>
                </li>
                <li [routerLinkActive]="['link-active']">
                    <a [routerLink]="['/fetch-data']">
                        <span class='glyphicon glyphicon-th-
list'></span> Fetch data
                    </a>
                </li>
            </ul>
```

```
        </div>
    </div>
</div>
```

With the above change in place, when I go ahead and check my page, it will appear like this:

Adding the Bootstrap Form

Next, we will add the bootstrap form to our page. Currently, I have just pasted the skeleton code from **https://bootsnipp.com/snippets/r1kjW**. I have used this design and improvised it based on our need. Here is the code snippet.

```html
<h3>Movies List</h3>
<div class="container">
    <div class="row">
        <div class="row">
            <div class="col-xs-12 col-sm-9 col-md-9">
                <div class="list-group">
                    <div class="list-group-item">
                        <div class="row-content">
                            <div class="list-group-item-heading">
                                <a href="#" title="movieName">
                                    <small>Movie Name</small>
                                </a>
                            </div>
                            <small>
                                <i class="glyphicon glyphicon-time"></i> Release Year
                                <i class="glyphicon glyphicon-user"></i> Director Name
                                <br>
                                <span class="explore"><i
```

```
class="glyphicon glyphicon-th"></i> <a href="#">Movie
Reviews </a></span>
                                        </small>
                                </div>
                        </div>
                    </div>
                </div>
            </div>
        <hr>
    </div>
</div>
```

And then in the corresponding CSS file, I have pasted the following snippet.

```
.list-group {
border-radius: 0;
}

.list-group.list-group-item {
background-color: transparent;
overflow: hidden;
border: 0;
border-radius: 0;
padding: 016px;
    }

.list-group.list-group-item.row-picture,
.list-group.list-group-item.row-action-primary {
float: left;
display: inline-block;
padding-right: 16px;
padding-top: 8px;
        }

.list-group.list-group-item.row-pictureimg,
.list-group.list-group-item.row-action-primaryimg,
.list-group.list-group-item.row-picturei,
.list-group.list-group-item.row-action-primaryi,
.list-group.list-group-item.row-picturelabel,
.list-group.list-group-item.row-action-primarylabel {
display: block;
width: 56px;
height: 56px;
        }

.list-group.list-group-item.row-pictureimg,
.list-group.list-group-item.row-action-primaryimg {
```

```css
background: rgba(0,0,0,0.1);
padding: 1px;
        }

.list-group.list-group-item.row-pictureimg.circle,
.list-group.list-group-item.row-action-primaryimg.circle
{
border-radius: 100%;
            }

.list-group.list-group-item.row-picturei,
.list-group.list-group-item.row-action-primaryi {
background: rgba(0,0,0,0.25);
border-radius: 100%;
text-align: center;
line-height: 56px;
font-size: 20px;
color: white;
        }

.list-group.list-group-item.row-picturelabel,
.list-group.list-group-item.row-action-primarylabel {
margin-left: 7px;
margin-right:7px;
margin-top: 5px;
margin-bottom:5px;
        }

.list-group.list-group-item.row-content {
display: inline-block;
width: calc(100%-92px);
min-height: 66px;
        }

.list-group.list-group-item.row-content.action-secondary
{
position: absolute;
right: 16px;
top: 16px;
            }

.list-group.list-group-item.row-content.action-secondaryi
{
font-size: 20px;
color: rgba(0,0,0,0.25);
cursor: pointer;
            }
```

```css
.list-group.list-group-item.row-content.action-
secondary~* {
max-width: calc(100%-30px);
                }

.list-group.list-group-item.row-content.least-content {
position: absolute;
right: 16px;
top: 0px;
color: rgba(0,0,0,0.54);
font-size: 14px;
            }

.list-group.list-group-item.list-group-item-heading {
color: rgba(0,0,0,0.77);
font-size: 20px;
line-height: 29px;
        }

.list-group.list-group-separator {
clear: both;
overflow: hidden;
margin-top: 10px;
margin-bottom: 10px;
    }

.list-group.list-group-separator:before {
content: "";
width: calc(100%-90px);
border-bottom: 1pxsolidrgba(0,0,0,0.1);
float: right;
        }

.bg-profile {
background-color: #3498DB!important;
height: 150px;
z-index: 1;
}

.bg-bottom {
height: 100px;
margin-left: 30px;
}

.img-profile {
display: inline-block!important;
background-color: #fff;
```

```
border-radius: 6px;
margin-top:50%;
padding: 1px;
vertical-align: bottom;
border: 2pxsolid#fff;
-moz-box-sizing: border-box;
box-sizing: border-box;
color: #fff;
z-index: 2;
}

.row-float {
margin-top:40px;
}

.explorea {
color: green;
font-size: 13px;
font-weight: 600
}

.twittera {
color: #4099FF
}

.img-box {
box-shadow: 03px6pxrgba(0,0,0,.16),03px6pxrgba(0,0,0,.23)
;
border-radius: 2px;
border: 0;
}
```

Bootsnipp is one of the shortcuts of designing layouts. Here, I can quickly search for the layout and then apply the design accordingly. With the above change in place, now my movies list page looks like this.

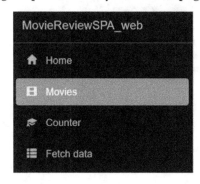

One point to note here is that this is just the hardcoded values. There is no data binding at the moment.

Creating Angular Service

In this section, we will create service for making any API calls. This is the thumb rule one should stick to. One should not try calling APIs directly from components. Here, I have created the new services folder inside our app folder.

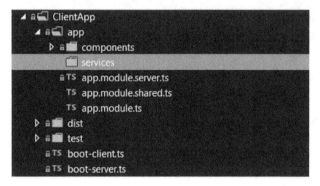

Here, I will create my service using the **ng g s movies** command.

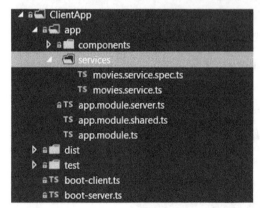

It generates a spec file as well which we don't need at the moment. Hence, we can delete this file. And, here we have nice boiler plate code for the service.

```
movies.service.ts  ⊬ ✕
🗗 MovieReviewSPA.web (tsconfig project)          ▾ () "movies.service"
  1     import { Injectable } from '@angular/core';
  2
  3     @Injectable()
  4   ⊟export class MoviesService {
  5
  6       constructor() { }
  7
  8     }
```

I will import a few dependencies here like **Http**. Here is the code snippet.

```
import { Injectable } from '@angular/core';
import { Http } from '@angular/http';
import 'rxjs/add/operator/map';

@Injectable()
Export class MoviesService {

//In order to use any injectable, pass it via ctor
constructor(private http:Http) { }

    getMovies() {
returnthis.http.get('/api/movies')
//Once, we get the response back, it has to get mapped to
json
            .map(res => res.json());
    }
}
```

Let me explain the code a bit. In order to use the Http service, first I need to import it, and then in order to use it in the code, I need to inject it as a private variable in the code.

Then, I need to create one function, which simply makes an Api call to movies. However, when the data is getting returned, the Json data needs to be mapped again. For this, we need to use an operator map which is part of RxJS. Now, we need to register this service as a provider. Here is the code snippet.

```
import { NgModule } from '@angular/core';
import { BrowserModule } from '@angular/platform-browser';
import { FormsModule } from '@angular/forms';
import { HttpModule } from '@angular/http';
import { sharedConfig } from './app.module.shared';
import { MoviesComponent } from './components/movies/
movies.component';
import { MoviesService } from './services/movies.service';

@NgModule({
    bootstrap: sharedConfig.bootstrap,
    declarations: [...sharedConfig.declarations,
```

```
MoviesComponent],
    imports: [
        BrowserModule,
        FormsModule,
        HttpModule,
        ...sharedConfig.imports
    ],
    providers: [
        { provide: 'ORIGIN_URL', useValue: location.
origin },
        MoviesService
    ]
})
export class AppModule {
}
```

Here, I have registered it in the **app.module.ts** file. You can notice that I have registered the service under the providers section. Now, in order to consume the service in the component, I need to use it in my movies component file. Here is the snippet for the same.

```
import { Component, OnInit } from' @angular/core';
import { MoviesService} from'../../services/movies.
service';

@Component({
    selector: 'app-movies',
    templateUrl: './movies.component.html',
    styleUrls: ['./movies.component.css']
})
export class MoviesComponent implements OnInit {

    movies;
constructor(private moviesService: MoviesService) { }

    ngOnInit() {
this.moviesService.getMovies().subscribe(movies => {
this.movies = movies;
            console.log("Movies: ", this.movies);
        });

    }
}
```

Let me explain the code a bit. First of all, I have injected the movie service in constructor and therefore, I have resolved the file reference for the same. Then, I have declared a field called movies and then initialized the same in the **ngOnInit** function.

Here, via the movies service, I have called my endpoint, subscribed to the observable and then used that to initialize my movies field. Then, in order to test the same, I have also logged the output in the console just to make sure that my service call is happening correctly.

One more point to note here is that since this is an asynchronous call, there is a time lag until my movies field gets initialized. Therefore, if I don't wrap this call inside the code block, my movies field will show as undefined. By wrapping it inside the code block, we make sure that the console.log executes only after it receives a response from the server.

With the above changes in place, when I inspect my console, it will look like this.

Now, I will go to the movies.component.html file and do data binding as shown below.

```html
<h3>Movies List</h3>
<div class="container">
    <div class="row">
        <div class="row">
            <div class="col-xs-12 col-sm-9 col-md-9">
                <div class="list-group">
                    <div class="list-group-item">
                        <div class="row-content" *ngFor="let m of movies">
                            <div class="list-group-item-heading">
                                <a href="#" title="movieName">
                                    <small>Movie Name: {{m.movieName}}</small>
                                </a>
                            </div>
                            <small>
                                <i class="glyphicon glyphicon-time"></i> Release Year: {{m.releaseYear}}
                                <i class="glyphicon glyphicon-user"></i> Director Name: {{m.directorName}}
                                <br>
                                <span class="explore"><i class="glyphicon glyphicon-th"></i> <a href="#">Movie Reviews: {{m.noOfReviews}} </a></span>
                            </small>
                            <hr>
```

```
            </div>
          </div>
        </div>
      </div>
    </div>
  </div>
</div>
```

Here, I have used the ***ngFor** built-in directive to loop through the collection and then simply binded the corresponding values. With the above change in place, it will look like this.

Creating a New Movie

In this section, we will use the same steps to post a new movie. In order to isolate it as a different view, I have created a new component.

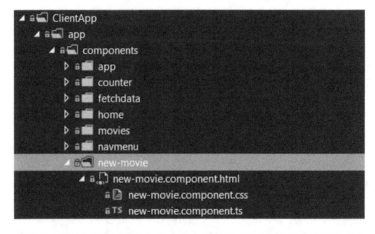

My markup looks like this.

Enter New Movie

Here is the code snippet.

```
<div class="container">
    <div class="row">
        <form (ngSubmit)="onSubmit(f)" #f="ngForm"
role="form" class="col-md-9 go-right">
            <h2>Enter New Movie</h2>
            <div class="form-group">
                <input id="movieName" name="movieName"
type="text" class="form-control" required
[(ngModel)]="movie.movieName">
                <label for="movieName">Movie Name</label>
            </div>
            <div class="form-group">
                <input id="directorName"
name="directorName" type="text" class="form-control"
required [(ngModel)]="movie.directorName">
                <label for="directorName">Director Name</
label>
            </div>
            <div class="form-group">
                <input id="releaseYear"
name="releaseYear" type="text" class="form-control"
required [(ngModel)]="movie.releaseYear">
                <label for="releaseYear">Release Year</
label>
            </div>
            <p class="bg-success"
style="padding:10px;margin-top:20px;clear:both"> <button
type="submit" class="btn btn-primary">Submit</button></p>
        </form>
    </div>
</div>
```

Again, I have borrowed the sample form from **https://bootsnipp.com/**. In order to grab the input values, I have used my local variable as **ngForm** and then I have passed the same instance to submit the action. Apart from that, in order to do data-binding, I have also used **ngModel** and passed the property name there. The corresponding CSS looks like this.

```
@importurl(http://fonts.googleapis.com/
css?family=Open+Sans:400,600);

.form-control {
background: transparent;
}

form {
width: 320px;
margin: 20px;
    }

form>div {
position: relative;
overflow: hidden;
    }

forminput, formtextarea {
width: 100%;
border: 2pxsolidgray;
background: none;
position: relative;
top: 0;
left: 0;
z-index: 1;
padding: 8px12px;
outline: 0;
    }

forminput:valid, formtextarea:valid {
background: white;
      }

forminput:focus, formtextarea:focus {
border-color: #357EBD;
      }

forminput:focus+label, formtextarea:focus+label {
background: #357EBD;
color: white;
font-size: 70%;
padding: 1px6px;
z-index: 2;
```

```
text-transform: uppercase;
            }
formlabel {
-webkit-transition: background0.2s, color0.2s, top0.2s,
bottom0.2s, right0.2s, left0.2s;
transition: background0.2s, color0.2s, top0.2s,
bottom0.2s, right0.2s, left0.2s;
position: absolute;
color: #999;
padding: 7px6px;
font-weight: normal;
     }
formtextarea {
display: block;
resize: vertical;
     }
form.go-bottominput, form.go-bottomtextarea {
padding: 12px12px12px12px;
     }
form.go-bottomlabel {
top: 0;
bottom: 0;
left: 0;
width: 100%;
     }
form.go-bottominput:focus, form.go-bottomtextarea:focus {
padding: 4px6px20px6px;
     }
form.go-bottominput:focus+label, form.go-
bottomtextarea:focus+label {
top: 100%;
margin-top:16px;
       }
form.go-rightlabel {
border-radius: 05px5px0;
height: 100%;
top: 0;
right: 100%;
width: 100%;
margin-right:100%;
     }
```

```
form.go-rightinput:focus+label, form.go-
righttextarea:focus+label {
right: 0;
margin-right: 0;
width: 40%;
padding-top: 5px;
    }
```

No need to explain this. My typescript file looks like this.

```
import { Component, OnInit, ElementRef } from'@angular/
core';
import { NgForm } from'@angular/forms';
import { MoviesService } from'../../services/movies.
service';
import { Movie } from'./../../models/movie';
@Component({
    selector: 'app-new-movie',
    templateUrl: './new-movie.component.html',
    styleUrls: ['./new-movie.component.css']
})
export class NewMovieComponent implements OnInit {

    movie: Movie =new Movie();
    constructor(private moviesService: MoviesService) { }
    ngOnInit() {
    }

    onSubmit(form: NgForm) {
var formData = this.movie;
        formData.id = 0;
        formData.movieName = this.movie.movieName.
toString();
        formData.directorName = this.movie.directorName.
toString();
        formData.releaseYear = this.movie.releaseYear.
toString();
        console.log(formData);
this.moviesService.createMovie(formData)
            .subscribe(x => console.log(x));
    }
}
```

The code is pretty straightforward here. First of all, I have grabbed all the required references for the form, service and newly created model which I'll explain in a while. Then I have injected the service in the constructor in order to call the same.

Before that, I have actually initialized my **movie** model as this model class will be filled by the form data. Lastly, for the submit action, I have fetched all the form values and then passed the **createMovie** action. Since I am using forms here, they need to be imported in my **app.module.ts** file as well. Here is the code snippet.

```
import { NgModule } from'@angular/core';
import { BrowserModule } from'@angular/platform-browser';
import { FormsModule } from'@angular/forms';
import { HttpModule } from'@angular/http';
import { sharedConfig } from'./app.module.shared';
import { MoviesComponent } from'./components/movies/
movies.component';
import { MoviesService } from'./services/movies.service';
import { NewMovieComponent } from'./components/new-movie/
new-movie.component';

@NgModule({
    bootstrap: sharedConfig.bootstrap,
    declarations: [...sharedConfig.declarations,
MoviesComponent, NewMovieComponent],
    imports: [
        BrowserModule,
        FormsModule,
        HttpModule,
        ...sharedConfig.imports
    ],
    providers: [
        { provide: 'ORIGIN_URL', useValue: location.
origin },

        MoviesService
]
    })
export class AppModule {
}
```

Here, I have pasted the code snippet for my movie model, which basically acts as a data carrier here.

```
export class Movie {
    public id: number =null;
    public movieName: string="";
    public directorName: string="";
    public releaseYear: string="";
}
```

I have also updated the service code as well with the post method.

```
import { Injectable } from' @angular/core';
import { Http } from' @angular/http';
import' rxjs/add/operator/map';

@Injectable()
export class MoviesService {

//In order to use any injectable, pass it via ctor
constructor(private http:Http) { }

    getMovies() {
returnthis.http.get('/api/movies')
//Once, we get the response back, it has to get mapped to
json
        .map(res => res.json());
    }

    createMovie(movie) {
returnthis.http.post('/api/movies', movie)
        .map(res => res.json());
    }
}
```

Therefore, these things are pretty straightforward. Now, let's go ahead and see the same in action.

Enter New Movie

Jurassic World

Colin Trevorrow

2015

Submit

As soon as I clicked on Submit, it successfully created one record in db and logged the same in the console as well. You can also see that it also returned the created status as 201.

Now, if I see the list of my movies list, it will appear like this.

Movies List

Movie Name:- Godzilla

◷ Release Year:- 2014 ♟ Director Name:- Gareth Edwards
▥ Movie Reviews:- 3

Movie Name:- Jurassic World

◷ Release Year:- 2015 ♟ Director Name:- Colin Trevorrow
▥ Movie Reviews:- 0

Movie Name:- Avatar

◷ Release Year:- 2017 ♟ Director Name:- James Cameron
▥ Movie Reviews:- 0

Movie Name:- Titanic

◷ Release Year:- 1997 ♟ Director Name:- James Cameron
▥ Movie Reviews:- 0

Movie Name:- Die Another Day

◷ Release Year:- 2002 ♟ Director Name:- Lee Tamahori
▥ Movie Reviews:- 0

Questions

1. What is Angular CLI and why it is useful?
2. How to create a new Component via CLI?
3. How to create a new Module via CLI?
4. What is the command to create a new service?
5. Why services are needed?
6. How to define routes in Angular?
7. Where to register the routes and navigation?

Summary

In this section, we learned a couple of things like how to get started with Angular components and how to fix the scaffolding project in order to align the same with Angular CLI. We first created a component just to list all the movies. We then utilized the ready-made bootstrap form. After this, we created one more action, which was basically to create a new movie. In the next section, we will complete all the CRUD implementation.

CHAPTER 6

Deeper into Angular

Introduction

In the last section, we covered the basics of AngularJS. In this section, we will delve further into enhancing our app by implementing client-side validation. Then, we'll improvise the app by adding toast notifications on different actions. We will also see how to log an error and innovative ways of logging errors. Finally, we will end this chapter by completing our CRUD functionality.

Client-Side Validation

In this section, we will add client-side validation. For the required input fields, I will apply the required attribute of HTML5. I have pasted the code snippet for the movie name.

```
<div class="form-group">
        <input id="movieName" name="movieName" type="text"
class="form-control" required [(ngModel)]="movie.
movieName" #movieName ="ngModel">
        <label for="movieName">Movie Name</label>
        <div class="alert alert-danger" *ngIf="movieName.
touched && !movieName.valid">Please specify the Movie
Name!</div>
    </div>
```

Here, I have also created a separate **div** for outputting error messages. In order to understand whether the control is valid or not, we need to read the control state of the required control. Therefore, whenever we build Angular forms, there is always a control state associated with the input control. This control object knows whether the input field has been touched or the value has been changed or checks whether the value is valid or not.

It also keeps the current value of the object. Since we are using the template-driven form and we have already applied ngModel for data binding, Angular will automatically create the control object for it. In order to fetch this control object, we need to use the **#movie="ngModel"** template variable. When Angular sees this, it will set the movie variable to the control object which is linked to this input field. Here is a glimpse of that. Here, I have just clicked on the movie name and it displayed the following error message:

Enter New Movie

Movie Name

Please specify the Movie Name!

Director Name

Release Year

Submit

Here is the code snippet of the markup.

```
<div class="container">
    <div class="row">
        <form (ngSubmit)="onSubmit(f)" #f="ngForm"
role="form" class="col-md-9 go-right">
        <h2>Enter New Movie</h2>
        <div class="form-group">
            <input id="movieName" name="movieName"
type="text" class="form-control" required
[(ngModel)]="movie.movieName" #movieName="ngModel">
            <label for="movieName">Movie Name</label>
            <div class="alert alert-danger"
*ngIf="movieName.touched && !movieName.valid">Please
specify the Movie Name!</div>
        </div>
        <div class="form-group">
            <input id="directorName" name="directorName"
type="text" class="form-control" required
[(ngModel)]="movie.directorName" #directorName="ngModel">
            <label for="directorName">Director Name</
label>
            <div class="alert alert-danger"
```

```
*ngIf="directorName.touched && !directorName.
valid">Please specify the Director Name!</div>
            </div>
            <div class="form-group">
                <input id="releaseYear" name="releaseYear"
type="text" class="form-control" required
[(ngModel)]="movie.releaseYear" #releaseYear="ngModel">
                <label for="releaseYear">Release Year</
label>
                <div class="alert alert-danger"
*ngIf="releaseYear.touched && !releaseYear.valid">Please
specify the Release Year!</div>
        </div>
        <p class="bg-success" style="padding:10px;margin-
top:20px;clear:both"> <button type="submit" class="btn
btn-primary" [disabled]="!f.valid">Submit</button></p>
        </form>
    </div>
</div>
```

Once done, it will look like this.

Enter New Movie

Movie Name

Please specify the Movie Name!

Director Name

Please specify the Director Name!

Release Year

Please specify the Release Year!

Submit

Now, I will enable this **Submit** button, only when all the fields are valid. I already have the **#f="ngForm"** form variable. We can check the status of the form. Here is the simple code snippet.

```
<pclass="bg-success"style="padding:10px;margin-top:2
```

```
0px;clear:both"><buttontype="submit"class="btn btn-
primary"[disabled]="!f.valid">Submit</button></p>
```

Here, I have used the **[disabled]** attribute binding, which says disable the button until the form becomes valid. With the above change in place, when I see the change, it will appear like this.

Enter New Movie

Movie Name

Director Name

Release Year

Submit

Displaying Toast Notification

Till now, we have been displaying messages on the console. That's good during development. But in the actual production scenario, something more meaningful is required. For this kind of scenario, we will use toast notification. In order to use this, first we need to install it using the **npm install ng2-toasty@2.5.0 --save** command. @2.5.0 is the version, which worked for me. Next, we need to include this ng2-toasty in the vendor bundle to use the same inside application. I have pasted the code snippet for the **webpack.config.vendor.js** file.

```
const path = require('path');
const webpack = require('webpack');
const ExtractTextPlugin = require('extract-text-webpack-
plugin');
const merge = require('webpack-merge');

module.exports = (env) => {
    const extractCSS = new ExtractTextPlugin('vendor.
css');
    const isDevBuild = !(env && env.prod);
    const sharedConfig = {
        stats: { modules: false },
        resolve: { extensions: [ '.js' ] },
        module: {
            rules: [
                { test: /\.(png|woff|woff2|eot|ttf|svg)
(\?|$)/, use: 'url-loader?limit=100000' }
```

```
                ]
            },
            entry: {
                vendor: [
                    '@angular/animations',
                    '@angular/common',
                    '@angular/compiler',
                    '@angular/core',
                    '@angular/forms',
                    '@angular/http',
                    '@angular/platform-browser',
                    '@angular/platform-browser-dynamic',
                    '@angular/router',
                    'bootstrap',
                    'bootstrap/dist/css/bootstrap.css',
                    'es6-shim',
                    'es6-promise',
                    'event-source-polyfill',
                    'ng2-toasty',
                    'ng2-toasty/bundles/style-bootstrap.css',
                    'jquery',
                    'zone.js',
                ]
            },
            output: {
                publicPath: '/dist/',
                filename: '[name].js',
                library: '[name]_[hash]'
            },
            plugins: [
                new webpack.ProvidePlugin({ $: 'jquery',
jQuery: 'jquery' }), // Maps these identifiers to the
jQuery package (because Bootstrap expects it to be a
global variable)
                new webpack.ContextReplacementPlugin(/\@
angular\b.*\b(bundles|linker)/, path.join(__dirname,
'./ClientApp')), // Workaround for https://github.com/
angular/angular/issues/11580
                new webpack.ContextReplacementPlugin(/
angular(\\|\/)core(\\|\/)@angular/, path.join(__dirname,
'./ClientApp')), // Workaround for https://github.com/
angular/angular/issues/14898
                new webpack.IgnorePlugin(/^vertx$/) //
Workaround for https://github.com/stefanpenner/es6-
promise/issues/100
```

```
        ]
    };
    const clientBundleConfig = merge(sharedConfig, {
        output: { path: path.join(__dirname, 'wwwroot',
'dist') },
        module: {
            rules: [
                { test: /\.css(\?|$)/, use: extractCSS.
extract({ use: isDevBuild ? 'css-loader' : 'css-
loader?minimize' }) }
            ]
        },
        plugins: [
            extractCSS,
            new webpack.DllPlugin({
                path: path.join(__dirname, 'wwwroot',
'dist', '[name]-manifest.json'),
                name: '[name]_[hash]'
            })
        ].concat(isDevBuild ? [] : [
            new webpack.optimize.UglifyJsPlugin()
        ])
    });
    const serverBundleConfig = merge(sharedConfig, {
        target: 'node',
        resolve: { mainFields: ['main'] },
        output: {
            path: path.join(__dirname, 'ClientApp',
'dist'),
            libraryTarget: 'commonjs2',
        },
        module: {
            rules: [ { test: /\.css(\?|$)/, use: ['to-
string-loader', isDevBuild ? 'css-loader' : 'css-
loader?minimize' ] } ]
        },
        entry: { vendor: ['aspnet-prerendering'] },
        plugins: [
            new webpack.DllPlugin({
                path: path.join(__dirname, 'ClientApp',
'dist', '[name]-manifest.json'),
                name: '[name]_[hash]'
            })
        ]
```

```
    });
    return [clientBundleConfig, serverBundleConfig];
}
```

Whenever we edit or add anything in the bundle, we need to bundle the command to regenerate the bundle. Before running the bundle, it is recommended that you stop all the IIS processes related to the application else the bundle won't take effect and you will get a weird error. The command that I am going to run is "**webpack --config webpack.config.vendor.js**". On successful completion, it will show the following message:

After this, I will run the **webpack** command to create the main bundle as well. This will also show the confirmation after completion, as shown in the following screenshot.

In order to use this module, we need to add the same to **app.module.shared. ts** as shown below. Before that, I would like to share one tip here. Let's say you are going to use any third party or any Angular module, and you are not aware of the complete list of offerings the module is going to present. You can take a quick look at the library as shown below.

```
import { NgModule } from '@angular/core';
import { RouterModule } from '@angular/router';
import { FormsModule } from '@angular/forms';
import { } from 'ng2-toasty';
import {   ToastyModule                    Class ToastyModule
import {   ToastData                       s/navmenu/navmenu.component';
import {   ToastOptions                    ome/home.component';
import {   ToastyComponent                 nts/fetchdata/fetchdata.component';
import {   ToastyConfig                    s/counter/counter.component';
import {   ToastyEvent                     /movies/movies.component';
import {   ToastyEventType                 ts/new-movie/new-movie.component';
export c   ToastyService
    boot:  providers (in index.d.ts)
    decl   toastyServiceFactory (in toasty.service.d.ts)

        NavMenuComponent,
        CounterComponent,
        FetchDataComponent,
        HomeComponent,
        MoviesComponent,
        NewMovieComponent
    ],
    imports: [
        FormsModule,
        ToastyModule.forRoot(),
        RouterModule.forRoot([
            { path: '', redirectTo: 'home', pathMatch: 'full' },
            { path: 'movies', component: MoviesComponent },
            { path: 'movies/new', component: NewMovieComponent },
            { path: 'home', component: HomeComponent },
            { path: 'counter', component: CounterComponent },
            { path: 'fetch-data', component: FetchDataComponent },
            { path: '**', redirectTo: 'home' }
        ])
    ]
};
```

Here, I have written the imported statement and inside the curly brackets, I have entered "Ctrl + Enter". It gives me an entire list, which is a nice way of delving into the library. This is the power of using static typing over dynamic. Anyways, here I will use **ToastyModule** and import it in our import section. Here is the code snippet for this module.

```
import { NgModule } from '@angular/core';
import { RouterModule } from '@angular/router';
import { FormsModule } from '@angular/forms';
import { ToastyModule } from 'ng2-toasty';
import { AppComponent } from './components/app/app.
component'
import { NavMenuComponent } from './components/navmenu/
navmenu.component';
import { HomeComponent } from './components/home/home.
component';
import { FetchDataComponent } from './components/
fetchdata/fetchdata.component';
import { CounterComponent } from './components/counter/
counter.component';
```

```
import { MoviesComponent } from './components/movies/
movies.component';
import { NewMovieComponent } from './components/new-
movie/new-movie.component';

export const sharedConfig: NgModule = {
    bootstrap: [ AppComponent ],
    declarations: [
            AppComponent,
            NavMenuComponent,
            CounterComponent,
            FetchDataComponent,
            HomeComponent,
            MoviesComponent,
            NewMovieComponent
    ],
    imports: [
            FormsModule,
            ToastyModule.forRoot(),
            RouterModule.forRoot([
                { path: '', redirectTo: 'home',
pathMatch: 'full' },
                { path: 'movies', component:
MoviesComponent },
                { path: 'movies/new', component:
NewMovieComponent },
                { path: 'home', component: HomeComponent
},
                { path: 'counter', component:
CounterComponent },
                { path: 'fetch-data', component:
FetchDataComponent },
                { path: '**', redirectTo: 'home' }
        ])
    ]
};
```

With this, we can inject the toasty module in our components and use it. Here is the code snippet.

```
import { Component, OnInit, ElementRef } from '@angular/
core';
import { NgForm } from '@angular/forms';
import { MoviesService } from '../../services/movies.
service';
import { Movie } from './../../models/movie';
import { ToastyService } from "ng2-toasty";
```

```
@Component({
    selector: 'app-new-movie',
    templateUrl: './new-movie.component.html',
    styleUrls: ['./new-movie.component.css']
})
export class NewMovieComponent implements OnInit {

    movie: Movie =new Movie();
    constructor(private moviesService: MoviesService,
private toastyService:ToastyService) { }
    ngOnInit() {
    }

    onSubmit(form: NgForm) {
        var formData = this.movie;
        formData.id = 0;
        formData.movieName = this.movie.movieName.
toString();
        formData.directorName = this.movie.directorName.
toString();
        formData.releaseYear = this.movie.releaseYear.
toString();
        console.log(formData);
        this.moviesService.createMovie(formData)
            .subscribe(x => {
                this.toastyService.success({
                    title: 'Success',
                    msg: 'New Movie Created!',
                    theme: 'bootstrap',
                    showClose: true,
                    timeout: 5000
                });
            },
                err => {
                    this.toastyService.error({
                        title: 'Error',
                        msg: 'An unexpected error occured
while creating new Movie!',
                        theme: 'bootstrap',
                        showClose: true,
                        timeout: 5000
                    });
                });
    }
}
```

First of all, I have resolved the dependency for toasty, thereafter I have injected it via the constructor so that I can use it. I have used toasty to show both successful and failure scenarios. Now, in order to understand the complete overloaded values of ng2-toasty, I recommend that you check the library at **https://github.com/akserg/ng2-toasty**. Now, to make this work, we need to add something to the DOM, basically to the **app.component.html** file.

```
<ng2-toasty [position]="'bottom-right'"></ng2-toasty>
<div class='container-fluid'>
    <div class='row'>
        <div class='col-sm-3'>
            <nav-menu></nav-menu>
        </div>
        <div class='col-sm-9 body-content'>
            <router-outlet></router-outlet>
        </div>
    </div>
</div>
```

Here, right at the top, I have added one element saying position of toasty and have used the binding property to set the position. With the above change in place, let's test the same.

Enter New Movie

| Top Gun |
| Tony Scott |
| 1986 |

Submit

When you click on Submit, the following toast message appears at the bottom of the screen.

In order to test the failure scenario, I have purposely thrown the exception from API as shown below.

```
[HttpPost("")]
```

```
public int Post([FromBody]Movie movie)
{
      throw new Exception("Some Exception");
      UOW.Movies.Add(movie);
      UOW.Commit();
      return Response.StatusCode = (int)
HttpStatusCode.Created;
}
```

With the above change in place, when I go ahead and test the app, it will display the following error:

Enter New Movie

Titanic

James Cameron

1997

Submit

Error X
An unexpected error occured while creating new Movie!

This was just for demonstration purpose. I will undo my controller change.

Logging Errors

In this section, we will focus on logging errors. It's always a nice idea to log errors at some place that can be easily accessible to developers. Different developers can have different choices of logging errors. But I prefer to use cloud for the same. This is the place where **sentry** comes into picture. This is a cloud system used for storing logs and its super easy to set this up. You can do free registration on the site as an individual user. Once you log in, you will see the following dashboard:

Here, you can click on the New Project button and select the following options as shown below.

On the next page, we will get a variety of options.

When I click on the Frontend tab, it will display the following choices.

Here, I will select the first option and on clicking the tab, it will open the documentation page as shown below.

Configure Angular

Full Documentation

This is a quick getting started guide. For in-depth instructions on integrating Sentry with Angular, view our complete documentation.

Installation

Raven.js should be installed via npm.

```
$ npm install raven-js --save
```

Configuration

Configuration depends on which module loader/packager you are using to build your Angular application.

Below are instructions for SystemJS, followed by instructions for Webpack, Angular CLI, and other module loaders/packagers.

SystemJS

First, configure SystemJS to locate the Raven.js package:

```
System.config({
  packages: {
    /* ...existing package config... */
    'raven-js': {
      main: 'dist/raven.js'
    }
  },
  paths: {
```

The documentation is very easy. However, let me show you how to configure this in our application. First, I will do **npm install raven-js --save** in my web project.

```
C:\Dell\Books\ASPNETCorePlusAngular4\MovieReviewSPA\MovieReviewSPA.web (Another) (MovieReviewSPA_web@0.0.0)
λ npm install raven-js --save
```

Once it gets installed successfully, we need to include it in the **webpack. config.vendor.js** file. Here is the code snippet.

```
const path = require('path');
const webpack = require('webpack');
const ExtractTextPlugin = require('extract-text-webpack-
plugin');
const merge = require('webpack-merge');

module.exports = (env) => {
    const extractCSS = new ExtractTextPlugin('vendor.
css');
    const isDevBuild = !(env && env.prod);
    const sharedConfig = {
        stats: { modules: false },
        resolve: { extensions: [ '.js' ] },
        module: {
            rules: [
                { test: /\.(png|woff|woff2|eot|ttf|svg)
(\?|$)/, use: 'url-loader?limit=100000' }
            ]
        },
        entry: {
            vendor: [
                '@angular/animations',
                '@angular/common',
                '@angular/compiler',
                '@angular/core',
                '@angular/forms',
                '@angular/http',
                '@angular/platform-browser',
                '@angular/platform-browser-dynamic',
                '@angular/router',
                'bootstrap',
                'bootstrap/dist/css/bootstrap.css',
                'es6-shim',
                'es6-promise',
                'event-source-polyfill',
                'ng2-toasty',
```

```
                    'ng2-toasty/bundles/style-bootstrap.css',
                    'jquery',
                    'raven-js',
                    'zone.js',
                ]
        },
        output: {
            publicPath: '/dist/',
            filename: '[name].js',
            library: '[name]_[hash]'
        },
        plugins: [
            new webpack.ProvidePlugin({ $: 'jquery',
jQuery: 'jquery' }), // Maps these identifiers to the
jQuery package (because Bootstrap expects it to be a
global variable)
            new webpack.ContextReplacementPlugin(/\@
angular\b.*\b(bundles|linker)/, path.join(__dirname,
'./ClientApp')), // Workaround for https://github.com/
angular/angular/issues/11580
            new webpack.ContextReplacementPlugin(/
angular(\\|\/)core(\\|\/)@angular/, path.join(__dirname,
'./ClientApp')), // Workaround for https://github.com/
angular/angular/issues/14898
            new webpack.IgnorePlugin(/^vertx$/) //
Workaround for https://github.com/stefanpenner/es6-
promise/issues/100
        ]
    };

    const clientBundleConfig = merge(sharedConfig, {
        output: { path: path.join(__dirname, 'wwwroot',
'dist') },
        module: {
            rules: [
                { test: /\.css(\?|$)/, use: extractCSS.
extract({ use: isDevBuild ? 'css-loader' : 'css-
loader?minimize' }) }
            ]
        },
        plugins: [
            extractCSS,
            new webpack.DllPlugin({
                path: path.join(__dirname, 'wwwroot',
'dist', '[name]-manifest.json'),
                name: '[name]_[hash]'
            })
```

```
    ].concat(isDevBuild ? [] : [
        new webpack.optimize.UglifyJsPlugin()
    ])
});


const serverBundleConfig = merge(sharedConfig, {
    target: 'node',
    resolve: { mainFields: ['main'] },
    output: {
        path: path.join(__dirname, 'ClientApp',
'dist'),
        libraryTarget: 'commonjs2',
    },
    module: {
        rules: [ { test: /\.css(\?|$)/, use: ['to-
string-loader', isDevBuild ? 'css-loader' : 'css-
loader?minimize' ] } ]
    },
    entry: { vendor: ['aspnet-prerendering'] },
    plugins: [
        new webpack.DllPlugin({
            path: path.join(__dirname, 'ClientApp',
'dist', '[name]-manifest.json'),
            name: '[name]_[hash]'
        })
    ]
});


return [clientBundleConfig, serverBundleConfig];
}
```

raven-js is the name of the folder in the nodes module. Since we have added a new vendor to the webpack module, we need to build the webpack again. Therefore, we need to stop all the dotnet processes from the taskbar, and then we need to execute **webpack --config webpack.config.vendor.js**.

Finally, we need to run **webpack** again.

Once done, we can go ahead with the code integration. I have pasted the code snippet for the **app.module.shared.ts** file.

```
import * as Raven from 'raven-js';
import { NgModule } from '@angular/core';
import { RouterModule } from '@angular/router';
import { FormsModule } from '@angular/forms';
import { ToastyModule } from 'ng2-toasty';
import { AppComponent } from './components/app/app.
component'
import { NavMenuComponent } from './components/navmenu/
navmenu.component';
import { HomeComponent } from './components/home/home.
component';
import { FetchDataComponent } from './components/
fetchdata/fetchdata.component';
import { CounterComponent } from './components/counter/
counter.component';
import { MoviesComponent } from './components/movies/
movies.component';
import { NewMovieComponent } from './components/new-
movie/new-movie.component';

Raven

.config('https://7579eaef4acc46bab3ffd87d3d85f3ea@sentry.
io/203240')
        .install();

export const sharedConfig: NgModule = {
        bootstrap: [ AppComponent ],
        declarations: [
            AppComponent,
            NavMenuComponent,
            CounterComponent,
```

```
            FetchDataComponent,
            HomeComponent,
            MoviesComponent,
            NewMovieComponent
        ],
        imports: [
            FormsModule,
            ToastyModule.forRoot(),
            RouterModule.forRoot([
                { path: '', redirectTo: 'home',
pathMatch: 'full' },
                { path: 'movies', component:
MoviesComponent },
                { path: 'movies/new', component:
NewMovieComponent },
                { path: 'home', component: HomeComponent
},
                { path: 'counter', component:
CounterComponent },
                { path: 'fetch-data', component:
FetchDataComponent },
                { path: '**', redirectTo: 'home' }
            ])
        ]
};
```

Here, I have done a couple of things. First, I have imported the Raven to the top in my file and then I have copied the raven setting from the documentation and pasted if before export.

Then, in your main module file (where @NgModule is called, e.g. app.module.ts):

```
import Raven = require('raven-js');
import { BrowserModule } from '@angular/platform-browser';
import { NgModule, ErrorHandler } from '@angular/core';
import { AppComponent } from './app.component';

Raven
  .config('https://7579eaef4acc46bab3ffd87d3d85f3ea@sentry.io/203240')
  .install();

export class RavenErrorHandler implements ErrorHandler {
  handleError(err:any) : void {
    Raven.captureException(err.originalError || err);
  }
}

@NgModule({
  imports: [ BrowserModule ],
  declarations: [ AppComponent ],
  bootstrap: [ AppComponent ],
  providers: [ { provide: ErrorHandler, useClass: RavenErrorHandler } ]
})
export class AppModule { }
```

You can also get this Url from the project settings. Make sure to use the public key. Next, we will go to our **new-movie-component.ts** file and make the following changes as shown below.

```
import * as Raven from 'raven-js';
import { Component, OnInit, ElementRef } from '@angular/
core';
import { NgForm } from '@angular/forms';
import { MoviesService } from '../../services/movies.
service';
import { Movie } from './../../models/movie';
import { ToastyService } from "ng2-toasty";

@Component({
        selector: 'app-new-movie',
        templateUrl: './new-movie.component.html',
        styleUrls: ['./new-movie.component.css']
})
export class NewMovieComponent implements OnInit {

        movie: Movie =new Movie();
        constructor(private moviesService: MoviesService,
private toastyService:ToastyService) { }
        ngOnInit() {
        }

        onSubmit(form: NgForm) {
            var formData = this.movie;
            formData.id = 0;
            formData.movieName = this.movie.movieName.
toString();
            formData.directorName = this.movie.
directorName.toString();
            formData.releaseYear = this.movie.
releaseYear.toString();
            console.log(formData);
            this.moviesService.createMovie(formData)
                .subscribe(x => {
                    console.log(x);
            this.toastyService.success({
                title: 'Success',
                msg: 'New Movie Created!',
                theme: 'bootstrap',
                showClose: true,
                timeout: 5000
            });
        },
        err => {
            Raven.captureException(err.originalError ||
err);
                        this.toastyService.error({
                            title: 'Error',
```

```
                    msg: 'An unexpected error occured
while creating new Movie!',
                    theme: 'bootstrap',
                    showClose: true,
                    timeout: 5000
            });
        });
    }
}
```

This code is pretty straightforward. First, I have imported raven-js in my file and then used it under the error block to log the error. First, I am trying to capture the original error. If that is null, then the actual error object itself; I am logging. In order to test this, I will throw an exception purposely from my controller as shown below.

```
// Create a new movie
        // POST /api/movies
        [HttpPost("")]
        public int Post([FromBody]Movie movie)
        {
            throw new Exception("Some Exception");
            UOW.Movies.Add(movie);
            UOW.Commit();
            return Response.StatusCode = (int)
HttpStatusCode.Created;
        }
```

With the above change in place, when I go ahead and run the app and try to add the new movie, it will display the following toasty message and also log the error in sentry.

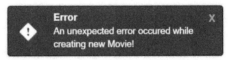

Now, under the dashboard, we can see the error as shown below.

Select a project ∨		
ORGANIZATION	**Assigned to me**	View more ⟲
Dashboard		
Projects & Teams	No issues have been assigned to you.	
Stats		
	New this week	⟲
ISSUES		
Assigned to Me	⊕ Response with status: 500 Internal Server Error for URL: http://localho...	
Bookmarks	Movie-Review-SPA	
History	**Recent activity**	⟲
MANAGE	Nothing to show here, move along.	
Members		

When I click on it, it will display the detailed error as shown below.

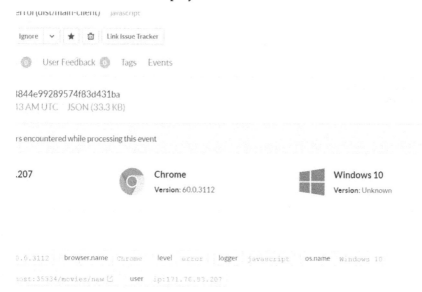

error (dist/main-client)   javascript

Ignore   ∨   ★   🗑   Link Issue Tracker

User Feedback   Tags   Events

8844e99289574f83d431ba
13 AM UTC   JSON (33.3 KB)

rs encountered while processing this event

.207   Chrome   Windows 10
                    Version: 60.0.3112   Version: Unknown

0.0.3112   browser.name Chrome   level error   logger   javascript   os.name Windows 10
host:35334/movies/new   user   ip:171.76.93.207

Therefore, this is great way of logging exceptions in your application.

Editing a Movie

In this section, we will go ahead and create another action for editing a movie. This will be very similar to creating a new movie. For editing a movie, we need a link from some page where movieId gets passed in the route. In order to achieve this, we can add the links to the movie list page itself. I have pasted the improvised code snippet for **movies.component.html**.

```html
<h3>Movies List</h3>
<form>
    <div class="container">
        <div class="row">
            <div class="row">
                <div class="col-xs-12 col-sm-9 col-md-9">
                    <div class="list-group">
                        <div class="list-group-item">
                            <div class="row-content"
*ngFor="let m of movies">
                                <div class="list-group-
item-heading">
                                    <a href="#"
title="movieName">
                                        <small>Movie
Name: {{m.movieName}}</small>
                                    </a>
```

```
                                        </div>
                                        <small>
                                            <i class="glyphicon
glyphicon-time"></i> Release Year: {{m.releaseYear}}
                                            <i class="glyphicon
glyphicon-user"></i> Director Name: {{m.directorName}}
                                            <br>
                                            <span class="btn btn-
info"><i class="glyphicon glyphicon-th"></i> <a href="#"
style="color: black">Movie Reviews: {{m.noOfReviews}} </
a></span>
                                            <span class="btn
btn-primary"><i class="glyphicon glyphicon-edit"></i> <a
href="#" style="color: black">Edit Movie </a></span>
                                            <span class="btn btn-
danger"><i class="glyphicon glyphicon-remove"></i> <a
href="#" style="color: black">Delete Movie </a></span>
                                        </small>
                                        <hr>
                                    </div>
                                </div>
                            </div>
                        </div>
                    </div>
                </div>
            </div>
        </div>
    </div>
</form>
```

Here, I have just added two buttons for editing and deleting the movie and made some style changes. For editing a movie, we will need the edit movie component. I have created the component here.

```
Cmder                                                              —  □  ×

C:\Dell\Books\ASPNETCorePlusAngular4\MovieReviewSPA\MovieReviewSPA.web (Another) (MovieReviewSPA_web@0.0.0)
λ cd ClientApp\app\components\

C:\Dell\Books\ASPNETCorePlusAngular4\MovieReviewSPA\MovieReviewSPA.web\ClientApp\app\components (Another)
λ ng g c edit-movie
installing component
  create ClientApp\app\components\edit-movie\edit-movie.component.css
  create ClientApp\app\components\edit-movie\edit-movie.component.html
  create ClientApp\app\components\edit-movie\edit-movie.component.spec.ts
  create ClientApp\app\components\edit-movie\edit-movie.component.ts
  update ClientApp\app\app.module.ts

C:\Dell\Books\ASPNETCorePlusAngular4\MovieReviewSPA\MovieReviewSPA.web\ClientApp\app\components (Another)
λ
```

Note: One point to note here is that **app.module.ts** might get updated by the wrong path. Hence, you need to fix that path manually. I have pasted the code snippet below.

```
import { NgModule } from '@angular/core';
import { BrowserModule } from '@angular/platform-
browser';
import { FormsModule } from '@angular/forms';
import { HttpModule } from '@angular/http';
import { sharedConfig } from './app.module.shared';
import { MoviesComponent } from './components/movies/
movies.component';
import { MoviesService } from './services/movies.
service';
import { NewMovieComponent } from './components/new-
movie/new-movie.component';
import { EditMovieComponent } from './components/edit-
movie/edit-movie.component';

@NgModule({
    bootstrap: sharedConfig.bootstrap,
    declarations: [...sharedConfig.declarations,
MoviesComponent, NewMovieComponent, EditMovieComponent],
    imports: [
        BrowserModule,
        FormsModule,
        HttpModule,
        ...sharedConfig.imports
    ],
    providers: [
        { provide: 'ORIGIN_URL', useValue: location.
origin },
        MoviesService
    ]
})
export class AppModule {
}
```

At this moment, components look like this.

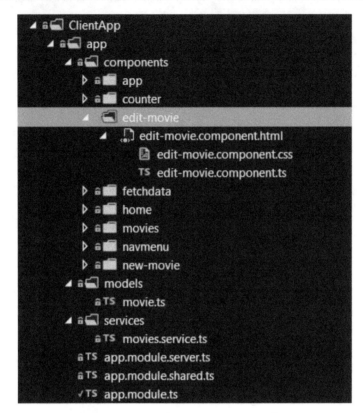

In order to get to this page, we will need route. Therefore, we need to go to the **app.module.shared.ts** file and make the following changes.

```
import * as Raven from 'raven-js';
import { NgModule } from '@angular/core';
import { RouterModule } from '@angular/router';
import { FormsModule } from '@angular/forms';
import { ToastyModule } from 'ng2-toasty';
import { AppComponent } from './components/app/app.
component'
import { NavMenuComponent } from './components/navmenu/
navmenu.component';
import { HomeComponent } from './components/home/home.
component';
import { FetchDataComponent } from './components/
fetchdata/fetchdata.component';
import { CounterComponent } from './components/counter/
counter.component';
import { MoviesComponent } from './components/movies/
movies.component';
import { NewMovieComponent } from './components/new-
movie/new-movie.component';
```

```
import { EditMovieComponent } from './components/edit-
movie/edit-movie.component';
import { MoviesService } from './services/movies.
service';

Raven

.config('https://7579eaef4acc46bab3ffd87d3d85f3ea@sentry.
io/203240')
    .install();

export const sharedConfig: NgModule = {
        bootstrap: [ AppComponent ],
        declarations: [
            AppComponent,
            NavMenuComponent,
            CounterComponent,
            FetchDataComponent,
            HomeComponent,
            MoviesComponent,
            NewMovieComponent,
            EditMovieComponent
        ],
    imports: [
        FormsModule,
        ToastyModule.forRoot(),
        RouterModule.forRoot([
            { path: '', redirectTo: 'home', pathMatch:
'full' },
            { path: 'movies', component: MoviesComponent
},
            { path: 'movies/new', component:
NewMovieComponent },
            { path: 'movies/:id', component:
EditMovieComponent },
            { path: 'home', component: HomeComponent },
            { path: 'counter', component: CounterComponent
},
            { path: 'fetch-data', component: FetchDataComponent },
            { path: '**', redirectTo: 'home' }
        ])
    ],
    providers: [MoviesService]
};
```

Now, we go to the **edit-movie.component.ts** file and make the following changes.

```
import { Component, OnInit } from '@angular/core';
import { ActivatedRoute, Router } from '@angular/router';
import { Movie } from './../../models/movie';
import { MoviesService } from '../../services/movies.
service';

@Component({
    selector: 'app-edit-movie',
    templateUrl: './edit-movie.component.html',
    styleUrls: ['./edit-movie.component.css']
})
export class EditMovieComponent implements OnInit {
    movie: Movie = new Movie();

constructor(private route: ActivatedRoute,
        private router: Router, private moviesService:
MoviesService) {
        route.params.subscribe(p => {
            this.movie.id = +p['id'];
        });
    }
    ngOnInit() {
        if (this.movie.id) {
            this.moviesService.getMovie(this.movie.id)
                .subscribe(m => {
                    this.movie = m;
                },
                err => {
                    if (err.status == 404) {
                        this.router.navigate(['/not-
found']);
                    }
                });
        }
    }
}
```

Let me explain the code here. First, in the constructor, I have added the reference to the activated route. We can use this to read the route parameters. And then, I have added router to help the user navigate to different pages if route doesn't match or if the user passes an invalid id. Next, in the constructor, I have subscribed to the **route.params** observable. This is the place where we get the parameters. Here, I have used the + symbol just to convert the incoming id to the number.

Then, I have created a method in my existing service to fetch the movie by its id. Here is the code snippet.

```
import { Injectable } from '@angular/core';
import { Http } from '@angular/http';
import 'rxjs/add/operator/map';

@Injectable()
export class MoviesService {
        //In order to use any injectable, pass it via
ctor
        constructor(private http:Http) { }

        getMovies() {
            return this.http.get('/api/movies')
            //Once, we get the response back, it has to
get mapped to json
            .map(res => res.json());
    }

    createMovie(movie) {
        return this.http.post('/api/movies', movie)
            .map(res => res.json());
    }
    getMovie(id) {
        return this.http.get('/api/movies/' + id)
            .map(res => res.json());
    }
}
```

The **edit-movie-component.html** markup looks exactly the same as the new movie markup. Here is the code snippet for the markup.

```
import { Component, OnInit } from '@angular/core';
import { ActivatedRoute, Router } from '@angular/router';
import { Movie } from './../../models/movie';
import { MoviesService } from '../../services/movies.
service';

@Component({
    selector: 'app-edit-movie',
    templateUrl: './edit-movie.component.html',
    styleUrls: ['./edit-movie.component.css']
})
export class EditMovieComponent implements OnInit {
    movie: Movie = new Movie();
    constructor(private route: ActivatedRoute,
        private router: Router, private moviesService:
MoviesService) {
        route.params.subscribe(p => {
            this.movie.id = +p['id'];
```

```
        });
    }

    ngOnInit() {
        if (this.movie.id) {
            this.moviesService.getMovie(this.movie.id)
                .subscribe(m => {
                        this.movie = m;
                    },
                    err => {
                        if (err.status == 404) {
                            this.router.navigate(['/not-found']);
                        }
                    });
        }
    }
}
```

Similarly, the corresponding CSS file

```
@import url(http://fonts.googleapis.com/
css?family=Open+Sans:400,600);

.form-control {
    background: transparent;
}

form {
    width: 320px;
    margin: 20px;
}
    form > div {
        position: relative;
        overflow: hidden;
    }
    form input, form textarea {
        width: 100%;
        border: 2px solid gray;
        background: none;
        position: relative;
        top: 0;
        left: 0;
        z-index: 1;
        padding: 8px 12px;
        outline: 0;
    }
```

```
    form input:valid, form textarea:valid {
        background: white;
    }

    form input:focus, form textarea:focus {
        border-color: #357EBD;
    }

        form input:focus + label, form textarea:focus + label {
            background: #357EBD;
            color: white;
            font-size: 70%;
            padding: 1px 6px;
            z-index: 2;
            text-transform: uppercase;
        }
form label {
    -webkit-transition: background 0.2s, color 0.2s,
top 0.2s, bottom 0.2s, right 0.2s, left 0.2s;
    transition: background 0.2s, color 0.2s, top
0.2s, bottom 0.2s, right 0.2s, left 0.2s;
    position: absolute;
    color: #999;
    padding: 7px 6px;
    font-weight: normal;
}

form textarea {
    display: block;
    resize: vertical;
}

form.go-bottom input, form.go-bottom textarea {
    padding: 12px 12px 12px 12px;
}

form.go-bottom label {
    top: 0;
    bottom: 0;
    left: 0;
    width: 100%;
}
form.go-bottom input:focus, form.go-bottom
textarea:focus {
    padding: 4px 6px 20px 6px;
}

        form.go-bottom input:focus + label, form.go-
```

```
bottom textarea:focus + label {
           top: 100%;
           margin-top:16px;
       }

   form.go-right label {
       border-radius: 0 5px 5px 0;
       height: 100%;
       top: 0;
       right: 100%;
       width: 100%;
       margin-right:100%;
   }
   form.go-right input:focus + label, form.go-right
textarea:focus + label {
       right: 0;
       margin-right: 0;
       width: 40%;
       padding-top: 5px;
   }
```

I have also made a minor change in the movies.component.html file. Here, I have introduced the router link. Here is the code snippet for the markup.

```
<h3>Movies List</h3>
<form>
    <div class="container">
        <div class="row">
            <div class="row">
                <div class="col-xs-12 col-sm-9 col-md-9">
                    <div class="list-group">
                        <div class="list-group-item">
                            <div class="row-content"
*ngFor="let m of movies">
                                <div class="list-group-item-
heading">
                                    <a href="#"
title="movieName">
                                        <small>Movie Name:
{{m.movieName}}</small>
                                    </a>
                                </div>
                                <small>
                                    <i class="glyphicon
glyphicon-time"></i> Release Year: {{m.releaseYear}}
                                    <i class="glyphicon
```

```
glyphicon-user"></i> Director Name: {{m.directorName}}
                                <br>
                                <span class="btn btn-info"><i
class="glyphicon glyphicon-th"></i> <a href="#" style="color:
black">Movie Reviews: {{m.noOfReviews}} </a></span>
                                <span class="btn btn-
primary"><i class="glyphicon glyphicon-edit"></i>
<a [routerLink]="['/movies/', m.id]" style="color:
black">Edit Movie </a></span>
                                <span class="btn btn-
danger"><i class="glyphicon glyphicon-remove"></i> <a
href="#" style="color: black">Delete Movie </a></span>
                            </small>
                            <hr>
                        </div>
                    </div>
                </div>
            </div>
        </div>
    </div>
</form>
```

With the above change in place, when I go ahead and test my app, it will look like this.

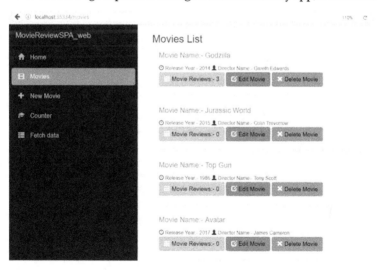

Here, if I hover over any movie, it will appear as shown below.

localhost:35334/movies/4

Basically, the route appears at the bottom of the page. Therefore, when I click on the link, it will take me to the corresponding page as shown below.

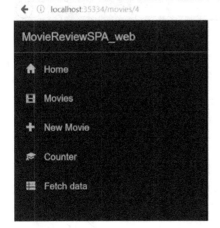

Now, we need to implement the submit action. In order to do this, first we need to make the following changes in the **edit-movie-component.ts** file.

```
import * as Raven from 'raven-js';
import { Component, OnInit } from '@angular/core';
import { ActivatedRoute, Router } from '@angular/router';
import { Movie } from './../../models/movie';
import { MoviesService } from '../../services/movies.
service';
import { ToastyService } from "ng2-toasty";

@Component({
    selector: 'app-edit-movie',
    templateUrl: './edit-movie.component.html',
    styleUrls: ['./edit-movie.component.css']
})
export class EditMovieComponent implements OnInit {
    movie: Movie = new Movie();

    constructor(private route: ActivatedRoute,
        private router: Router, private moviesService:
MoviesService, private toastyService: ToastyService) {
        route.params.subscribe(p => {
            this.movie.id = +p['id'];
        });
}

ngOnInit() {
    if (this.movie.id) {
        this.moviesService.getMovie(this.movie.id)
            .subscribe(m => {
                this.movie = m;
            },
            err => {
                if (err.status == 404) {
```

```
                    this.router.navigate(['/']);
                }
            });
    }
}
onSubmit() {
    if (this.movie.id) {
        this.moviesService.updateMovie(this.movie)
            .subscribe(x => {
                console.log(x);
                this.toastyService.success({
                    title: 'Success',
                    msg: 'Movie Updated!',
                    theme: 'bootstrap',
                    showClose: true,
                    timeout: 5000
                });
                this.router.navigate(['/movies'])
            },
            err => {
Raven.captureException(err.originalError || err);
                this.toastyService.error({
                    title: 'Error',
                    msg: 'An unexpected error while
updating the record!',
                    theme: 'bootstrap',
                        showClose: true,
                        timeout: 5000
                });
            });
        }
    }
}
```

This is a fairly simple code. Here, first I am grabbing the route param value and then checking whether the value exists. Then on loading, it should fetch all the data related to the movie against that id. Afterwards, if the user wants to edit the movie, then the user can use the **onSumbit()** function.

Here, on successful action, it redirects this page to the movies list else it logs the error message. Here, I have also created a new method in service just to call my updated API. I made the following changes in the **movie.service.ts** file.

```
import { Injectable } from '@angular/core';
import { Http } from '@angularv/http';
import 'rxjs/add/operator/map';

@Injectable()
```

```
export class MoviesService {

    //In order to use any injectable, pass it via ctor
    constructor(private http:Http) { }

    getMovies() {
        return this.http.get('/api/movies')
            //Once, we get the response back, it has to
get mapped to json
            .map(res => res.json());
    }

    createMovie(movie) {
        return this.http.post('/api/movies', movie)
            .map(res => res.json());
    }

    getMovie(id) {
        return this.http.get('/api/movies/' + id)
            .map(res => res.json());
    }
    updateMovie(movie) {
        return this.http.put('/api/movies/', movie)
            .map(res => res.json());
    }
}
```

With the above change in place, when I go ahead and test the app, it will look like this.

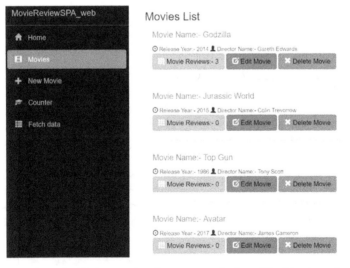

Here, when I click on the first record, it will display the following screenshot:

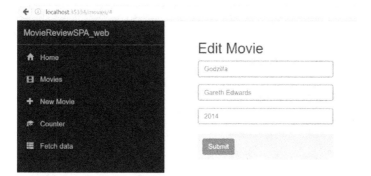

Now, I will go ahead and change the release year from **2014** to **2016**.

When I click on the Submit button, it will show the following toast message and get redirected to the movies list page.

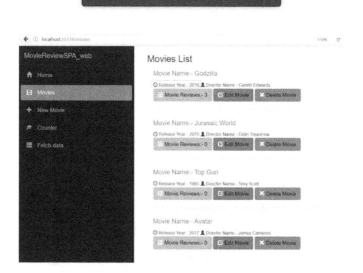

Fixing Multiple selections

In this section, we will fix multiple selections of menus. This problem occurs after we introduce two routes with **movies** and **movies/new**. As soon as I select the **New-Movie** route, both the links get activated.

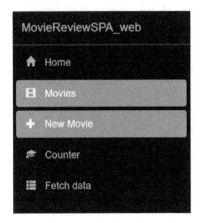 

The reason for this is that both the links start from the same route **movies**. Therefore, in order to fix this issue, we need to apply **[routerLinkActiveOptions] ="{exact:true}"** to the navmenu item as shown below. Here we are saying that we need to activate the link only when the route matches. Here is the code snippet for the **navmenu.component.html** page.

```
<div class='main-nav'>
    <div class='navbar navbar-inverse'>
        <div class='navbar-header'>
            <button type='button' class='navbar-toggle'
data-toggle='collapse' data-target='.navbar-collapse'>
                <span class='sr-only'>Toggle navigation</
span>
                <span class='icon-bar'></span>
                <span class='icon-bar'></span>
                <span class='icon-bar'></span>
            </button>
            <a class='navbar-brand' [routerLink]="['/
home']">MovieReviewSPA_web</a>
        </div>
        <div class='clearfix'></div>
        <div class='navbar-collapse collapse'>
        <ul class='nav navbar-nav'>
            <li [routerLinkActive]="['link-active']">
                <a [routerLink]="['/home']">
                    <span class='glyphicon glyphicon-
home'></span> Home
                </a>
```

```
                    </li>
                    <li [routerLinkActive]="['link-active']"
[routerLinkActiveOptions]="{exact:true}">
                        <a [routerLink]="['/movies']">
                            <span class='glyphicon glyphicon-
film'></span> Movies
                        </a>
                    </li>
                    <li [routerLinkActive]="['link-active']">
                        <a [routerLink]="['/movies/new']">
                            <span class='glyphicon glyphicon-
plus'></span> New Movie
                        </a>
                    </li>
                    <li [routerLinkActive]="['link-active']">
                        <a [routerLink]="['/counter']">
                            <span class='glyphicon glyphicon-
education'></span> Counter
                        </a>
                    </li>
                    <li [routerLinkActive]="['link-active']">
                        <a [routerLink]="['/fetch-data']">
                            <span class='glyphicon glyphicon-
th-list'></span> Fetch data
                        </a>
                    </li>
                </ul>
            </div>
        </div>
</div>
```

With the above change in place, when I go ahead and test the app again, it behaves normally as shown below.

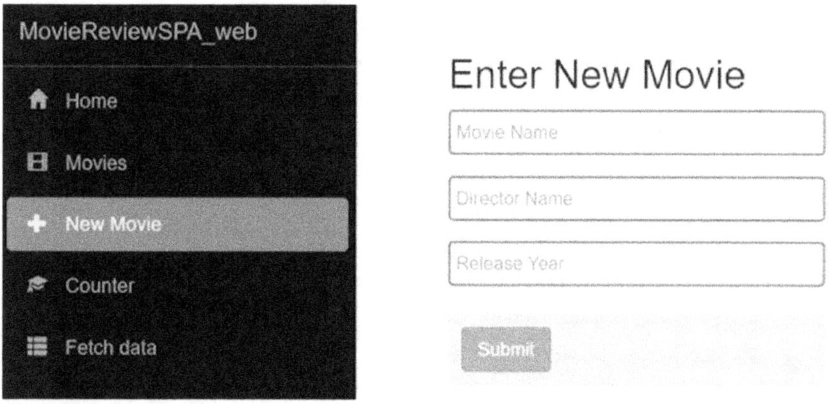

Removing a Movie

In this section, we will implement the Remove Movie feature. This is also a straightforward feature. I have pasted the code snippet for the markup. I have done the improvisation in the **movies.component.html** file.

```html
<h3>Movies List</h3>
<form>
    <div class="container">
        <div class="row">
            <div class="row">
                <div class="col-xs-12 col-sm-9 col-md-9">
                    <div class="list-group">
                        <div class="list-group-item">
                            <div class="row-content" *ngFor="let m of movies">
                                <div class="list-group-item-heading">
                                    <a href="#" title="movieName">
                                        <small>Movie Name: {{m.movieName}}</small>
                                    </a>
                                </div>
                                <small>
                                    <i class="glyphicon glyphicon-time"></i> Release Year: {{m.releaseYear}}
                                    <i class="glyphicon glyphicon-user"></i> Director Name: {{m.directorName}}
                                    <br>
                                    <span class="btn btn-info"><i class="glyphicon glyphicon-th"></i> <a href="#" style="color: black">Movie Reviews: {{m.noOfReviews}} </a></span>
                                    <span class="btn btn-primary"><i class="glyphicon glyphicon- edit"></i> <a [routerLink]="['/movies/', m.id]" style="color: black">Edit Movie </a></span>
                                    <button class="btn btn-danger" style="color: black" type="button" (click)="delete(m.id)"><i class="glyphicon glyphicon-remove"></i> Delete Movie</button>
                                </small>
                                <hr>
                            </div>
                        </div>
```

```
                </div>
              </div>
            </div>
          </div>
       </div>
    </div>
</form>
```

Basically, for the delete action, I have introduced a button with the delete method that takes the id as a parameter and I have made the corresponding changes in the **movies.component.ts** file.

```typescript
import * as Raven from 'raven-js';
import { Component, OnInit } from '@angular/core';
import { MoviesService } from '../../services/movies.
service';
import { Router } from '@angular/router';
import { ToastyService } from "ng2-toasty";

@Component({
    selector: 'app-movies',
    templateUrl: './movies.component.html',
    styleUrls: ['./movies.component.css']
})
export class MoviesComponent implements OnInit {

    movies;
    movie: {};
    constructor(
        private moviesService: MoviesService, private
router: Router, private toastyService: ToastyService) {
    }
    ngOnInit() {
        this.moviesService.getMovies().subscribe(movies
=> {
            this.movies = movies;
            console.log("Movies: ", this.movies);
        });
}

submit() {
    this.moviesService.createMovie(this.movie)
        .subscribe(x => console.log(x));
}

delete(id) {
    if (confirm("Are you sure?")) {
        this.moviesService.deleteMovie(id)
```

```
            .subscribe(x => {
                this.toastyService.success({
                    title: 'Success',
                    msg: 'Movie Deleted!',
                    theme: 'bootstrap',
                    showClose: true,
                    timeout: 5000
                });
                this.router.navigate(['/home']);
            },
            err => {

Raven.captureException(err.originalError || err);
                this.toastyService.error({
                    title: 'Error',
                    msg: 'An unexpected error while
deleting the record!',
                    theme: 'bootstrap',
                    showClose: true,
                    timeout: 5000
                });
            });
        }
    }
}
```

The code is pretty straightforward and self-explanatory. Here, I have first imported all the required imports at the top, then injected my service, router and toasty there. Lastly, I have made the API call to delete the record. This again contains both the success and failure scenarios. There is a corresponding service change as well. Here is the code snippet for the same.

```
import { Injectable } from '@angular/core';
import { Http } from '@angular/http';
import 'rxjs/add/operator/map';

@Injectable()
export class MoviesService {

    //In order to use any injectable, pass it via ctor
    constructor(private http:Http) { }

    getMovies() {
        return this.http.get('/api/movies')
            //Once, we get the response back, it has to
get mapped to json
            .map(res => res.json());
```

```
    }

    createMovie(movie) {
        return this.http.post('/api/movies', movie)
            .map(res => res.json());
    }

    getMovie(id) {
        return this.http.get('/api/movies/' + id)
            .map(res => res.json());
    }

    updateMovie(movie) {
        return this.http.put('/api/movies/', movie)
            .map(res => res.json());
    }
    deleteMovie(id) {
        return this.http.delete('/api/movies/' + id)
            .map(res => res.json());
    }
}
```

With the above change in place, when I go ahead and test my app, it behaves as shown below. Here, when I click on the delete button next to the **Titanic** movie, it pops up a simple JavaScript confirmation box. Currently, I have just kept the simple JavaScript confirmation box here. I might replace it with a beautiful bootstrap class later on. But for now, this is fine.

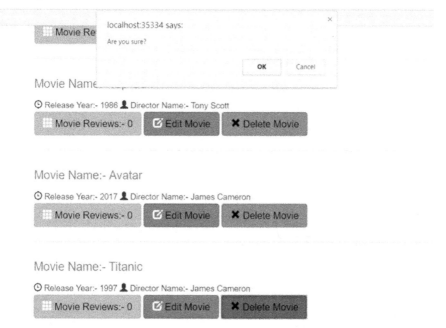

On clicking Ok, it will delete the record and get redirected to the home page.

Questions

1. How to enable Client Side Validations in Angular Form?
2. What are the steps involved to install third part libraries?
3. How to wire up toast notifications with the application?
4. How to log errors?
5. How to fix multiple selection scenario?
6. How do you make sure that toast notification should appear at bottom right?

Summary

In this section, we extended Angular to Movies' CRUD functionality. Here, we started with creating client-side validation and then introduced toast notification as well. We also saw innovative and clean ways of logging errors. Then, we covered other functionalities like editing and deleting a movie. Apart from this, we also saw how to get rid of multiple menu selections.

CHAPTER 7

Adding More Features using Angular

Introduction

In the last section, we have implemented one set of CRUD Operations using AngularJS. In this section, we will delve further into enhancing our app by implementing similar features to reviews first and then implementing different features like filtering, paging, sorting and other related options to make the app more robust and user friendly. Hence, without wasting time, let's get started.

Listing reviews

In this section, we will create the Reviews feature. First of all, we need to create components around the same.

```
C:\Dell\Books\ASPNETCorePlusAngular4\MovieReviewSPA\MovieReviewSPA.web (Another) (MovieReviewSPA_web@0.0.0)
λ cd ClientApp\app\components\

C:\Dell\Books\ASPNETCorePlusAngular4\MovieReviewSPA\MovieReviewSPA.web\ClientApp\app\components (Another)
λ ng g c reviews
installing component
  create ClientApp\app\components\reviews\reviews.component.css
  create ClientApp\app\components\reviews\reviews.component.html
  create ClientApp\app\components\reviews\reviews.component.spec.ts
  create ClientApp\app\components\reviews\reviews.component.ts
  update ClientApp\app\app.module.ts

C:\Dell\Books\ASPNETCorePlusAngular4\MovieReviewSPA\MovieReviewSPA.web\ClientApp\app\components (Another)
λ
```

Now, I will go ahead and fix the app.module.ts file with correct references as auto resolve updates the wrong references here.

```
import { NgModule } from '@angular/core';
import { BrowserModule } from '@angular/platform-
browser';
import { FormsModule } from '@angular/forms';
import { HttpModule } from '@angular/http';
import { sharedConfig } from './app.module.shared';
import { MoviesComponent } from './components/movies/
movies.component';
import { MoviesService } from './services/movies.
service';
import { NewMovieComponent } from './components/new-
movie/new-movie.component';
import { EditMovieComponent } from './components/edit-
movie/edit-movie.component';
import { NotFoundComponent } from './components/not-
found/not-found.component';
import { ReviewsComponent } from './components/reviews/
reviews.component';

@NgModule({
    bootstrap: sharedConfig.bootstrap,
    declarations: [...sharedConfig.declarations,
MoviesComponent, NewMovieComponent, EditMovieComponent,
NotFoundComponent, ReviewsComponent],
    imports: [
        BrowserModule,
        FormsModule,
        HttpModule,
        ...sharedConfig.imports
    ],
    providers: [
        { provide: 'ORIGIN_URL', useValue: location.
origin },
        MoviesService
    ]
})
export class AppModule {
}
```

Then, I will go ahead and delete the test file as it's not needed. Now, I will go ahead and create another service that will be dedicated for movie reviews using the **ng g s movie-reviews** command.

```
C:\Dell\Books\ASPNETCorePlusAngular4\MovieReviewSPA\MovieReviewSPA.web\ClientApp\app\services (Another)
λ ng g s reviews
installing service
   create ClientApp\app\services\reviews.service.spec.ts
   create ClientApp\app\services\reviews.service.ts
   WARNING Service is generated but not provided, it must be provided to be used

C:\Dell\Books\ASPNETCorePlusAngular4\MovieReviewSPA\MovieReviewSPA.web\ClientApp\app\services (Another)
λ
```

I will now register the service with the module as shown below.

```
import { NgModule } from '@angular/core';
import { BrowserModule } from '@angular/platform-
browser';
import { FormsModule } from '@angular/forms';
import { HttpModule } from '@angular/http';
import { sharedConfig } from './app.module.shared';
import { MoviesComponent } from './components/movies/
movies.component';
import { MoviesService } from './services/movies.
service';
import { ReviewsService } from './services/reviews.
service';
import { NewMovieComponent } from './components/new-
movie/new-movie.component';
import { EditMovieComponent } from './components/edit-
movie/edit-movie.component';
import { NotFoundComponent } from './components/not-
found/not-found.component';
import { ReviewsComponent } from './components/reviews/
reviews.component';

@NgModule({
    bootstrap: sharedConfig.bootstrap,
    declarations: [...sharedConfig.declarations,
MoviesComponent, NewMovieComponent, EditMovieComponent,
NotFoundComponent, ReviewsComponent],
    imports: [
        BrowserModule,
        FormsModule,
        HttpModule,
        ...sharedConfig.imports
    ],
    providers: [
        { provide: 'ORIGIN_URL', useValue: location.
origin },
```

```
        MoviesService,
        ReviewsService
    ]
})
export class AppModule {
}
```

Similarly, we need to make changes in the **app.module.shared.ts** file to include the new route. Here is the code snippet.

```
import * as Raven from 'raven-js';
import { NgModule } from '@angular/core';
import { RouterModule } from '@angular/router';
import { FormsModule } from '@angular/forms';
import { ToastyModule } from 'ng2-toasty';
import { AppComponent } from './components/app/app.
component'
import { NavMenuComponent } from './components/navmenu/
navmenu.component';
import { HomeComponent } from './components/home/home.component';
import { FetchDataComponent } from './components/
fetchdata/fetchdata.component';
import { CounterComponent } from './components/counter/
counter.component';
import { MoviesComponent } from './components/movies/
movies.component';
import { ReviewsComponent } from './components/reviews/
reviews.component';
import { NewMovieComponent } from './components/new-
movie/new-movie.component';
import { EditMovieComponent } from './components/edit-
movie/edit-movie.component';
import { MoviesService } from './services/movies.service';
import { ReviewsService } from './services/reviews.service';

Raven

.config('https://7579eaef4acc46bab3ffd87d3d85f3ea@sentry.
io/203240')
    .install();

export const sharedConfig: NgModule = {
    bootstrap: [ AppComponent ],
    declarations: [
        AppComponent,
        NavMenuComponent,
        CounterComponent,
        FetchDataComponent,
```

```
        HomeComponent,
        MoviesComponent,
        NewMovieComponent,
        EditMovieComponent,
        ReviewsComponent
    ],
    imports: [
        FormsModule,
        ToastyModule.forRoot(),
        RouterModule.forRoot([
            { path: '', redirectTo: 'home', pathMatch:
'full' },
            { path: 'movies', component: MoviesComponent
},
            { path: 'movies/new', component: NewMovieComponent },
            { path: 'movies/:id', component: EditMovieComponent },
            { path: 'reviews/:id', component: ReviewsComponent },
            { path: 'home', component: HomeComponent },
            { path: 'counter', component: CounterComponent },
            { path: 'fetch-data', component: FetchDataComponent },
            { path: '**', redirectTo: 'home' }
        ])
    ],
    providers: [MoviesService, ReviewsService]
};
```

After this, I have implemented my reviews service to fetch reviews associated with movie as shown below.

```
import { Injectable } from '@angular/core';
import { Http } from '@angular/http';
import 'rxjs/add/operator/map';

@Injectable()
export class ReviewsService {

    constructor(private http: Http) { }

    getReviewById(id) {
        return this.http.get('/api/moviereviews/' + id)
            .map(res => res.json());
    }
}
```

Similarly, to consume the same, I have made corresponding changes in my **reviews.component.ts** file as shown below.

```
import * as Raven from 'raven-js';
import { Component, OnInit } from '@angular/core';
import { ReviewsService } from '../../services/reviews.service';
import { Router, ActivatedRoute } from '@angular/router';
import { ToastyService } from "ng2-toasty";
import { Review } from './../../models/review';

@Component({
    selector: 'app-reviews',
    templateUrl: './reviews.component.html',
    styleUrls: ['./reviews.component.css']
})
export class ReviewsComponent implements OnInit {

    reviews;
    review: Review= new Review();

    constructor(private reviewsService: ReviewsService,
        private route: ActivatedRoute,
        private router: Router,
        private toastyService: ToastyService) {
        route.params.subscribe(p => {
            this.review.movieId = +p['id'];
        });
    }

    ngOnInit() {
this.reviewsService.getReviewById(this.review.movieId).
subscribe(reviews => {
            this.reviews = reviews;
            console.log("Reviews: ", this.reviews);
        });
    }
}
```

I would like to point out that this is exactly the same model that we had seen earlier to create the movie features. Here, I am just replicating the same for reviews. Hence no need to explain the logic again. I have also created a new model to get it mapped against review. Here is the code snippet.

```
export class Review {
    public id: number = null;
    public reviewerName: string = "";
    public reviewerComments: string = "";
    public reviewerRating: number = null;
    public movieId: number = null;
}
```

Similarly, the **reviews.component.html** file looks like this.

```
<br />
<p>
    <a [routerLink]="['/reviews/new/',review.movieId]"
class="btn btn-primary"> <i class="glyphicon glyphicon-
plus"></i> Post New review</a>
    <a [routerLink]="['/movies/']" class="btn btn-
info"><i class="glyphicon glyphicon-backward"></i> Back</
a>backward"></i> Back</a>
</p>
<h3>Reviews List</h3>
<form>
    <div class="container">
        <div class="row">
            <div class="row">
                <div class="col-xs-12 col-sm-9 col-md-9">
                    <div class="list-group">
                        <div class="list-group-item">
                            <div class="row-content"
*ngFor="let r of reviews">
                                <div class="list-group-
item-heading">
                                    <a href="#"
title="reviewerName">
                                        <small>Reviewer
Name: {{r.reviewerName}}</small>
                                    </a>
                                </div>
                                <small>
                                    <i class="glyphicon
glyphicon-time"></i> Reviewer Comments: {{r.
reviewerComments}}
                                    <i class="glyphicon
glyphicon-user"></i> Reviewer Rating: {{r.
reviewerRating}}
                                    <br>
                                    <span class="btn
btn-primary"><i class="glyphicon glyphicon-edit"></
i> <a [routerLink]="['/reviews/', r.id]" style="color:
black">Edit Review </a></span>
                                    <button class="btn
btn-danger" data-toggle="confirmation" style="color:
black" type="button" (click)="delete(r.id)"><i
class="glyphicon glyphicon-remove"></i> Delete Review</
button>
```

```
                                        </small>
                                        <hr>
                            </div>
                        </div>
                    </div>
                </div>
            </div>
        </div>
    </div>
</form>
```

Again, the corresponding CSS will just be a copy paste of the earlier one. Here is the code snippet.

```css
.list-group {
border-radius: 0;
}

    .list-group .list-group-item {
        background-color: transparent;
        overflow: hidden;
        border: 0;
        border-radius: 0;
        padding: 0 16px;
    }

        .list-group .list-group-item .row-picture,
        .list-group .list-group-item .row-action-primary
{
            float: left;
            display: inline-block;
            padding-right: 16px;
            padding-top: 8px;
        }

            .list-group .list-group-item .row-picture img,
            .list-group .list-group-item .row-action-
primary img,
            .list-group .list-group-item .row-picture i,
            .list-group .list-group-item .row-action-primary i,
            .list-group .list-group-item .row-picture label,
            .list-group .list-group-item .row-action-
primary label {
                display: block;
                width: 56px;
```

```css
                        height: 56px;
            }

            .list-group .list-group-item .row-picture img,
            .list-group .list-group-item .row-action-
primary img {
                        background: rgba(0, 0, 0, 0.1);
                        padding: 1px;
            }
            .list-group .list-group-item .row-picture
img.circle,
            .list-group .list-group-item .row-action-
primary img.circle {
                        border-radius: 100%;
            }
        .list-group .list-group-item .row-picture i,
        .list-group .list-group-item .row-action-primary i {
                        background: rgba(0, 0, 0, 0.25);
                        border-radius: 100%;
                        text-align: center;
                        line-height: 56px;
                        font-size: 20px;
                        color: white;
            }

            .list-group .list-group-item .row-picture label,
            .list-group .list-group-item .row-action-
primary label {
                        margin-left: 7px;
                        margin-right:7px;
                        margin-top: 5px;
                        margin-bottom:5px;
            }

            .list-group .list-group-item .row-content {
                        display: inline-block;
                        width: calc(100% - 92px);
                        min-height: 66px;
            }
            .list-group .list-group-item .row-content
.action-secondary {
                        position: absolute;
                        right: 16px;
                        top: 16px;
```

```css
            }
            .list-group .list-group-item .row-content
.action-secondary i {
                font-size: 20px;
                color: rgba(0, 0, 0, 0.25);
                cursor: pointer;
            }
            .list-group .list-group-item .row-content
.action-secondary ~ * {
                max-width: calc(100% - 30px);
            }
        .list-group .list-group-item .row-content .least-content {
                position: absolute;
                right: 16px;
                top: 0px;
                color: rgba(0, 0, 0, 0.54);
                font-size: 14px;
            }
        .list-group .list-group-item .list-group-item-heading {
            color: rgba(0, 0, 0, 0.77);
            font-size: 20px;
            line-height: 29px;
        }
    .list-group .list-group-separator {
        clear: both;
        overflow: hidden;
        margin-top: 10px;
        margin-bottom: 10px;
    }
        .list-group .list-group-separator:before {
            content: "";
            width: calc(100% - 90px);
            border-bottom: 1px solid rgba(0, 0, 0, 0.1);
            float: right;
        }
.bg-profile {
    background-color: #3498DB !important;
    height: 150px;
```

```
        z-index: 1;
}
.bg-bottom {
    height: 100px;
    margin-left: 30px;
}
.img-profile {
    display: inline-block !important;
    background-color: #fff;
    border-radius: 6px;
    margin-top:50%;
    padding: 1px;
    vertical-align: bottom;
    border: 2px solid #fff;
    -moz-box-sizing: border-box;
    box-sizing: border-box;
    color: #fff;
    z-index: 2;
}
.row-float {
    margin-top:40px;
}
.explore a {
    color: green;
    font-size: 13px;
    font-weight: 600
}
.twitter a {
    color: #4099FF
}
.img-box {
    box-shadow: 0 3px 6px rgba(0,0,0,.16),0 3px 6px
rgba(0,0,0,.23);
    border-radius: 2px;
    border: 0;
}
```

With the above change in place, when, I hover over any reviews, they will show the exact route as shown below.

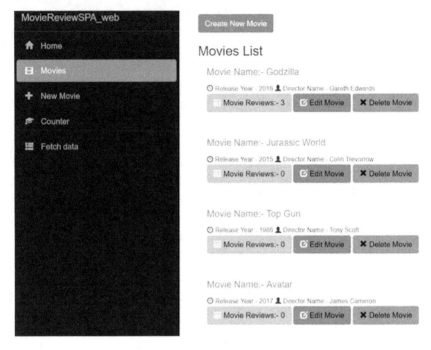

Then, it will show the exact route as shown below.

localhost:35334/reviews/4

When I click on it, it will appear like this.

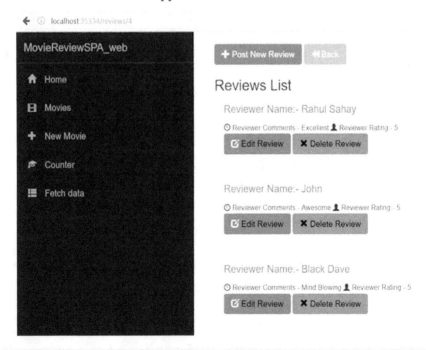

Therefore, listing of reviews is working fine. Let's go ahead and implement other features.

Fixing URL Refresh Issues

One point you may have noticed during development is that if you refresh your page say movies or any other new route, it gives the error saying node module failed for some reason.

The reason is that when it comes via a route, the service is available. However, while refreshing the page, it's not available. The easy way to fix this is using the complete URL. Hence, I need to go ahead and modify my service as shown below.

```
import { Injectable, Inject } from '@angular/core';
import { Http } from '@angular/http';
import 'rxjs/add/operator/map';

@Injectable()
export class ReviewsService {

    constructor(private http: Http, @Inject('ORIGIN_URL')
private originUrl: string) { }

    getReviewById(id) {
        return this.http.get(this.originUrl +'/api/
moviereviews/' + id)
            .map(res => res.json());
    }
}
```

Here, I have appended the code with the complete domain URL. Now, I have already provided this **ORIGIN_URL** in the **app.module.ts** under the providers section. I am using the same here. Apart from the above change, we also need to include service in one more place and that is in the **app.module.server.ts** file. Here is the code snippet for the same.

```
import { NgModule } from '@angular/core';
import { ServerModule } from '@angular/platform-server';
import { sharedConfig } from './app.module.shared';
import { MoviesService } from './services/movies.service';
import { ReviewsService } from './services/reviews.
service';
```

```
@NgModule({
    bootstrap: sharedConfig.bootstrap,
    declarations: sharedConfig.declarations,
    imports: [
        ServerModule,
        ...sharedConfig.imports
    ],
    providers: [MoviesService, ReviewsService]
})
Export class AppModule {
}
```

As you can see, here I have already implemented the same for the movie service as well. With the above change in place, when I refresh the page, it will display the screen as expected.

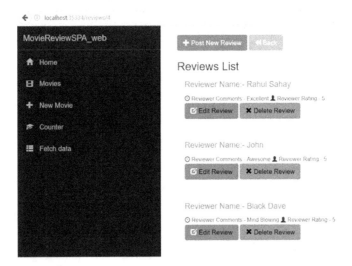

Creating reviews

In this section, we will allow the user to post new reviews against the movie. Hence, we will create a new screen for the same. I have already introduced the **Add New Review** link at the top of the screen. This time, I will go ahead and create a component via **ng g c new-review --spec false**. If we use this command, the test file will not get generated.

```
C:\Dell\Books\ASPNETCorePlusAngular4\MovieReviewSPA\MovieReviewSPA.web\ClientApp\app\components (Another)
λ ng g c new-review --spec false
installing component
    create ClientApp\app\components\new-review\new-review.component.css
    create ClientApp\app\components\new-review\new-review.component.html
    create ClientApp\app\components\new-review\new-review.component.ts
    update ClientApp\app\app.module.ts
```

As I said, my components folder looks like this.

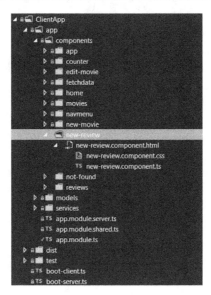

Now, I will go ahead and fix my file reference in the **app.module.ts** file as shown below.

```
import { NgModule } from '@angular/core';
import { BrowserModule } from '@angular/platform-
browser';
import { FormsModule } from '@angular/forms';
import { HttpModule } from '@angular/http';
import { sharedConfig } from './app.module.shared';
import { MoviesComponent } from './components/movies/
movies.component';
import { MoviesService } from './services/movies.
service';
import { ReviewsService } from './services/reviews.
service';
import { NewMovieComponent } from './components/new-
movie/new-movie.component';
import { EditMovieComponent } from './components/edit-
movie/edit-movie.component';
import { NotFoundComponent } from './components/not-
found/not-found.component';
import { ReviewsComponent } from './components/reviews/
reviews.component';
import { NewReviewComponent } from './components/new-
review/new-review.component';

@NgModule({
    bootstrap: sharedConfig.bootstrap,
    declarations: [...sharedConfig.declarations,
```

```
        MoviesComponent,
        NewMovieComponent,
        EditMovieComponent,
        NotFoundComponent,
        ReviewsComponent,
        NewReviewComponent],
    imports: [
        BrowserModule,
        FormsModule,
        HttpModule,
        ...sharedConfig.imports
    ],
    providers: [
        { provide: 'ORIGIN_URL', useValue: location.
origin },
        MoviesService,
        ReviewsService
    ]
})
export class AppModule {
}
```

Now, we need to add the new route to the **app.module.shared.ts** file as shown below. All the steps are the usual steps that we have done multiple times already.

```
import * as Raven from 'raven-js';
import { NgModule } from '@angular/core';
import { RouterModule } from '@angular/router';
import { FormsModule } from '@angular/forms';
import { ToastyModule } from 'ng2-toasty';
import { AppComponent } from './components/app/app.
component'
import { NavMenuComponent } from './components/navmenu/
navmenu.component';
import { HomeComponent } from './components/home/home.
component';
import { FetchDataComponent } from './components/
fetchdata/fetchdata.component';
import { CounterComponent } from './components/counter/
counter.component';
import { MoviesComponent } from './components/movies/
movies.component';
import { ReviewsComponent } from './components/reviews/
reviews.component';
import { NewMovieComponent } from './components/new-
movie/new-movie.component';
```

```
import { EditMovieComponent } from './components/edit-
movie/edit-movie.component';
import { NewReviewComponent } from './components/new-
review/new-review.component';
import { MoviesService } from './services/movies.service';
import { ReviewsService } from './services/reviews.service';

Raven

.config('https://7579eaef4acc46bab3ffd87d3d85f3ea@sentry.
io/203240')
    .install();

export const sharedConfig: NgModule = {
    bootstrap: [ AppComponent ],
    declarations: [
        AppComponent,
        NavMenuComponent,
        CounterComponent,
        FetchDataComponent,
        HomeComponent,
        MoviesComponent,
        NewMovieComponent,
        EditMovieComponent,
        ReviewsComponent,
        NewReviewComponent
    ],
    imports: [
        FormsModule,
        ToastyModule.forRoot(),
        RouterModule.forRoot([
            { path: '', redirectTo: 'home', pathMatch: 'full' },
            { path: 'movies', component: MoviesComponent },
            { path: 'movies/new', component: NewMovieComponent },
            { path: 'movies/:id', component: EditMovieComponent },
            { path: 'reviews/:id', component: ReviewsComponent },
            { path: 'reviews/new/:id', component: NewReviewComponent },
            { path: 'home', component: HomeComponent },
            { path: 'counter', component: CounterComponent },
            { path: 'fetch-data', component: FetchDataComponent },
            { path: '**', redirectTo: 'home' }
        ])
    ],
    providers: [MoviesService, ReviewsService]
};
```

Once done, my **new-review.component.html** will look like this.

```html
<div class="container">
    <div class="row">
        <form (ngSubmit)="onSubmit(f)" #f="ngForm"
role="form" class="col-md-9 go-right">
            <h2>Enter New Review</h2>
            <div class="form-group">
                <input id="reviewerName"
name="reviewerName" type="text" class="form-
control" required [(ngModel)]="review.reviewerName"
#reviewerName="ngModel">
                <label for="reviewName">Reviewer Name</
label>
                <div class="alert alert-danger"
*ngIf="reviewerName.touched && !reviewerName.
valid">Please specify the Reviewer Name!</div>
            </div>
            <div class="form-group">
                <textarea id="reviewerComments"
name="reviewerComments" type="text" class="form-
control" required [(ngModel)]="review.reviewerComments"
#reviewerComments="ngModel"></textarea>
                <label for="reviewerComments">Reviewer
Comments</label>
                <div class="alert alert-danger"
*ngIf="reviewerComments.touched && !reviewerComments.
valid">Please specify the Reviewer Comments!</div>
            </div>
            <div class="form-group">
                <input id="reviewerRating"
name="reviewerRating" type="text" class="form-
control" required [(ngModel)]="review.reviewerRating"
#reviewerRating="ngModel">
                <label for="reviewerRating">Reviewer
Rating</label>
                <div class="alert alert-danger"
*ngIf="reviewerRating.touched && !reviewerRating.
valid">Please specify the Reviewer Rating!</div>
            </div>
<p class="bg-success" style="padding:10px;margin-
top:20px;clear:both">
                <button type="submit" class="btn btn-primary"
[disabled]="!f.valid">Submit</button>
                <a [routerLink]="['/movies/']" class="btn
btn-info"><i class="glyphicon glyphicon-backward"></i>
```

```
Back</a>
          </p> </form>
     </div>
</div>
```

And the corresponding CSS file will look like this.

```
@import url(http://fonts.googleapis.com/
css?family=Open+Sans:400,600);

.form-control {
    background: transparent;
    }

form {
    width: 320px;
    margin: 20px;
}

    form > div {
    position: relative;
    overflow: hidden;
}

form input, form textarea {
    width: 100%;
    border: 2px solid gray;
    background: none;
    position: relative;
    top: 0;
    left: 0;
    z-index: 1;
    padding: 8px 12px;
    outline: 0;
}

    form input:valid, form textarea:valid {
        background: white;
    }

    form input:focus, form textarea:focus {
        border-color: #357EBD;
    }

        form input:focus + label, form textarea:focus +
label {
            background: #357EBD;
            color: white;
            font-size: 70%;
            padding: 1px 6px;
```

```css
        z-index: 2;
        text-transform: uppercase;
    }
    form label {
        -webkit-transition: background 0.2s, color 0.2s,
top 0.2s, bottom 0.2s, right 0.2s, left 0.2s;
        transition: background 0.2s, color 0.2s, top
0.2s, bottom 0.2s, right 0.2s, left 0.2s;
        position: absolute;
        color: #999;
        padding: 7px 6px;
        font-weight: normal;
    }

    form textarea {
        display: block;
        resize: vertical;
    }

    form.go-bottom input, form.go-bottom textarea {
        padding: 12px 12px 12px 12px;
    }

    form.go-bottom label {
        top: 0;
        bottom: 0;
        left: 0;
        width: 100%;
    }

    form.go-bottom input:focus, form.go-bottom
textarea:focus {
        padding: 4px 6px 20px 6px;
    }

        form.go-bottom input:focus + label, form.go-
bottom textarea:focus + label {
            top: 100%;
            margin-top:16px;
        }

    form.go-right label {
        border-radius: 0 5px 5px 0;
        height: 100%;
        top: 0;
        right: 100%;
        width: 100%;
        margin-right:100%;
    }

    form.go-right input:focus + label, form.go-right
```

```
textarea:focus + label {
        right: 0;
        margin-right: 0;
        width: 40%;
        padding-top: 5px;
    }
```

With the above changes in place, when I click on the **Post New Review** Link, the following page will be displayed.

Now, let's go ahead and write the Submit logic. This will be very similar to the earlier ones. Here is the code snippet for **new-review.component.ts**.

```
import * as Raven from 'raven-js';
import { Component, OnInit } from '@angular/core';
import { NgForm } from '@angular/forms';
import { ReviewsService } from '../../services/reviews.service';
import { Review } from './../../models/review';
import { ToastyService } from "ng2-toasty";
import { Router, ActivatedRoute } from '@angular/router';

@Component({
    selector: 'app-new-review',
    templateUrl: './new-review.component.html',
    styleUrls: ['./new-review.component.css']
})
export class NewReviewComponent implements OnInit {

    review:Review=new Review();
    constructor(private reviewsService: ReviewsService,
        private toastyService: ToastyService,
        private route: ActivatedRoute,
        private router: Router) {
```

```
    route.params.subscribe(p => {
        this.review.movieId = +p['id'];
    });
}

ngOnInit() {
}
    onSubmit(form: NgForm) {
        var formData = this.review;
        formData.id = 0;
        formData.reviewerName = this.review.
reviewerName.toString();
        formData.reviewerComments = this.review.
reviewerComments.toString();
        formData.reviewerRating = this.review.
reviewerRating;
        formData.movieId = this.review.movieId;
        console.log(formData);

this.reviewsService.createReview(this.review.movieId, formData)
            .subscribe(x => {
                console.log(x);
                this.toastyService.success({
                    title: 'Success',
                    msg: 'New Review Created!',
                    theme: 'bootstrap',
                    showClose: true,
                    timeout: 5000
                });
                this.router.navigate(['/movies']);
            },
            err => {
                Raven.captureException(err.
originalError || err);
                this.toastyService.error({
                    title: 'Error',
                    msg: 'An unexpected error occured
while creating new Review!',
                    theme: 'bootstrap',
                    showClose: true,
                    timeout: 5000
                });
            });
    }
}
```

Corresponding to this, I have also created an equivalent method in **reviews. service.ts**.

```
import { Injectable, Inject } from '@angular/core';
import { Http } from '@angular/http';
import 'rxjs/add/operator/map';

@Injectable()
export class ReviewsService {

    constructor(private http: Http, @Inject('ORIGIN_URL')
private originUrl: string) { }

    getReviewById(id) {
        return this.http.get(this.originUrl +'/api/
moviereviews/' + id)
        .map(res => res.json());
    }

    createReview(id,review) {
        return this.http.post('/api/moviereviews/' +id,
review)
            .map(res => res.json());
    }
}
```

With the above change in place, when I go ahead and enter a new review, it will work as expected.

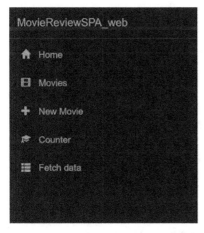

Once it is submitted successfully, it will get redirected to the movies page with the confirmation message.

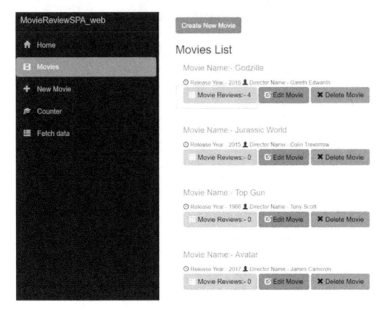

Here, you can see that the Movie Reviews tab shows **4**. So, when I click on my Movie Reviews as highlighted above, it will show my new record as well.

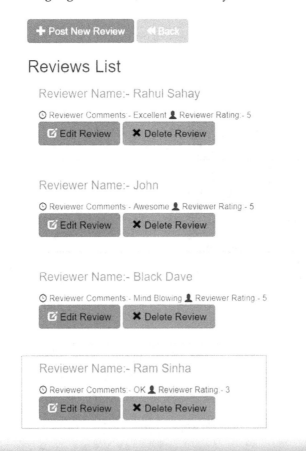

Editing reviews

In the previous section, we learned how to create a new review. In this section, we will learn how to edit an existing review. For this, we need to create the **ng g c edit-review --spec false** component.

I need to again fix my **app.module.ts** file references. Here is the code snippet for the same.

```typescript
import { NgModule } from '@angular/core';
import { BrowserModule } from '@angular/platform-browser';
import { FormsModule } from '@angular/forms';
import { HttpModule } from '@angular/http';
import { sharedConfig } from './app.module.shared';
import { MoviesComponent } from './components/movies/movies.component';
import { MoviesService } from './services/movies.service';
import { ReviewsService } from './services/reviews.service';
import { NewMovieComponent } from './components/new-movie/new-movie.component';
import { EditMovieComponent } from './components/edit-movie/edit-movie.component';
import { NotFoundComponent } from './components/not-found/not-found.component';
import { ReviewsComponent } from './components/reviews/reviews.component';
import { NewReviewComponent } from './components/new-review/new-review.component';
import { EditReviewComponent } from './components/edit-review/edit-review.component';

@NgModule({
    bootstrap: sharedConfig.bootstrap,
    declarations: [...sharedConfig.declarations,
        MoviesComponent,
        NewMovieComponent,
        EditMovieComponent,
```

```
        NotFoundComponent,
        ReviewsComponent,
        NewReviewComponent,
        EditReviewComponent],
    imports: [
        BrowserModule,
        FormsModule,
        HttpModule,
        ...sharedConfig.imports
    ],
    providers: [
        { provide: 'ORIGIN_URL', useValue: location.origin },
        MoviesService,
        ReviewsService
    ]
})
export class AppModule {
}
```

Here, I also need to introduce a new route in the **app.module.shared.ts** file as shown below.

```
import * as Raven from 'raven-js';
import { NgModule } from '@angular/core';
import { RouterModule } from '@angular/router';
import { FormsModule } from '@angular/forms';
import { ToastyModule } from 'ng2-toasty';
import { AppComponent } from './components/app/app.component'
import { NavMenuComponent } from './components/navmenu/
navmenu.component';
import { HomeComponent } from './components/home/home.
component';
import { FetchDataComponent } from './components/
fetchdata/fetchdata.component';
import { CounterComponent } from './components/counter/
counter.component';
import { MoviesComponent } from './components/movies/
movies.component';
import { ReviewsComponent } from './components/reviews/
reviews.component';
import { NewMovieComponent } from './components/new-
movie/new-movie.component';
import { EditMovieComponent } from './components/edit-
movie/edit-movie.component';
import { NewReviewComponent } from './components/new-
review/new-review.component';
```

```
import { EditReviewComponent } from './components/edit-
review/edit-review.component';
import { MoviesService } from './services/movies.service';
import { ReviewsService } from './services/reviews.service';

Raven

.config('https://7579eaef4acc46bab3ffd87d3d85f3ea@sentry.
io/203240')
    .install();

export const sharedConfig: NgModule = {
    bootstrap: [ AppComponent ],
    declarations: [
        AppComponent,
        NavMenuComponent,
        CounterComponent,
        FetchDataComponent,
        HomeComponent,
        MoviesComponent,
        NewMovieComponent,
        EditMovieComponent,
        ReviewsComponent,
        NewReviewComponent,
        EditReviewComponent
    ],
    imports: [
        FormsModule,
        ToastyModule.forRoot(),
        RouterModule.forRoot([
            { path: '', redirectTo: 'home', pathMatch: 'full' },
            { path: 'movies', component: MoviesComponent },
            { path: 'movies/new', component: NewMovieComponent },
            { path: 'movies/:id', component: EditMovieComponent },
            { path: 'reviews/:id', component: ReviewsComponent },
            { path: 'editreview/:id', component: EditReviewComponent },
            { path: 'reviews/new/:id', component: NewReviewComponent },
            { path: 'home', component: HomeComponent },
            { path: 'counter', component: CounterComponent },
            { path: 'fetch-data', component: FetchDataComponent },
            { path: '**', redirectTo: 'home' }
        ])
    ],
    providers: [MoviesService, ReviewsService]

};
```

I also need to change reviews.component.html. I have changed the edit link.

```html
<br />
<p>
    <a [routerLink]="['/reviews/new/',review.movieId]"
class="btn btn-primary"> <i class="glyphicon glyphicon-
plus"></i> Post New Review</a>
    <a [routerLink]="['/movies/']" class="btn btn-
info"><i class="glyphicon glyphicon-backward"></i> Back</
a>
</p>
<h3>Reviews List</h3>
<form>
    <div class="container">
        <div class="row">
            <div class="row">
                <div class="col-xs-12 col-sm-9 col-md-9">
                    <div class="list-group">
                        <div class="list-group-item">
                            <div class="row-content"
*ngFor="let r of reviews">
                                <div class="list-group-
item-heading">
                                    <a href="#"
title="reviewerName">
                                        <small>Reviewer
Name: {{r.reviewerName}}</small>
                                    </a>
                                </div>
                                <small>
                                    <i class="glyphicon
glyphicon-time"></i> Reviewer Comments: {{r.
reviewerComments}}
                                    <i class="glyphicon
glyphicon-user"></i> Reviewer Rating: {{r.
reviewerRating}}
                                    <br>
                                    <span class="btn
btn-primary"><i class="glyphicon glyphicon-edit"></i>
<a [routerLink]="['/editreview/', r.id]" style="color:
black">Edit Review </a></span>
                                    <button class="btn
btn-danger" data-toggle="confirmation" style="color:
black" type="button" (click)="delete(r.id)"><i
class="glyphicon glyphicon-remove"></i> Delete Review</
button>
```

```
                              </small>
                              <hr>
                        </div>
                    </div>
                </div>
            </div>
        </div>
    </div>
</form>
```

Now, I can simply copy the **new-review** markup and paste it in the **edit-review** markup and then make the necessary changes as shown below.

```
<div class="container">
    <div class="row">
        <form (ngSubmit)="onSubmit(f)" #f="ngForm"
role="form" class="col-md-9 go-right">
            <h2>Edit Review</h2>
            <div class="form-group">
                <input id="reviewerName"
name="reviewerName" type="text" class="form-
control" required [(ngModel)]="review.reviewerName"
ngControl="reviewerName" #reviewerName="ngModel">
                <label for="reviewerName">Reviewer Name</
label>
                <div class="alert alert-danger"
*ngIf="reviewerName.touched && !reviewerName.
valid">Please specify the Reviewer Name!</div>
            </div>
            <div class="form-group">
                <textarea id="reviewerComments"
name="reviewerComments" type="text" class="form-
control" required [(ngModel)]="review.
reviewerComments" ngControl="reviewerComments"
#reviewerComments="ngModel"></textarea>
                <label for="reviewerComments">Reviewer
Comments</label>
                <div class="alert alert-danger"
*ngIf="reviewerComments.touched && !reviewerComments.
valid">Please specify the Reviewer Comments!</div>
            </div>
            <div class="form-group">
                <input id="reviewerRating"
name="reviewerRating" type="text" class="form-
control" required [(ngModel)]="review.reviewerRating"
```

```
ngControl="reviewerRating" #reviewerRating="ngModel">
                    <label for="reviewerRating">Reviewer
Rating</label>
                <div class="alert alert-danger"
*ngIf="reviewerRating.touched && !reviewerRating.
valid">Please specify the Reviewer Rating!</div>
            </div>
            <p class="bg-success"
style="padding:10px;margin-top:20px;clear:both">
                <button type="submit" class="btn btn-
primary" [disabled]="!f.valid">Submit</button>
                <a [routerLink]="['/movies/']" class="btn
btn-info"><i class="glyphicon glyphicon-backward"></i>
Back</a>
            </p>
        </form>
    </div>
</div>
```

And its corresponding CSS file will look like this.

```
@import url(http://fonts.googleapis.com/
css?family=Open+Sans:400,600);

.form-control {
    background: transparent;
}

form {
    width: 320px;
    margin: 20px;
}

    form > div {
        position: relative;
        overflow: hidden;
    }

    form input, form textarea {
        width: 100%;
        border: 2px solid gray;
        background: none;
        position: relative;
        top: 0;
        left: 0;
        z-index: 1;
```

```
        padding: 8px 12px;
        outline: 0;
    }

    form input:valid, form textarea:valid {
        background: white;
    }

    form input:focus, form textarea:focus {
        border-color: #357EBD;
    }

    form input:focus + label, form textarea:focus + label {
        background: #357EBD;
        color: white;
        font-size: 70%;
        padding: 1px 6px;
        z-index: 2;
        text-transform: uppercase;
    }

form label {
    -webkit-transition: background 0.2s, color 0.2s,
top 0.2s, bottom 0.2s, right 0.2s, left 0.2s;
    transition: background 0.2s, color 0.2s, top
0.2s, bottom 0.2s, right 0.2s, left 0.2s;
    position: absolute;
    color: #999;
    padding: 7px 6px;
    font-weight: normal;
}

form textarea {
    display: block;
    resize: vertical;
}

form.go-bottom input, form.go-bottom textarea {
    padding: 12px 12px 12px 12px;
}

form.go-bottom label {
    top: 0;
    bottom: 0;
    left: 0;
    width: 100%;
}
```

```
    form.go-bottom input:focus, form.go-bottom
textarea:focus {
        padding: 4px 6px 20px 6px;
    }

        form.go-bottom input:focus + label, form.go-
bottom textarea:focus + label {
            top: 100%;
            margin-top:16px;
        }

    form.go-right label {
        border-radius: 0 5px 5px 0;
        height: 100%;
        top: 0;
        right: 100%;
        width: 100%;
        margin-right:100%;
    }

    form.go-right input:focus + label, form.go-right
textarea:focus + label {
        right: 0;
        margin-right: 0;
        width: 40%;
    padding-top: 5px;
}
```

Then, I have implemented the following logic in the edit-review.component.
ts file to populate the input fields.

```
import * as Raven from 'raven-js';
import { Component, OnInit } from '@angular/core';
import { ActivatedRoute, Router } from '@angular/router';
import { Review } from './../../models/review';
import { ReviewsService } from '../../services/reviews.service';
import { ToastyService } from "ng2-toasty";

@Component({
    selector: 'app-edit-review',
    templateUrl: './edit-review.component.html',
    styleUrls: ['./edit-review.component.css']
})
export class EditReviewComponent implements OnInit {

    review: Review = new Review();
    constructor(private route: ActivatedRoute,
        private router: Router,
```

```
        private reviewsService: ReviewsService,
        private toastyService: ToastyService) {

        route.params.subscribe(p => {
            this.review.id = +p['id'];
        });
    }

    ngOnInit() {
        if (this.review.id) {
            this.reviewsService.editReview(this.review.id)
                .subscribe(m => {
                    this.review = m;
                        console.log("Review:", this.review);
                    },
                    err => {
                        if (err.status == 404) {
this.router.navigate(['/movies']);
                        }
                    });
        }
    }
}
```

After this, I have created the required action in my service.

```
import { Injectable, Inject } from '@angular/core';
import { Http } from '@angular/http';
import 'rxjs/add/operator/map';

@Injectable()
export class ReviewsService {

    constructor(private http: Http, @Inject('ORIGIN_URL')
private originUrl: string) { }
    getReviewById(id) {
        return this.http.get(this.originUrl +'/api/
moviereviews/' + id)
            .map(res => res.json());
    }

    createReview(id, review) {
        return this.http.post('/api/moviereviews/' +id, review)
            .map(res => res.json());
    }
    editReview(id) {
        return this.http.get('/api/moviereviews/
GetByReviewId?id=' +id)
```

```
        .map(res => res.json());
    }
}
```

One point to note here is that I have designed the new API implementation to fetch the review. I have pasted the code snippet for **MovieReviewsController.cs**.

```csharp
using System;
using System.Collections.Generic;
using System.Linq;
using System.Net;
using System.Net.Http;
using Microsoft.AspNetCore.Authorization;
using Microsoft.AspNetCore.Mvc;
using MovieReviewSPA.Data.Contracts;
using MovieReviewSPA.Model;

namespace MovieReviewSPA.Web.Controllers.API
{
    [Route("api/[controller]")]

    public class MovieReviewsController : Controller
    {
        private readonly IMovieReviewUow UOW;

        public MovieReviewsController(IMovieReviewUow uow)
        {
            UOW = uow;
        }
        [HttpGet("")]
        public IEnumerable<MovieReview> Get()
        {
            return UOW.MovieReviews.GetAll().OrderBy(m =>
m.MovieId);
        }
        [HttpGet("{id}")]
        public IEnumerable<MovieReview> Get(int Id)
        {
            return UOW.MovieReviews.GetAll().Where(m =>
m.MovieId == Id);
        }

        [HttpGet("[action]")]
        public MovieReview GetByReviewId(int id)
        {
            return UOW.MovieReviews.GetAll().
FirstOrDefault(m => m.Id == id);
```

```
        }

        // /api/MovieReviews/getbyreviewername?value=rahul
        [HttpGet("[action]")]
        public MovieReview GetByReviewerName(string value)
        {
            var review = UOW.MovieReviews.GetAll().
FirstOrDefault(m => m.ReviewerName.StartsWith(value));

            if (review != null) return review;
            throw new Exception(new HttpResponseMessage(H
ttpStatusCode.NotFound).ToString());
        }

        // Update an existing review
        // PUT /api/MovieReviews/
        [HttpPut("")]
        public HttpResponseMessage Put([FromBody]
MovieReview review)
        {
            //review.Id = Id;
            UOW.MovieReviews.Update(review);
            UOW.Commit();
            return new HttpResponseMessage(HttpStatusCo
de.NoContent);
        }

        // Create a new review
        // POST /api/MovieReviews
        [HttpPost("{id}")]
        public int Post(int Id, [FromBody]MovieReview
review)
        {
            review.MovieId = Id;
            UOW.MovieReviews.Add(review);
            UOW.Commit();

            return Response.StatusCode = (int)
HttpStatusCode.Created;
        }

        //Delete a review
        //Delete /api/MovieReviews/5
        [HttpDelete("{id}")]
        public HttpResponseMessage Delete(int id)
        {
            UOW.MovieReviews.Delete(id);
            UOW.Commit();
```

```
            return new HttpResponseMessage(HttpStatusCo
de.NoContent);
        }
    }
}
```

With the above change in place, when I click on Edit Review, it will display the following screen.

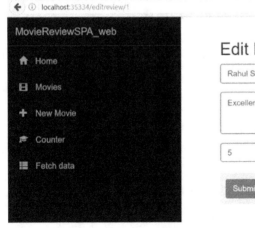

Now, let's get started with editing the review. I have pasted the code snippet for the same.

```
import * as Raven from 'raven-js';
import { Component, OnInit } from '@angular/core';
import { ActivatedRoute, Router } from '@angular/router';
import { Review } from './../../models/review';
import { ReviewsService } from '../../services/reviews.
service';
import { ToastyService } from "ng2-toasty";

@Component({
    selector: 'app-edit-review',
    templateUrl: './edit-review.component.html',
    styleUrls: ['./edit-review.component.css']
})
export class EditReviewComponent implements OnInit {
        review: Review = new Review();
        constructor(private route: ActivatedRoute,
        private router: Router,
        private reviewsService: ReviewsService,
        private toastyService: ToastyService) {

        route.params.subscribe(p => {
            this.review.id = +p['id'];
        });
    }

ngOnInit() {
    if (this.review.id) {
        this.reviewsService.editReview(this.review.id)
            .subscribe(m => {
                this.review = m;
                    console.log("Review:", this.review);
                },
                err => {
                    if (err.status == 404) {
this.router.navigate(['/movies']);
                    }
                });
        }
}

    onSubmit() {
```

```
        if (this.review.id) {
            this.reviewsService.updateReview(this.review)
                .subscribe(x => {
                    console.log(x);
                    this.toastyService.success({
                        title: 'Success',
                        msg: 'Review Updated!',
                        theme: 'bootstrap',
                        showClose: true,
                        timeout: 5000
                    });
                    this.router.navigate(['/movies']);
                },
                err => {
Raven.captureException(err.originalError || err);
                    this.toastyService.error({
                        title: 'Error',
                        msg: 'An unexpected error while
updating the record!',
                        theme: 'bootstrap',
                        showClose: true,
                        timeout: 5000
                    });
                });
        }
    }
}
```

And the corresponding change in service is as shown below.

```
import { Injectable, Inject } from '@angular/core';
import { Http } from '@angular/http';
import 'rxjs/add/operator/map';

@Injectable()
export class ReviewsService {

    constructor(private http: Http, @Inject('ORIGIN_URL')
private originUrl: string) { }

    getReviewById(id) {
        return this.http.get(this.originUrl +'/api/
moviereviews/' + id)
            .map(res => res.json());
    }
```

```
createReview(id,review) {
    return this.http.post('/api/moviereviews/' +id, review)
        .map(res => res.json());
}
editReview(id) {
    return this.http.get('/api/moviereviews/
GetByReviewId?id=' +id)
        .map(res => res.json());
}

updateReview(review) {
    return this.http.put('/api/moviereviews/',
review)
        .map(res => res.json());
}
}
```

Here, I am changing the rating to 4.

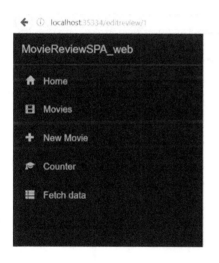

On successful edit, it will get redirected to the movies page and show the following toast message.

We can verify the review by clicking on the reviews page again.

Reviews List

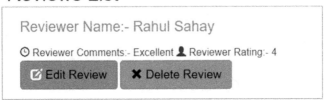

Reviewer Name:- Rahul Sahay

🕑 Reviewer Comments:- Excellent 👤 Reviewer Rating:- 4

> 🖉 Edit Review   ✖ Delete Review

Reviewer Name:- John

🕑 Reviewer Comments:- Awesome 👤 Reviewer Rating:- 5

> 🖉 Edit Review   ✖ Delete Review

Reviewer Name:- Black Dave

🕑 Reviewer Comments:- Mind Blowing 👤 Reviewer Rating:- 5

> 🖉 Edit Review   ✖ Delete Review

Reviewer Name:- Ram Sinha

🕑 Reviewer Comments:- OK 👤 Reviewer Rating:- 3

> 🖉 Edit Review   ✖ Delete Review

Deleting Reviews

In this section, we will learn how to implement the delete feature. This is a straight forward method. Here is the code snippet for **reviews.component.ts**.

```
import * as Raven from 'raven-js';
import { Component, OnInit } from '@angular/core';
import { ReviewsService } from '../../services/reviews.
service';
import { Router, ActivatedRoute } from '@angular/router';
import { ToastyService } from "ng2-toasty";
import { Review } from './../../models/review';

@Component({
```

```
    selector: 'app-reviews',
    templateUrl: './reviews.component.html',
    styleUrls: ['./reviews.component.css']
})
export class ReviewsComponent implements OnInit {

    reviews;
    review: Review= new Review();

    constructor(private reviewsService: ReviewsService,
        private route: ActivatedRoute,
        private router: Router,
        private toastyService: ToastyService) {
        route.params.subscribe(p => {
            this.review.movieId = +p['id'];
        });
    }

    ngOnInit() {

this.reviewsService.getReviewById(this.review.movieId).
subscribe(reviews => {
            this.reviews = reviews;
            this.toastyService.success({
                title: 'Success',
                msg: 'Reviewes fetched successfully!',
                theme: 'bootstrap',
                showClose: true,
                timeout: 5000
            });
        });
    }
    delete(id) {
        if (confirm("Are you sure, you want delete review?")) {
            this.reviewsService.deleteReview(id)
                .subscribe(x => {
                    this.toastyService.success({
                        title: 'Success',
                        msg: 'Review Deleted!',
                        theme: 'bootstrap',
                        showClose: true,
                        timeout: 5000
                    });
                    this.router.navigate(['/movies']);
                },
                err => {
```

```
Raven.captureException(err.originalError || err);
                    this.toastyService.error({
                         title: 'Error',
                         msg: 'An unexpected error while
deleting the record!',
                         theme: 'bootstrap',
                         showClose: true,
                         timeout: 5000
                    });
               });
          }
     }
}
```

And the corresponding service change in **reviews.service.ts** is shown below.

```
import { Injectable, Inject } from '@angular/core';
import { Http } from '@angular/http';
import 'rxjs/add/operator/map';

@Injectable()
export class ReviewsService {

    constructor(private http: Http, @Inject('ORIGIN_URL')
private originUrl: string) { }

    getReviewById(id) {
        return this.http.get(this.originUrl +'/api/
moviereviews/' + id)
            .map(res => res.json());
    }

    createReview(id, review) {
        return this.http.post('/api/moviereviews/' +id,
review)
            .map(res => res.json());
    }

    editReview(id) {
        return this.http.get('/api/moviereviews/
GetByReviewId?id=' +id)
            .map(res => res.json());
    }

    updateReview(review) {
        return this.http.put('/api/moviereviews/',
review)
```

```
            .map(res => res.json());
    }
    deleteReview(id) {
        return this.http.delete('/api/moviereviews/' +
id)
            .map(res => res.json());
    }
}
```

Once done, when I click on the delete button for **Ram Sinha review**, it will display the following screenshot:

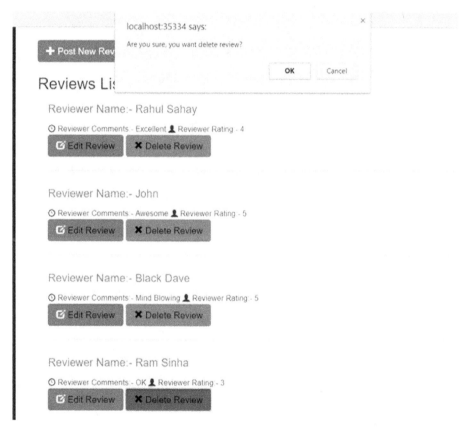

When I click on OK, the review will get deleted and get redirected to the movies page and display the following toast message.

Questions

1. How to pass data to routes?
2. How route params work?
3. What is default Observable from Angular in routing?
4. How components send data to WEB API?
5. What are @Injectables()?
6. How to inject constants into service?

Summary

In this section, we did a couple of things. First, we started with listing reviews. Then, we saw how to fix the direct URL navigation issue or Page refresh issue. We also implemented features like creating, editing and deleting of reviews. In the next section, we will see how to implement pagination and other important features.

CHAPTER 8

Adding More Features to the App

Introduction

In this section, we will get started with adding more features to the app. First, we will add filters to the app, then will see that how they interact with the client and server-side. Then, we will move on to add new features to the app like paging and image upload functionality. During this course, we will see how to create a new tabbed view.

Adding a Movie Filter

In this section, we will add a filter to filter the movies based on name. This is a pretty straightforward change. I have pasted the markup for **movies.component.html**.

```
<br />
<p>
    <a [routerLink]="['/movies/new']" class="btn btn-
primary">Create New Movie</a>
</p>
<div class="well">
    <div class="form-group">
```

```
        <label for="movie">Filter Movie</label>
        <select id="movie" class="form-control"
[(ngModel)]="filter.id" (change)="onDropdownChange()">
            <option value=""></option>
            <option *ngFor="let m of movies" value="{{m.
id}}">{{m.movieName}}</option>
        </select>
    </div>
    <button class="btn btn-danger" (click)="onResetFilter
()">Reset</button>
</div>
<h3>Movies List</h3>
<form>
    <div class="container">
        <div class="row">
            <div class="row">
                <div class="col-xs-12 col-sm-9 col-md-9">
                    <div class="list-group">
                        <div class="list-group-item">
                            <div class="row-content"
*ngFor="let m of movies">
                                <div class="list-group-
item-heading">
                                    <a title="movieName">
                                        <small>Movie
Name: {{m.movieName}}</small>
                                    </a>
                                </div>
                                <small>
                                    <i class="glyphicon
glyphicon-time"></i> Release Year: {{m.releaseYear}}
                                    <i class="glyphicon
glyphicon-user"></i> Director Name: {{m.directorName}}
                                    <br>
                                    <span class="btn
btn-info"><i class="glyphicon glyphicon-th"></i> <a
[routerLink]="['/reviews/', m.id]" style="color:
black">Movie Reviews: {{m.noOfReviews}} </a></span>
                                    <span class="btn
btn-primary"><i class="glyphicon glyphicon-edit"></
i> <a [routerLink]="['/movies/', m.id]" style="color:
black">Edit Movie </a></span>
                                    <button class="btn
btn-danger" data-toggle="confirmation" style="color:
black" type="button" (click)="delete(m.id)"><i
```

```
class="glyphicon glyphicon-remove"></i> Delete Movie</
button>
                                    </small>
                                    <hr>
                                </div>
                            </div>
                        </div>
                    </div>
                </div>
            </div>
        </div>
</form>
```

Let me explain the code snippet. Here, I have added a drop-down menu and added binding with the movie id, displaying the movie name in the drop down. Here is the corresponding component change.

```
import * as Raven from 'raven-js';
import { Component, OnInit } from '@angular/core';
import { MoviesService } from '../../services/movies.
service';
import { Router } from '@angular/router';
import { ToastyService } from "ng2-toasty";

@Component({
    selector: 'app-movies',
    templateUrl: './movies.component.html',
    styleUrls: ['./movies.component.css']
})
export class MoviesComponent implements OnInit {

    movies;
    allMovies;
    movie: {};
    filter:any={};

    constructor(
        private moviesService: MoviesService, private
router: Router, private toastyService: ToastyService) {

    }

    ngOnInit() {
        this.moviesService.getMovies().subscribe(movies
=> {
            this.movies = this.allMovies= movies;
            console.log("Movies: ", this.movies);
        });
```

```
    }

    submit() {
        this.moviesService.createMovie(this.movie)
            .subscribe(x => console.log(x));
    }

    delete(id) {
        if (confirm("Are you sure?")) {
            this.moviesService.deleteMovie(id)
                .subscribe(x => {
                    this.toastyService.success({
                        title: 'Success',
                        msg: 'Movie Deleted!',
                        theme: 'bootstrap',
                        showClose: true,
                        timeout: 5000
                    });
                    this.router.navigate(['/home']);
                },
                err => {
Raven.captureException(err.originalError || err);
                    this.toastyService.error({
                        title: 'Error',
                        msg: 'An unexpected error while
deleting the record!',
                        theme: 'bootstrap',
                        showClose: true,
                        timeout: 5000
                    });
                });
        }
    }
    onDropdownChange() {
        var movies = this.allMovies;
        if (this.filter.id) {
            movies = movies.filter(m => m.id == this.filter.id);
        }
        this.movies = movies;
    }
    onResetFilter() {
        this.filter = {};
        this.onDropdownChange();
    }
}
```

Here, when I am getting movies on page load, I am storing them in **allMovies** as well. Therefore, we will have a separate field where we will store all the movies that we retrieve from the server and we use this list while applying filters. Therefore, in **onDropdownChange**, we store the values locally first and then check whether the id is there or not. If the id is there, then we apply the filters.

I have assigned a global variable to the filtered list. Similarly, in **onResetFilter()**, I have set the filter object with an empty object and then called the function. Once done, it will appear like this.

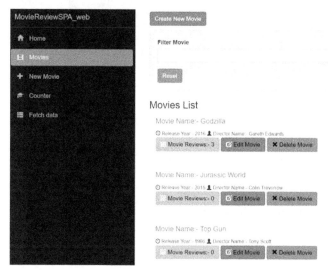

Here when I click on the drop-down menu, it will show all the movies as shown below.

Now, when I select **Godzilla**, it will only show **Godzilla** in the list.

Adding the Review Filter

In this section, I have applied the same logic, but here I have filtered with the rating. I have pasted the code snippet for **reviews.component.html.**

```html
<br />
<p>
    <a [routerLink]="['/reviews/new/',review.movieId]"
class="btn btn-primary"> <i class="glyphicon glyphicon-
plus"></i> Post New Review</a>
    <a [routerLink]="['/movies/']" class="btn btn-
info"><i class="glyphicon glyphicon-backward"></i> Back</
a>
</p>
<h3>Reviews List</h3>
<div class="well">
    <div class="form-group">
        <label for="reviewerRating">Filter Reviews by
Rating</label>
        <select id="reviewerRating" class="form-
control" [(ngModel)]="filter.reviewerRating"
(change)="onDropdownChange()">
            <option value=""></option>
            <option *ngFor="let r of reviews" value="{{r.
reviewerRating}}">{{r.reviewerRating}}</option>
        </select>
    </div>
    <button class="btn btn-danger" (click)="onResetFilter
()">Reset</button>
</div>
<form>
    <div class="container">
        <div class="row">
            <div class="row">
                <div class="col-xs-12 col-sm-9 col-md-9">
                    <div class="list-group">
                        <div class="list-group-item">
                            <div class="row-content"
*ngFor="let r of reviews">
                                <div class="list-group-
item-heading">
                                    <a href="#"
title="reviewerName">
                                        <small>Reviewer
Name: {{r.reviewerName}}</small>
                                    </a>
```

```
                                   </div>
                                   <small>
                                      <i
class="glyphicon glyphicon-time"></i> Reviewer Comments:
{{r.reviewerComments}}
                                            <i
class="glyphicon glyphicon-user"></i> Reviewer Rating:
{{r.reviewerRating}}
                                         <br>
                                         <span class="btn
btn-primary"><i class="glyphicon glyphicon-edit"></i>
<a [routerLink]="['/editreview/', r.id]" style="color:
black">Edit Review </a></span>
                                         <button
class="btn btn-danger" style="color: black" type="button"
(click)="delete(r.id)"><i class="glyphicon glyphicon-
remove"></i> Delete Review</button>
                                   </small>
                                   <hr>
                          </div>
                       </div>
                    </div>
                 </div>
              </div>
           </div>
        </div>
</form>
```

And the corresponding **reviews.component.ts** file is as shown below.

```
import * as Raven from 'raven-js';
import { Component, OnInit } from '@angular/core';
import { ReviewsService } from '../../services/reviews.service';
import { Router, ActivatedRoute } from '@angular/router';
import { ToastyService } from "ng2-toasty";
import { Review } from './../../models/review';

@Component({
    selector: 'app-reviews',
    templateUrl: './reviews.component.html',
    styleUrls: ['./reviews.component.css']
})
export class ReviewsComponent implements OnInit {

    reviews;
    review: Review = new Review();
    allReviews;
    filter: any = {};

    constructor(private reviewsService: ReviewsService,
```

```
        private route: ActivatedRoute,
        private router: Router,
        private toastyService: ToastyService) {
        route.params.subscribe(p => {
            this.review.movieId = +p['id'];
        });
    }
    ngOnInit() {
this.reviewsService.getReviewById(this.review.movieId).
subscribe(reviews => {
            this.reviews = this.allReviews= reviews;
            this.toastyService.success({
                title: 'Success',
                msg: 'Reviewes fetched successfully!',
                theme: 'bootstrap',
                showClose: true,
                timeout: 5000
            });
        });

    }
    delete(id) {
        if (confirm("Are you sure, you want delete review?")) {
            this.reviewsService.deleteReview(id)
                .subscribe(x => {
                    this.toastyService.success({
                        title: 'Success',
                        msg: 'Review Deleted!',
                        theme: 'bootstrap',
                        showClose: true,
                        timeout: 5000
                    });
                    this.router.navigate(['/movies']);
                },
                err => {
Raven.captureException(err.originalError || err);
                this.toastyService.error({
                    title: 'Error',
                        msg: 'An unexpected error while
deleting the record!',
                        theme: 'bootstrap',
                        showClose: true,
                        timeout: 5000
                });
            });
        }
    }
```

```
    onDropdownChange() {
        var reviews = this.allReviews;
        if (this.filter.reviewerRating) {
            reviews = reviews.filter(r => r.reviewerRating
== this.filter.reviewerRating);
        }
        this.reviews = reviews;
    }
    onResetFilter() {
        this.filter = {};
        this.onDropdownChange();
    }
}
```

Once done, when I click on Movie Reviews, it will display the following screenshot:

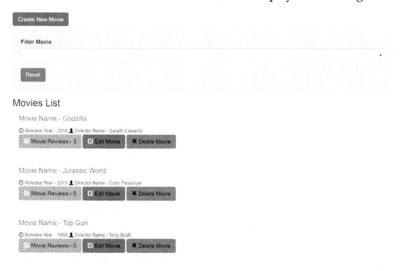

It will take me to the reviews page.

When I click on the drop-down menu, it will show the rating here.

Let's say here if I select 4 from the drop-down menu, it will appear like this.

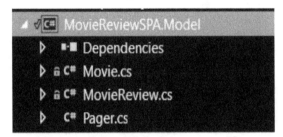

Adding Paging Control

In this section, we will add pagination to our app. For paging, obviously we will need two main components. They are **Page** and **PageSize**. I will add model to my model folder with the name **Pager**.

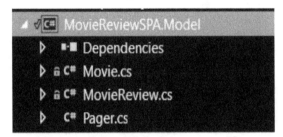

I have pasted the code snippet for the same.

```
using System;
using System.Collections.Generic;
using System.Text;

namespace MovieReviewSPA.Model
{
    public class Pager
    {
        public int Page { get; set; }
        public int PageSize { get; set; }
    }
}
```

Once done, I need to modify my IRepository.cs file. Here is the code snippet for the same.

```
using System.Linq;
using MovieReviewSPA.Model;

namespace MovieReviewSPA.Data.Contracts
{
    public interface IRepository<T> where T : class
    {
        //To query using LINQ
        IQueryable<T> GetAll(Pager queryObj);

        IQueryable<T> GetAll();

        //Returning Movie or Review by id
        T GetById(int id);

        //Adding Movie or Review
        void Add(T entity);

        //Updating Movie or Review
        void Update(T entity);

        //Deleting Moovie or Review
        void Delete(T entity);

        //Deleting Movie or Review by id
        void Delete(int id);

    }
}
```

Here I have created an overloaded version of **GetAll()**. The first one is with the Pager parameter, where in it can take the page and page size from the frontend. The other one is without a parameter. Let's go ahead and implement **IRepository**. Hence, my **EFRepository.cs** file will now look like this.

```
using System;
using System.Linq;
using Microsoft.EntityFrameworkCore;
using Microsoft.EntityFrameworkCore.ChangeTracking;
using MovieReviewSPA.Data.Contracts;
using MovieReviewSPA.Model;

namespace MovieReviewSPA.Data
{
    public class EFRepository<T> :IRepository<T> where T
: class
    {
        public EFRepository(DbContext dbContext)
```

```
        {
            if (dbContext == null)
                throw new ArgumentNullException("dbContext");
            DbContext = dbContext;
            DbSet = DbContext.Set<T>();
        }

        protected DbContext DbContext { get; set; }
        protected DbSet<T> DbSet { get; set; }
        public IQueryable<T> GetAll(Pager queryObj)
        {
            IQueryable<T> query = DbSet;

            if (queryObj.Page <= 0)
                queryObj.Page = 1;

            if (queryObj.PageSize <= 0)
                queryObj.PageSize = 10;
            query = query.Skip((queryObj.Page - 1) *
queryObj.PageSize).Take(queryObj.PageSize);

            return query;
        }

        public virtual IQueryable<T> GetAll()
        {
            return DbSet;
        }

        public virtual T GetById(int id)
        {
            return DbSet.Find(id);
        }

        public virtual void Add(T entity)
        {
            EntityEntry<T> dbEntityEntry = DbContext.
Entry(entity);
            if (dbEntityEntry.State != (EntityState)
EntityState.Detached)
            {
                dbEntityEntry.State = EntityState.Added;
            }
            else
            {
                DbSet.Add(entity);
            }
        }
```

```csharp
        public virtual void Update(T entity)
        {
                EntityEntry<T> dbEntityEntry = DbContext.
Entry(entity);
                if (dbEntityEntry.State != (EntityState)
EntityState.Detached)
                {
                    DbSet.Attach(entity);
                }
                dbEntityEntry.State = EntityState.Modified;
        }

        public void Delete(T entity)
        {
                EntityEntry<T> dbEntityEntry = DbContext.
Entry(entity);
                if (dbEntityEntry.State != (EntityState)
EntityState.Deleted)
                {
                    dbEntityEntry.State = EntityState.Deleted;
                }
                else
                {
                    DbSet.Attach(entity);
                    DbSet.Remove(entity);
                }
        }

        public void Delete(int id)
        {
            var entity = GetById(id);
            if (entity == null) return;

            Delete(entity);
        }

        /* public virtual object Include<TEntity,
TProperty>(Func<TEntity, TProperty> p) where TEntity : class
        {
            return DbSet;
        }*/
    }
}
```

Here, I have implemented the pager calculation logic in the overloaded version of the method. Lastly, I have also modified **MoviesController** and **LookupsController** to accommodate the changes. Here are the changes.

```csharp
using System;
using System.Linq;
using System.Net;
using System.Net.Http;
using Microsoft.AspNetCore.Mvc;
using MovieReviewSPA.Data.Contracts;
using MovieReviewSPA.Model;
using MovieReviewSPA.web.ViewModels.Movie;

namespace MovieReviewSPA.web.Controllers.API
{
    [Route("api/[controller]")]
    public class MoviesController : Controller
    {
        private IMovieReviewUow UOW;

        public MoviesController(IMovieReviewUow uow)
        {
            UOW = uow;
        }

        // GET api/movies
        [HttpGet("")]
        public IQueryable Get(Pager movieQuery)
        {
            var model = UOW.Movies.GetAll(movieQuery).
OrderByDescending(m => m.Reviews.Count())
                .Select(m => new MovieViewModel
                {
                    Id = m.Id,
                    MovieName = m.MovieName,
                    DirectorName = m.DirectorName,
                    ReleaseYear = m.ReleaseYear,
                    NoOfReviews = m.Reviews.Count()
                });
            return model;
        }

        // GET api/movies/1
        [HttpGet("{id}")]
        public Movie Get(int id)
        {
            var movie = UOW.Movies.GetById(id);
            if (movie != null) return movie;
            throw new Exception(new HttpResponseMessage(H
ttpStatusCode.NotFound).ToString());
        }
```

```
        // Update an existing movie
        // PUT /api/movie/
        [HttpPut("")]
        public HttpResponseMessage Put([FromBody]Movie movie)
        {
            UOW.Movies.Update(movie);
            UOW.Commit();
            return new HttpResponseMessage(HttpStatusCo
de.NoContent);
        }

        // Create a new movie
        // POST /api/movies
        [HttpPost("")]
        public int Post([FromBody]Movie movie)
        {
            UOW.Commit();
            return Response.StatusCode = (int)
HttpStatusCode.Created;
        }

        // DELETE api/movies/5
        [HttpDelete("{id}")]
        public HttpResponseMessage Delete(int id)
        {
            UOW.Movies.Delete(id);
            UOW.Commit();
            return new HttpResponseMessage(HttpStatusCo
de.NoContent);
        }
    }
}
```

And **LookupsController** looks like this.

```
using System.Collections.Generic;
using System.Linq;
using Microsoft.AspNetCore.Mvc;
using MovieReviewSPA.Data.Contracts;
using MovieReviewSPA.Model;

namespace MovieReviewSPA.web.Controllers.API
{
    [Route("api/[controller]")]
    public class LookupsController : Controller
    {
        private readonly IMovieReviewUow UOW;

        public LookupsController(IMovieReviewUow uow)
```

```
        {
            UOW = uow;
        }
        // GET: api/lookups/movies
        [HttpGet("movies")]
        public IEnumerable<Movie> GetMovies(Pager
movieQuery)
        {
            return UOW.Movies.GetAll(movieQuery).
OrderBy(m => m.Id);
        }

        // /api/Lookups/getbyreviewerid?id=1
        [HttpGet("getbyreviewerid")]
        public MovieReview GetByReviewerId(int id)
        {
            return UOW.MovieReviews.GetById(id);
        }
        #region OData Future: IQueryable<T>
        //[Queryable]
        // public IQueryable<Movie> Get()
        // public IQueryable<MovieReview> Get()

        #endregion

    }
}
```

Once done, I can go ahead and test the API. It will return the following results.

Here, I have given the page number as 1 and page size as 2. Similarly, if I don't give the page size, it will look like this.

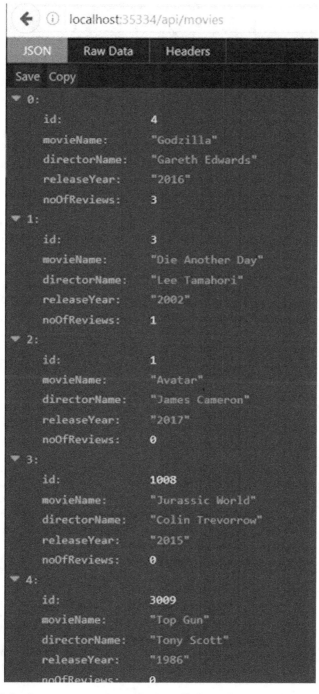

Even if I don't pass any parameter, it will then also pass the complete list as shown below. It means all the test cases are valid.

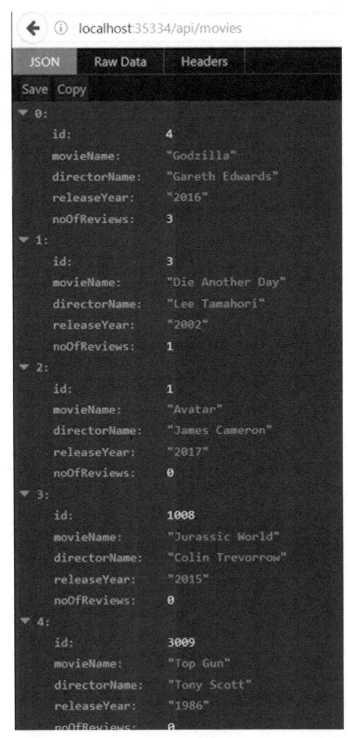

Now, let's implement the frontend part for the same. I have created the **utilities** folder in the **components** folder. Here, I'll create my pagination component.

```
▲ ✓🔲 MovieReviewSPA.web
      🔗 Connected Services
   ▷  ■■ Dependencies
   ▷ 🔧 Properties
   ▷ 🌐 wwwroot
   ▲ 📁 ClientApp
      ▲ 📁 app
         ▲ 📁 components
            ▷ 🔲 app
            ▷ 🔲 counter
            ▲ 📁 edit-movie
               ▷ 📄 edit-movie.component.html
            ▷ 🔲 edit-review
            ▷ 🔲 fetchdata
            ▷ 🔲 home
            ▷ 🔲 movies
            ▷ 🔲 navmenu
            ▷ 🔲 new-movie
            ▷ 🔲 new-review
            ▷ 🔲 not-found
            ▷ 🔲 reviews
            ▲ 📁 utilities
                +TS pagination.component.ts
         ▷ 🔲 models
         ▷ 🔲 services
            TS app.module.server.ts
            TS app.module.shared.ts
            TS app.module.ts
      ▷ 🔲 dist
      ▷ 🔲 test
         TS boot-client.ts
         TS boot-server.ts
```

Here is the code snippet.

```
import {
    Component,
    Input,
    Output,
    EventEmitter
    } from '@angular/core';
import { OnChanges } from '@angular/core';

@Component({
```

```
    selector: 'pager',
    template: `
    <nav *ngIf="totalItems > pageSize">
        <ul class="pagination">
            <li [class.disabled]="currentPage == 1">
                <a (click)="previous()" aria-
label="Previous">
                    <span aria-hidden="true">&laquo;</span>
                </a>
            </li>
            <li [class.active]="currentPage == page"
*ngFor="let page of pages" (click)="changePage(page)">
                <a>{{ page }}</a>
            </li>
            <li [class.disabled]="currentPage == pages.
length">
                <a (click)="next()" aria-label="Next">
                    <span aria-hidden="true">&raquo;</span>
                </a>
            </li>
        </ul>
    </nav>
    `
})
export class PaginationComponent implements OnChanges {
    @Input('total-items') totalItems;
    @Input('page-size') pageSize = 10;
    @Output('page-changed') pageChanged = new
EventEmitter();
    pages: any[];
    currentPage = 1;
    @Output('total-items') totalNoOfPages;
    ngOnChanges() {
        this.currentPage = 1;
    this.totalNoOfPages = this.totalItems;
        var pagesCount = Math.ceil(this.totalItems /
this.pageSize);
        this.pages = [];
        for (var i = 1; i <= pagesCount; i++)
            this.pages.push(i);

        console.log(this);
    }

    changePage(page) {
```

```
        this.currentPage = page;
        this.pageChanged.emit(page);
    }

    previous() {
        if (this.currentPage == 1)
            return;

        this.currentPage--;
        this.pageChanged.emit(this.currentPage);
    }

    next() {
        if (this.currentPage == this.pages.length)
            return;

        this.currentPage++;
        console.log("next", this);
        this.pageChanged.emit(this.currentPage);
    }
}
```

Let me explain the code snippet here. It's pretty straightforward if you would have implemented any paging earlier in your app. First of all, it has a selector with the name **pager**. Then, it has a couple of paging parameters like **currentPage, totalitems, pageSize,** etc. In the movies.component.html page, I have applied the pager control at the bottom of the page.

```
<pager [total-items]="totalMovies" [page-size]="3" (page-cha
nged)="onPageChange($event)"></pager>
```

Here is the code for the same.

```
<br />
<p>
    <a [routerLink]="['/movies/new']" class="btn btn-
primary">Create New Movie</a>
</p>
<div class="well">
    <div class="form-group">
        <label for="movie">Filter Movie</label>
        <select id="movie" class="form-control"
[(ngModel)]="filter.id" (change)="onDropdownChange()">
            <option value=""></option>
            <option *ngFor="let m of movies" value="{{m.
id}}">{{m.movieName}}</option>
        </select>
    </div>
    <button class="btn btn-danger" (click)="onResetFilter
```

```
()">Reset</button>
</div>
<h3>Movies List</h3>
<form>
    <div class="container">
        <div class="row">
            <div class="row">
                <div class="col-xs-12 col-sm-9 col-md-9">
                    <div class="list-group">
                        <div class="list-group-item">
                            <div class="row-content"
*ngFor="let m of movies">
                                <div class="list-group-
item-heading">
                                    <a title="movieName">
                                        <small>Movie
Name: {{m.movieName}}</small>
                                    </a>
                                </div>
                                <small>
                                    <i class="glyphicon
glyphicon-time"></i> Release Year: {{m.releaseYear}}
                                    <i class="glyphicon
glyphicon-user"></i> Director Name: {{m.directorName}}
                                    <br>
                                    <span class="btn
btn-info"><i class="glyphicon glyphicon-th"></i> <a
[routerLink]="['/reviews/', m.id]" style="color:
black">Movie Reviews: {{m.noOfReviews}} </a></span>
                                    <span class="btn
btn-primary"><i class="glyphicon glyphicon-edit"></
i> <a [routerLink]="['/movies/', m.id]" style="color:
black">Edit Movie </a></span>
                                    <button class="btn
btn-danger" data-toggle="confirmation" style="color: black"
type="button" (click)="delete(m.id)"><i class="glyphicon
glyphicon-remove"></i> Delete Movie</button>
                                </small>
                                <hr>
                            </div>
                        </div>
                    </div>
                </div>
            </div>
        </div>
    </div>
</div>
```

```
</form>
<pager [total-items]="totalMovies" [page-size]="3" (page-
changed)="onPageChange($event)"></pager>
```

As usual, first we need to include this component in both the **app.module.ts** and **app.module.shared.ts** files.

```
import { NgModule } from '@angular/core';
import { BrowserModule } from '@angular/platform-
browser';
import { FormsModule } from '@angular/forms';
import { HttpModule } from '@angular/http';
import { sharedConfig } from './app.module.shared';
import { MoviesComponent } from './components/movies/
movies.component';
import { MoviesService } from './services/movies.
service';
import { ReviewsService } from './services/reviews.
service';
import { NewMovieComponent } from './components/new-
movie/new-movie.component';
import { EditMovieComponent } from './components/edit-
movie/edit-movie.component';
import { NotFoundComponent } from './components/not-
found/not-found.component';
import { ReviewsComponent } from './components/reviews/
reviews.component';
import { NewReviewComponent } from './components/new-
review/new-review.component';
import { EditReviewComponent } from './components/edit-
review/edit-review.component';
import { PaginationComponent } from './components/
utilities/pagination.component';

@NgModule({
    bootstrap: sharedConfig.bootstrap,
    declarations: [...sharedConfig.declarations,
        MoviesComponent,
        NewMovieComponent,
        EditMovieComponent,
        NotFoundComponent,
        ReviewsComponent,
        NewReviewComponent,
        EditReviewComponent,
        PaginationComponent],
    imports: [
        BrowserModule,
```

```
        FormsModule,
        HttpModule,
        ...sharedConfig.imports
    ],
    providers: [
        { provide: 'ORIGIN_URL', useValue: location.
origin },
        MoviesService,
        ReviewsService
    ]
})
export class AppModule {
}
```

The code to be included in the **app.module.shared.ts** file is shown below.

```
import * as Raven from 'raven-js';
import { NgModule } from '@angular/core';
import { RouterModule } from '@angular/router';
import { FormsModule } from '@angular/forms';
import { ToastyModule } from 'ng2-toasty';
import { AppComponent } from './components/app/app.
component'
import { NavMenuComponent } from './components/navmenu/
navmenu.component';
import { HomeComponent } from './components/home/home.
component';
import { FetchDataComponent } from './components/
fetchdata/fetchdata.component';
import { CounterComponent } from './components/counter/
counter.component';
import { MoviesComponent } from './components/movies/
movies.component';
import { ReviewsComponent } from './components/reviews/
reviews.component';
import { NewMovieComponent } from './components/new-
movie/new-movie.component';
import { EditMovieComponent } from './components/edit-
movie/edit-movie.component';
import { NewReviewComponent } from './components/new-
review/new-review.component';
import { EditReviewComponent } from './components/edit-
review/edit-review.component';
import { PaginationComponent } from './components/
utilities/pagination.component';
import { MoviesService } from './services/movies.
```

```
service';
import { ReviewsService } from './services/reviews.
service';

Raven

.config('https://7579eaef4acc46bab3ffd87d3d85f3ea@sentry.
io/203240')
    .install();

export const sharedConfig: NgModule = {
    bootstrap: [ AppComponent ],
    declarations: [
        AppComponent,
        NavMenuComponent,
        CounterComponent,
        FetchDataComponent,
        HomeComponent,
        MoviesComponent,
        NewMovieComponent,
        EditMovieComponent,
        ReviewsComponent,
        NewReviewComponent,
        EditReviewComponent,
        PaginationComponent
    ],
    imports: [
        FormsModule,
        ToastyModule.forRoot(),
        RouterModule.forRoot([
            { path: '', redirectTo: 'home', pathMatch: 'full' },
            { path: 'movies', component: MoviesComponent },
            { path: 'movies/new', component: NewMovieComponent },
            { path: 'movies/:id', component: EditMovieComponent },
            { path: 'reviews/:id', component:
ReviewsComponent },
            { path: 'editreview/:id', component:
EditReviewComponent },
            { path: 'reviews/new/:id', component:
NewReviewComponent },
            { path: 'home', component: HomeComponent },
            { path: 'counter', component: CounterComponent },
            { path: 'fetch-data', component:
FetchDataComponent },
            { path: '**', redirectTo: 'home' }
        ])
```

```
    ],
    providers: [MoviesService, ReviewsService]
};
```

The corresponding change in **movies.service.ts** is shown below.

```
import { Injectable, Inject } from '@angular/core';
import { Http } from '@angular/http';
import 'rxjs/add/operator/map';

@Injectable()
export class MoviesService {

    //In order to use any injectable, pass it via ctor
    constructor(private http: Http, @Inject('ORIGIN_URL')
private originUrl: string) { }

    getMovies(filter) {
        return this.http.get(this.originUrl + '/api/
movies' + '?' + this.toQueryString(filter))
            //Once, we get the response back, it has to
get mapped to json
            .map(res => res.json());
    }

    getMoviesCount() {
        return this.http.get(this.originUrl + '/api/movies' )
            //Once, we get the response back, it has to
get mapped to json
            .map(res => res.json());
    }

    toQueryString(obj) {
        var parts = [];
        for (var property in obj) {
            var value = obj[property];
            if (value != null && value != undefined)
                parts.push(encodeURIComponent(property) +
'=' + encodeURIComponent(value));
        }
        return parts.join('&');
    }

    createMovie(movie) {
        return this.http.post('/api/movies', movie)
            .map(res => res.json());
    }
```

```
getMovie(id) {
    return this.http.get('/api/movies/' + id)
        .map(res => res.json());
}
updateMovie(movie) {
    return this.http.put('/api/movies/', movie)
    .map(res => res.json());
}
deleteMovie(id) {
    return this.http.delete('/api/movies/' + id)
        .map(res => res.json());
}
}
```

Here, in the service, you can see that I have applied the filter. Here, I have kept one more call just to fetch the complete record count from the server. I have implemented one helper method as well just to compose the URL. Lastly, I have applied the changes in my **movies.component.ts** page. Here is the code snippet for the same.

```
import * *as Raven from 'raven-js';
import { Component, OnInit } from '@angular/core';
import { MoviesService } from '../../services/movies.service';
import { Router } from '@angular/router';
import { ToastyService } from "ng2-toasty";

@Component({
    selector: 'app-movies',
    templateUrl: './movies.component.html',
    styleUrls: ['./movies.component.css']
})
export class MoviesComponent implements OnInit {

    movies;
    allMovies;
    movie: {};
    filter: any = {};
    totalMovies;
    query: any = {
        pageSize: 3,
        allMovies: 10
    }
    queryResult: any = {};

    constructor(
        private moviesService: MoviesService, private
router: Router, private toastyService: ToastyService) {
    }
```

```
    ngOnInit() {
this.moviesService.getMovies(this.query).subscribe(movies => {
        this.movies = this.allMovies = movies;
        console.log("Movies: ", this.movies);
    });
        this.moviesService.getMoviesCount().
subscribe(movies => {
            this.totalMovies = movies.length;
            console.log("Total Movies: ", this.totalMovies);
        });
    }
    submit() {
        this.moviesService.createMovie(this.movie)
            .subscribe(x => console.log(x));
    }

    delete(id) {
        if (confirm("Are you sure?")) {
            this.moviesService.deleteMovie(id)
                .subscribe(x => {
                    this.toastyService.success({
                        title: 'Success',
                        msg: 'Movie Deleted!',
                        theme: 'bootstrap',
                        showClose: true,
                        timeout: 5000
                    });
                    this.router.navigate(['/home']);
                },
                err => {
Raven.captureException(err.originalError || err);
                    this.toastyService.error({
                        title: 'Error',
                        msg: 'An unexpected error while
deleting the record!',
                        theme: 'bootstrap',
                        showClose: true,
                        timeout: 5000
                    });
                });
        }
    }
    private populateMovies() {
        this.moviesService.getMovies(this.query)
```

```
                .subscribe(result => this.movies = result);
    }
    onDropdownChange() {
        var movies = this.allMovies;
        if (this.filter.id) {
            movies = movies.filter(m => m.id == this.filter.id);
        }
        this.movies = movies;
    }
    onResetFilter() {
        this.filter = {};
        this.onDropdownChange();
    }

    onPageChange(page) {
        this.query.page = page;
        this.populateMovies();
    }
}
```

Once done, when I inspect the app, it will appear like this.

Movies List

Movie Name:- Godzilla

🕒 Release Year:- 2016 👤 Director Name:- Gareth Edwards

| ⚏ Movie Reviews:- 3 | ☑ Edit Movie | ✖ Delete Movie |

Movie Name:- Die Another Day

🕒 Release Year:- 2002 👤 Director Name:- Lee Tamahori

| ⚏ Movie Reviews:- 1 | ☑ Edit Movie | ✖ Delete Movie |

Movie Name:- Avatar

🕒 Release Year:- 2017 👤 Director Name:- James Cameron

| ⚏ Movie Reviews:- 0 | ☑ Edit Movie | ✖ Delete Movie |

« 1 2 »

Since I have set the page size in pager to 3, there will be 3 records per-page. You can change this as per your requirements. When I click on the second page, it will appear as shown in the following screenshot:

Creating a Detail View

In this section, we will create a new view for presenting the read-only view of Movies and later on, we will add features like uploading photos against Movies. So without wasting any time let's create the component first. I have created the component as shown below.

```
C:\Dell\Books\ASPNETCorePlusAngular4\MovieReviewSPA\MovieReviewSPA.web\ClientApp\app\components (Another)
λ ng g c detail-review --spec false
installing component
    create ClientApp\app\components\detail-review\detail-review.component.css
    create ClientApp\app\components\detail-review\detail-review.component.html
    create ClientApp\app\components\detail-review\detail-review.component.ts
    update ClientApp\app\app.module.ts

C:\Dell\Books\ASPNETCorePlusAngular4\MovieReviewSPA\MovieReviewSPA.web\ClientApp\app\components (Another)
λ
```

Now, let's fix its references in the respective files such as the **app.module.ts** and **app.module.shared.ts** files. I have pasted the code snippet for the same.

```
import { NgModule } from '@angular/core';
import { BrowserModule } from '@angular/platform-browser';
import { FormsModule } from '@angular/forms';
import { HttpModule } from '@angular/http';
import { sharedConfig } from './app.module.shared';
import { MoviesComponent } from './components/movies/
movies.component';
import { MoviesService } from './services/movies.service';
import { ReviewsService } from './services/reviews.service';
```

```
import { NewMovieComponent } from './components/new-
movie/new-movie.component';
import { EditMovieComponent } from './components/edit-
movie/edit-movie.component';
import { NotFoundComponent } from './components/not-
found/not-found.component';
import { ReviewsComponent } from './components/reviews/
reviews.component';
import { NewReviewComponent } from './components/new-
review/new-review.component';
import { EditReviewComponent } from './components/edit-
review/edit-review.component';
import { PaginationComponent } from './components/
utilities/pagination.component';
import { DetailViewComponent } from './components/detail-
view/detail-view.component';

@NgModule({
    bootstrap: sharedConfig.bootstrap,
    declarations: [...sharedConfig.declarations,
        MoviesComponent,
        NewMovieComponent,
        EditMovieComponent,
        NotFoundComponent,
        ReviewsComponent,
        NewReviewComponent,
        EditReviewComponent,
        PaginationComponent,
        DetailViewComponent
],
    imports: [
        BrowserModule,
        FormsModule,
        HttpModule,
        ...sharedConfig.imports
    ],
    providers: [
        { provide: 'ORIGIN_URL', useValue: location.origin },
        MoviesService,
        ReviewsService
    ]
})
export class AppModule {
}
And,
```

```
import * as Raven from 'raven-js';
import { NgModule } from '@angular/core';
import { RouterModule } from '@angular/router';
import { FormsModule } from '@angular/forms';
import { ToastyModule } from 'ng2-toasty';
import { AppComponent } from './components/app/app.component'
import { NavMenuComponent } from './components/navmenu/
navmenu.component';
import { HomeComponent } from './components/home/home.
component';
import { FetchDataComponent } from './components/
fetchdata/fetchdata.component';
import { CounterComponent } from './components/counter/
counter.component';
import { MoviesComponent } from './components/movies/
movies.component';
import { ReviewsComponent } from './components/reviews/
reviews.component';
import { NewMovieComponent } from './components/new-
movie/new-movie.component';
import { EditMovieComponent } from './components/edit-
movie/edit-movie.component';
import { NewReviewComponent } from './components/new-
review/new-review.component';
import { EditReviewComponent } from './components/edit-
review/edit-review.component';
import { PaginationComponent } from './components/
utilities/pagination.component';
import { DetailViewComponent } from './components/detail-
view/detail-view.component';
import { MoviesService } from './services/movies.service';
import { ReviewsService } from './services/reviews.service';

Raven

.config('https://7579eaef4acc46bab3ffd87d3d85f3ea@sentry.
io/203240')
    .install();

export const sharedConfig: NgModule = {
    bootstrap: [ AppComponent ],
    declarations: [
        AppComponent,
        NavMenuComponent,
        CounterComponent,
```

```
        FetchDataComponent,
        HomeComponent,
        MoviesComponent,
        NewMovieComponent,
        EditMovieComponent,
        ReviewsComponent,
        NewReviewComponent,
        EditReviewComponent,
        PaginationComponent,
        DetailViewComponent
    ],
    imports: [
        FormsModule,
        ToastyModule.forRoot(),
        RouterModule.forRoot([
            { path: '', redirectTo: 'home', pathMatch: 'full' },
            { path: 'movies', component: MoviesComponent },
            { path: 'movies/new', component:
NewMovieComponent },
            { path: 'movies/:id', component:
EditMovieComponent },
            { path: 'movies/detail/:id', component:
DetailViewComponent },
            { path: 'reviews/:id', component:
ReviewsComponent },
            { path: 'editreview/:id', component:
EditReviewComponent },
            { path: 'reviews/new/:id', component:
NewReviewComponent },
            { path: 'home', component: HomeComponent },
            { path: 'counter', component: CounterComponent },
            { path: 'fetch-data', component:
FetchDataComponent },
            { path: '**', redirectTo: 'home' }
        ])
    ],
    providers: [MoviesService, ReviewsService]

};
```

Creating a Tabbed View

Here, I have added the route as well. I have also modified the **movies. component.html** page to accommodate the change.

```
<br />
<p>
    <a [routerLink]="['/movies/new']" class="btn btn-
primary">Create New Movie</a>
</p>
<div class="well">
    <div class="form-group">
        <label for="movie">Filter Movie</label>
        <select id="movie" class="form-control"
[(ngModel)]="filter.id" (change)="onDropdownChange()">
            <option value=""></option>
            <option *ngFor="let m of movies" value="{{m.
id}}">{{m.movieName}}</option>
        </select>
    </div>
    <button class="btn btn-danger" (click)="onResetFilter
()">Reset</button>
</div>
<h3>Movies List</h3>
<form>
    <div class="container">
        <div class="row">
            <div class="row">
                <div class="col-xs-12 col-sm-9 col-md-9">
                    <div class="list-group">
                        <div class="list-group-item">
                            <div class="row-content"
*ngFor="let m of movies">
                                <div class="list-group-
item-heading">
                                    <a title="movieName">
                                        <small>Movie
Name: {{m.movieName}}</small>
                                    </a>
                                </div>
                                <small>
                                    <i class="glyphicon
glyphicon-time"></i> Release Year: {{m.releaseYear}}
                                    <i class="glyphicon
glyphicon-user"></i> Director Name: {{m.directorName}}
                                    <br>
                                    <span class="btn
btn-info"><i class="glyphicon glyphicon-th"></i> <a
[routerLink]="['/reviews/', m.id]" style="color:
black">Movie Reviews: {{m.noOfReviews}} </a></span>
```

```
                                     <span class="btn
btn-primary"><i class="glyphicon glyphicon-edit"></
i> <a [routerLink]="['/movies/', m.id]" style="color:
black">Edit Movie </a></span>
                                     <span class="btn btn-
success"><i class="glyphicon glyphicon-upload"></i> <a
[routerLink]="['/movies/detail/', m.id]" style="color:
black">Detail View </a></span>
                                     <button class="btn
btn-danger" data-toggle="confirmation" style="color:
black" type="button" (click)="delete(m.id)"><i
class="glyphicon glyphicon-remove"></i> Delete Movie</
button>
                               </small>
                               <hr>
                               </div>
                          </div>
                      </div>
                 </div>
             </div>
         </div>
</form>
<pager [total-items]="totalMovies" [page-size]="3" (page-
changed)="onPageChange($event)"></pager>
```

Here, I have just added one button with route. Once done, it will look like this.

After this, I have pasted the following markup in the **detail-view.component.html** page.

```html
<h1>Movie</h1>
<div>
    <!-- Nav tabs -->
    <ul class="nav nav-tabs" role="tablist">
        <li role="presentation" class="active"><a
href="#basic" aria-controls="basic" role="tab" data-
toggle="tab">Movie</a></li>
        <li role="presentation"><a href="#photos" aria-
controls="photos" role="tab" data-toggle="tab">Pics</a></
li>
    </ul>
    <!-- Tab panes -->
    <div class="tab-content" *ngIf="movie">
        <!-- Movie tab -->
        <div role="tabpanel" class="tab-pane active"
id="basic">
            <h2>About Movie</h2>
            <ul>
                <li>Name: {{ movie.movieName }}</li>
                <li>Director Name: {{ movie.directorName
}}</li>
                <li>Release Year: {{ movie.releaseYear }}
            </ul>
            <br />
            <p>
                <a class="btn btn-info" [routerLink]="['/
movies']">View All Movies</a>
            </p>
        </div>
        <!-- Photos tab -->
        <div role="tabpanel" class="tab-pane"
id="photos">
            <h2>Movie Pics</h2>

        </div>
    </div>
</div>
```

And the corresponding **detail-view.component.ts** file looks like this.

```ts
import * as Raven from 'raven-js';
import { Component, OnInit, ElementRef, ViewChild } from
'@angular/core';
```

```
import { ActivatedRoute, Router } from '@angular/router';
import { Movie } from './../../models/movie';
import { MoviesService } from '../../services/movies.
service';
import { ToastyService } from "ng2-toasty";

@Component({
    templateUrl: './detail-view.component.html',
    })
export class DetailViewComponent implements OnInit {
    @ViewChild('fileInput') fileInput: ElementRef;
    movie: Movie = new Movie();
    photos: any[];
    constructor(private route: ActivatedRoute,
        private router: Router,
        private moviesService: MoviesService,
        private toastyService: ToastyService) {
        route.params.subscribe(p => {
            this.movie.id = +p['id'];
        });
    }

    ngOnInit() {

        if (this.movie.id) {
            this.moviesService.getMovie(this.movie.id)
                .subscribe(m => {
                    this.movie = m;
                    console.log("Movie:", this.movie);
                },
                err => {
                    if (err.status == 404) {
                        this.router.navigate(['/']);
                    }
                });
    }
}

onSubmit() {
    if (this.movie.id) {
        this.moviesService.updateMovie(this.movie)
            .subscribe(x => {
                console.log(x);
                this.toastyService.success({
                    title: 'Success',
                    msg: 'Movie Updated!',
```

```
                        theme: 'bootstrap',
                        showClose: true,
                        timeout: 5000
                   });
                   this.router.navigate(['/movies']);
              },
              err => {
                   Raven.captureException(err.originalError
|| err);
                   this.toastyService.error({
                        title: 'Error',
                        msg: 'An unexpected error while
updating the record!',
                        theme: 'bootstrap',
                        showClose: true,
                        timeout: 5000
                   });
              });
         }
     }
}
```

Currently, nothing is new as far as the component logic is concerned. Therefore, with the above change in place, when I click on the detail view, it will appear like this.

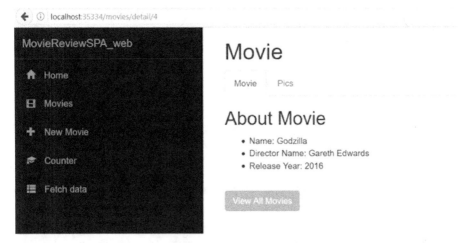

Now, it appears in tabs. You need to upload its pics so that it corresponds to the movie. However, when I click on the **Pics** tab, the page gets reloaded with a different URL http://localhost:35334/home#photos. I landed on the home page as it didn't find the matching route.

The problem is with the scaffolding template. Now, in order to quickly fix this, we need to add the following line import'bootstrap'; to the **boot.client.**

ts file. Here, I am importing bootstrap in the client. Here is the code snippet for the same.

```
import'bootstrap';
import'reflect-metadata';
import'zone.js';
import { enableProdMode } from' @angular/core';
import { platformBrowserDynamic } from' @angular/platform-
browser-dynamic';
import { AppModule } from'./app/app.module';

if (module['hot']) {
    module['hot'].accept();
    module['hot'].dispose(() => {
// Before restarting the app, we create a new root
element and dispose the old one
const oldRootElem = document.querySelector('app');
const newRootElem = document.createElement('app');
        oldRootElem.parentNode.insertBefore(newRootElem,
oldRootElem);
        modulePromise.then(appModule => appModule.destroy());
    });
} else {
    enableProdMode();
}

// Note: @ng-tools/webpack looks for the following
expression when performing production
// builds. Don't change how this line looks, otherwise
you may break tree-shaking.
const modulePromise = platformBrowserDynamic().
bootstrapModule(AppModule);
```

Once done, when I click on Pics, it will appear like this.

Adding An Image Model

In this section, we will go ahead and add the Image class first and then extend the model. Here, I have created a new class with the name **Image**.

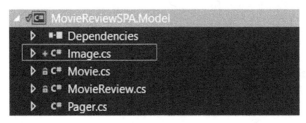

```
Using System;
using System.Collections.Generic;
using System.ComponentModel.DataAnnotations;
using System.Text;

namespace MovieReviewSPA.Model
    {
public class Image
    {
        public int Id { get; set; }

            [Required]
            [StringLength(255)]
            public string FileName { get; set; }

    }
}
```

Here, I have applied data annotations as well. Now, I will go to the Movie class and add the following. Basically, each movie should have a collection of photos.

```
using System;
using System.Collections.Generic;
using System.Collections.ObjectModel;
using System.ComponentModel.DataAnnotations;

namespace MovieReviewSPA.Model
{
    public class Movie
    {
        public int Id { get; set; }
        [Required]
        [StringLength(255)]
        public string MovieName { get; set; }
        [Required]
        [StringLength(255)]
```

```
        public string DirectorName { get; set; }
        [Required]
        [StringLength(10)]
        public string ReleaseYear { get; set; }
        public virtual ICollection<MovieReview> Reviews {
get; set; }
        public virtual ICollection<Image> Images { get;
set; }
        public Movie()
        {
        Images = new Collection<Image>();
        }
    }
}
```

As a good practice; I have initialized the collection inside the constructor. I will be using this in future just to avoid the null reference exception. Now, I will go ahead and add the model class to our **DbContext**, which is in the data project. I have pasted the code snippet for the same.

```
using Microsoft.EntityFrameworkCore;
using MovieReviewSPA.Model;

namespace MovieReviewSPA.Data
{
    public class MovieReviewDbContext :DbContext
    {
        public MovieReviewDbContext()
        {
            Database.EnsureCreated();
        }
        public DbSet<Movie> Movies { get; set; }
        public DbSet<MovieReview> MovieReviews { get;
set; }

        public DbSet<Image> Images { get; set; }

        protected override void OnConfiguring(DbContextOpt
ionsBuilder optionsBuilder)
        {
            if (!optionsBuilder.IsConfigured)
            {
                //While deploying to azure, make sure to
change the connection string based on azure settings
optionsBuilder.UseSqlServer(@"Server=(localdb)\mssqllocal
db;Database=MovieReviewSPA;Trusted_Connection=True;Multip
leActiveResultSets=true;");
            }
```

```
            }

        public MovieReviewDbContext(DbContextOptions<
MovieReviewDbContext> options) : base(options)
        {
            //It will look for connection string from
appsettings
        }
    }
}
```

Creating a New Migration

In this section, we will create a migration in order to push the changes to the database. So, we will execute the **dotnet ef migrations add AddImage** command.

It gave the same error and didn't add the table in the database as shown below.

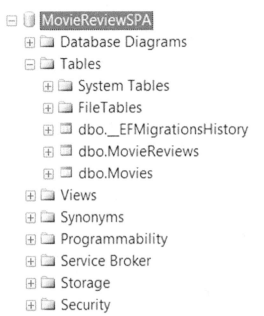

Although, we have implanted the solution in the startup file, it still gives the same problem. As per the Entity Framework Team, this issue is present in their backlog and will be fixed in the coming releases. I have already opened a ticket with them. You can track it at **http://bit.ly/EF-Core-Issues**. Now, in order to work-around this issue, we can drop the database and create it again with the following commands. First, we need to execute **dotnet ef database drop**.

```
X Cmder                                                                    —   □   ×

C:\Dell\Books\ASPNETCorePlusAngular4\MovieReviewSPA\MovieReviewSPA.web (Another) (MovieReviewSPA_web@0.0.0)
λ dotnet ef database drop

Build succeeded.
    0 Warning(s)
    0 Error(s)

Time Elapsed 00:00:07.20
Are you sure you want to drop the database 'MovieReviewSPA' on server '(localdb)\mssqllocaldb'? (y/N)
```

This will ask for confirmation. On typing Y, it will drop the database.

```
X Cmder                                                                    —   □   ×

C:\Dell\Books\ASPNETCorePlusAngular4\MovieReviewSPA\MovieReviewSPA.web (Another) (MovieReviewSPA_web@0.0.0)
λ dotnet ef database drop

Build succeeded.
    0 Warning(s)
    0 Error(s)

Time Elapsed 00:00:07.20
Are you sure you want to drop the database 'MovieReviewSPA' on server '(localdb)\mssqllocaldb'? (y/N)
y
Executed DbCommand (23ms) [Parameters=[], CommandType='Text', CommandTimeout='30']
IF EXISTS (SELECT * FROM INFORMATION_SCHEMA.TABLES WHERE TABLE_TYPE = 'BASE TABLE') SELECT 1 ELSE SELECT 0
Dropping database 'MovieReviewSPA'.
Executed DbCommand (15ms) [Parameters=[], CommandType='Text', CommandTimeout='60']
IF SERVERPROPERTY('EngineEdition') <> 5 EXEC(N'ALTER DATABASE [MovieReviewSPA] SET SINGLE_USER WITH ROLLBACK IMMEDIATE;'
);
Executed DbCommand (15ms) [Parameters=[], CommandType='Text', CommandTimeout='60']
IF SERVERPROPERTY('EngineEdition') <> 5 EXEC(N'ALTER DATABASE [MovieReviewSPA] SET SINGLE_USER WITH ROLLBACK IMMEDIATE;'
);
Executed DbCommand (62ms) [Parameters=[], CommandType='Text', CommandTimeout='60']
DROP DATABASE [MovieReviewSPA];
Executed DbCommand (62ms) [Parameters=[], CommandType='Text', CommandTimeout='60']
DROP DATABASE [MovieReviewSPA];
Successfully dropped database 'MovieReviewSPA'.

C:\Dell\Books\ASPNETCorePlusAngular4\MovieReviewSPA\MovieReviewSPA.web (Another) (MovieReviewSPA_web@0.0.0)
λ
```

Now, we can create a new one with the same old **dotnet ef migrations add AddImage** command.

```
A Cmder                                                                    —   □   ×

C:\Dell\Books\ASPNETCorePlusAngular4\MovieReviewSPA\MovieReviewSPA.web (Another) (MovieReviewSPA_web@0.0.0)
λ dotnet ef migrations add AddImage

Build succeeded.
    0 Warning(s)
    0 Error(s)

Time Elapsed 00:00:07.42
Your target project 'MovieReviewSPA.web' doesn't match your migrations assembly 'MovieReviewSPA.Data'. Either change you
r target project or change your migrations assembly.
Change your migrations assembly by using DbContextOptionsBuilder. E.g. options.UseSqlServer(connection, b => b.Migration
sAssembly("MovieReviewSPA.web")). By default, the migrations assembly is the assembly containing the DbContext.
Change your target project to the migrations project by using the Package Manager Console's Default project drop-down li
st, or by executing "dotnet ef" from the directory containing the migrations project.

C:\Dell\Books\ASPNETCorePlusAngular4\MovieReviewSPA\MovieReviewSPA.web (Another) (MovieReviewSPA_web@0.0.0)
λ
```

It will again give the same error, but this time, it will show the table there.

Since we dropped and re-created the database, we won't have records there. But, with our seed method in our application, when we run the app, it will push the seed data in the **Movie** and **MovieReviews** tables. So once we run the app, it will return to its original state as shown below.

Adding the Images Controller

In this section, we will add a new controller, which is meant for Images only.

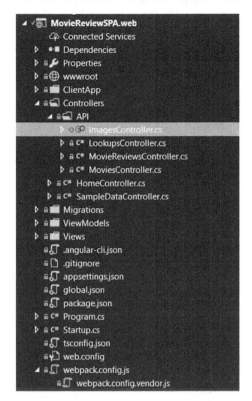

Here is the initial code snippet for Images controller.

```csharp
using System;
using System.IO;
using Microsoft.AspNetCore.Hosting;
using Microsoft.AspNetCore.Http;
using Microsoft.AspNetCore.Mvc;
using Microsoft.Extensions.Options;
using MovieReviewSPA.Data.Contracts;
using MovieReviewSPA.Model;

namespace MovieReviewSPA.web.Controllers.API
{
    [Route("/api/movies/{Id}/images")]
    public class ImagesController : Controller
    {
        private IHostingEnvironment _host;
        private IMovieReviewUow _uow;
        private ImageSettings _options;

        public ImagesController(IHostingEnvironment host,
IMovieReviewUow uow, IOptionsSnapshot<ImageSettings>
options)
```

```
        {
            _host = host;
            _uow = uow;
            _options = options.Value;
        }
        [HttpPost]
        public IActionResult Upload(int Id, IFormFile file)
        {
            var movie = _uow.Movies.GetById(Id);
            if (movie == null)
            {
                return NotFound();
            }
            if (file == null) return BadRequest("File not
valid");
            if (file.Length == 0) return BadRequest("Empty
File");
            if (file.Length > _options.MaxBytes) return
BadRequest("File exceeded 10 MB size!");
            if (!_options.IsSupported(file.FileName))
return BadRequest("Invalid File Type");
            var uploadsFolder = Path.Combine(_host.
WebRootPath, "uploads");
            if (!Directory.Exists(uploadsFolder))
                {
                    Directory.
CreateDirectory(uploadsFolder);
                }
                var fileName = Guid.NewGuid().ToString() +
Path.GetExtension(file.FileName);
                var filepath = Path.Combine(uploadsFolder,
fileName);
                using (var stream = new
FileStream(filepath, FileMode.Create))
                {
                    file.CopyTo(stream);
                }

                var image = new Image { FileName =
fileName };
                movie.Images.Add(image);
                _uow.Commit();
                return Ok(image);
        }
    }
}
```

Let me explain the code. Here, the upload method takes the Id, which is basically the Movie Id, and the file. Then, it checks a couple of things like first it checks for the movie with its id. If it's valid, it proceeds otherwise it will return a Bad Request. Similarly, it checks whether the file is valid, whether it's not an empty file and whether the file exceeds 10 MB in size. Here, I am reading these settings from the **appsettings.json** file.

```
{
        "Data": {
            "MovieReviewSPA": {
                "ConnectionString": "Server=(localdb)\\ms
sqllocaldb;Database=MovieReviewSPA;Trusted_Connection=Tru
e;MultipleActiveResultSets=true"
        }
    },
    "ImageSettings": {
        "MaxBytes": 10485760,
        "AcceptedFileTypes": [ ".jpg", ".jpeg", ".png" ]
    },
    "Logging": {
        "IncludeScopes": false,
        "LogLevel": {
        "Default": "Verbose",
        "System": "Information",
        "Microsoft": "Information"
        }
    }
}
```

In order to read these settings, I need to configure the same in the **startup.cs** file as shown below.

```
services.Configure<ImageSettings>(Configuration.
GetSection("ImageSettings"));
```

Basically, here I am reading the **ImageSettings** section. I have pasted the code snippet for the startup file.

```
using Microsoft.AspNetCore.Builder;
using Microsoft.AspNetCore.Hosting;
using Microsoft.AspNetCore.SpaServices.Webpack;
using Microsoft.EntityFrameworkCore;
using Microsoft.EntityFrameworkCore.Infrastructure;
using Microsoft.Extensions.Configuration;
using Microsoft.Extensions.DependencyInjection;
using Microsoft.Extensions.Logging;
using MovieReviewSPA.Data;
using MovieReviewSPA.Data.Contracts;
using MovieReviewSPA.Data.Helpers;
```

```
using MovieReviewSPA.Data.SampleData;
using MovieReviewSPA.Model;

namespace MovieReviewSPA.web
{
    public class Startup
    {
        public Startup(IHostingEnvironment env)
        {
        var builder = new ConfigurationBuilder()
                .SetBasePath(env.ContentRootPath)
                .AddJsonFile("appsettings.json",
optional: true, reloadOnChange: true)

.AddJsonFile($"appsettings.{env.EnvironmentName}.json",
optional: true)
                .AddEnvironmentVariables();
            Configuration = builder.Build();
        }

        public IConfigurationRoot Configuration { get; }

        // This method gets called by the runtime. Use
this method to add services to the container.
        public void ConfigureServices(IServiceCollection
services)
        {
            services.AddEntityFramework()
            .AddDbContext<MovieReviewDbContext>(options
=>

options.UseSqlServer(Configuration["Data:MovieReviewSPA:Co
nnectionString"],

                b => b.MigrationsAssembly("MovieRevie
wSPA.web")));

            // Add framework services.
            services.AddMvc();
            //Initiating Seed Data
            services.AddTransient<InitialData>();
            //DI Setup

services.Configure<ImageSettings>(Configuration.
GetSection("ImageSettings"));
            services.AddScoped<RepositoryFactories,
RepositoryFactories>();
            services.AddScoped<IRepositoryProvider,
RepositoryProvider>();
```

```
            services.AddScoped<IMovieReviewUow,
MovieReviewUow>();

        }

        // This method gets called by the runtime. Use
this method to configure the HTTP request pipeline.
        public void Configure(IApplicationBuilder app,
IHostingEnvironment env, ILoggerFactory loggerFactory,
InitialData seedDbContext)
        {
loggerFactory.AddConsole(Configuration.
GetSection("Logging"));
            loggerFactory.AddDebug();

            if (env.IsDevelopment())
            {
                app.UseDeveloperExceptionPage();
                app.UseWebpackDevMiddleware(new
WebpackDevMiddlewareOptions {
                    HotModuleReplacement = true
                });
            }
            else
            {
                app.UseExceptionHandler("/Home/Error");
            }

            app.UseStaticFiles();

            app.UseMvc(routes =>
            {
                routes.MapRoute(
                    name: "default",
                    template: "{controller=Home}/
{action=Index}/{id?}");

                routes.MapSpaFallbackRoute(
                name: "spa-fallback",
                defaults: new { controller = "Home",
action = "Index" });
            });
            //Initiating from here
            seedDbContext.SeedData();
        }
    }
}
```

Here, I have also created another **ImageSettings** class.

```
▲ ✓⊞  MovieReviewSPA.Model
  ▷  ▪▪■  Dependencies
  ▷  + C#  Image.cs
  ▷  + C#  ImageSettings.cs
  ▷  ✓ C#  Movie.cs
  ▷  â C#  MovieReview.cs
  ▷    C#  Pager.cs
```

Here is the code snippet for the same.

```csharp
using System.IO;
using System.Linq;

namespace MovieReviewSPA.Model
{
    public class ImageSettings
    {
        public int MaxBytes { get; set; }
        public string[] AcceptedFileTypes { get; set; }

        public bool IsSupported(string fileName)
        {
            return AcceptedFileTypes.Any(s => s == (Path.
GetExtension(fileName).ToLower()));
        }
    }
}
```

It contains all the fields that we are reading from the **appsettings** file. Apart from this, it also checks whether the image is supported or not? One point to note here is that I am using the **IOptionsSnapshot** interface for reading ImageSettings. This is a generic interface which has a value property that needs to be supplied to **IOptionsSnapshot**.

After this, there are simple C# File Handling features. Here, first I need to check whether the **uploads** folder exists in the **wwwroot** folder, which is public folder basically. If the uploads folder is not there, then we need to create it first. We then create our own Filename, which is basically a GUID and attach it with the file type. Then, we need to upload the file in the database.

Testing Upload Functionality

In this section, we will test the API, which we developed in the last section. Let's go ahead and open **postman**.

Make sure that you provide the same name in the key field as it's provided in the controller. So, I have given the name **file** and then in the value field, I have chosen the **Avatar** image. Now, when I click on the Send button, it will show the response back.

Therefore, as per logic, it created a new filename, stored the filename in the database and returned the id as 1. Now when I inspect the database, it will show the following result.

100 % ▾

▦ Results 📄 Messages

	Id	FileName	MovieId
1	1	75976734-d2ff-491b-8a9b-659ebfb594f1.jpg	1

Building Client Side

In this section, we will build client side for the same functionality. Therefore, I need to go to the movie-detail.component.html page and add an input type to upload a photo. Here is the code snippet for the same.

```
<h1>Movie</h1>
<div>
        <!-- Nav tabs -->
        <ul class="nav nav-tabs" role="tablist">
            <li role="presentation" class="active"><a
href="#basic" aria-controls="basic" role="tab" data-
toggle="tab">Movie</a></li>
```

```
            <li role="presentation"><a href="#photos"
aria-controls="photos" role="tab" data-toggle="tab">Pics</
a></li>
        </ul>
        <!-- Tab panes -->
        <div class="tvab-content" *ngIf="movie">
        <!-- Movie tab -->
        <div role="tabpanel" class="tab-pane active"
id="basic">
            <h2>About Movie</h2>
            <ul>
                <li>Name: {{ movie.movieName }}</li>
                <li>Director Name: {{ movie.directorName
}}</li>
                <li>Release Year: {{ movie.releaseYear }}
            </ul>
            <br />
            <p>
                <a class="btn btn-info" [routerLink]="['/
movies']">View All Movies</a>
            </p>
        </div>
        <!-- Photos tab -->
        <div role="tabpanel" class="tab-pane"
id="photos">
            <h2>Movie Pics</h2>
            <input type="file" (change)="uploadImage()"
#fileInput/>
        </div>
    </div>
</div>
```

Here, when the user selects a photo, it will get uploaded immediately, that is, we have the change event here. I also have the **#fileInput** template variable. This is used to gain the access of a file from the component.

```
import * as Raven from 'raven-js';
import { Component, OnInit, ElementRef, ViewChild } from
'@angular/core';
import { ActivatedRoute, Router } from '@angular/router';
import { Movie } from './../../models/movie';
import { MoviesService } from '../../services/movies.
service';
import { ImagesService } from '../../services/images.
service';
import { ToastyService } from "ng2-toasty";
@Component({
```

```
    templateUrl: './detail-view.component.html',
    })
    export class DetailViewComponent implements
OnInit {
    @ViewChild('fileInput') fileInput: ElementRef;
    movie: Movie = new Movie();
    photos: any[];

    constructor(private route: ActivatedRoute,
        private router: Router,
        private moviesService: MoviesService,
        private toastyService: ToastyService,
    private imagesService: ImagesService) {
        route.params.subscribe(p => {
            this.movie.id = +p['id'];
        });
    }

    ngOnInit() {

        if (this.movie.id) {
            this.moviesService.getMovie(this.movie.id)
                .subscribe(m => {
                    this.movie = m;
                    console.log("Movie:", this.movie);
                },
                err => {
                    if (err.status == 404) {
                        this.router.navigate(['/']);
                    }
                });
        }
}

onSubmit() {
        if (this.movie.id) {
            this.moviesService.updateMovie(this.movie)
                .subscribe(x => {
                    console.log(x);
                    this.toastyService.success({
                        title: 'Success',
                        msg: 'Movie Updated!',
                        theme: 'bootstrap',
                        showClose: true,
                        timeout: 5000
                    });
```

```
                    this.router.navigate(['/movies']);
            },
            err => {
                Raven.captureException(err.
originalError || err);
                this.toastyService.error({
                    title: 'Error',
                    msg: 'An unexpected error while
updating the record!',
                    theme: 'bootstrap',
                    showClose: true,
                    timeout: 5000
                });
            });
        }
    }

    uploadImage() {
        var nativeElement: HTMLInputElement = this.
fileInput.nativeElement;
        this.imagesService.upload(this.movie.id,
nativeElement.files[0]).subscribe(image => this.photos.
push(image));
        }
}
```

Let me explain the code snippet here. First, I have created a variable with the name fileInput which is basically referencing the DOM element, which is **ElementRef** here. Now, in order to link this with the template variable, we need to decorate it with the **ViewChild** decorator.

And as the argument, it takes the name of the template variable which is **fileInput**. Now, in the **uploadImage** method, we first gained access of the native element and stored it in the local variable. Now, we have a reference to this file; next, we need to upload this to the server.

Creating Image Service

In this section, we will execute **ng g s images --spec false**.

```
X Cmder                                                            —  □  ×

C:\Dell\Books\ASPNETCorePlusAngular4\MovieReviewSPA\MovieReviewSPA.web\ClientApp\app\services (Another)
λ ng g s images --spec false
installing service
  create ClientApp\app\services\images.service.ts
  WARNING Service is generated but not provided, it must be provided to be used

C:\Dell\Books\ASPNETCorePlusAngular4\MovieReviewSPA\MovieReviewSPA.web\ClientApp\app\services (Another)
λ
```

Once done, it will look like this.

Since I have created a new service, it needs to be registered under the provider section in the app.module.ts and app.module.shared.ts files.

```
import { NgModule } from '@angular/core';
import { BrowserModule } from '@angular/platform-browser';
import { FormsModule } from '@angular/forms';
import { HttpModule } from '@angular/http';
import { sharedConfig } from './app.module.shared';
```

```
import { MoviesComponent } from './components/movies/
movies.component';
import { MoviesService } from './services/movies.
service';
import { ReviewsService } from './services/reviews.
service';
import { ImagesService } from './services/images.
service';
import { NewMovieComponent } from './components/new-
movie/new-movie.component';
import { EditMovieComponent } from './components/edit-
movie/edit-movie.component';
import { NotFoundComponent } from './components/not-
found/not-found.component';
import { ReviewsComponent } from './components/reviews/
reviews.component';
import { NewReviewComponent } from './components/new-
review/new-review.component';
import { EditReviewComponent } from './components/edit-
review/edit-review.component';
import { PaginationComponent } from './components/
utilities/pagination.component';
import { DetailViewComponent } from './components/detail-
view/detail-view.component';

@NgModule({
    bootstrap: sharedConfig.bootstrap,
    declarations: [...sharedConfig.declarations,
        MoviesComponent,
        NewMovieComponent,
        EditMovieComponent,
        NotFoundComponent,
        ReviewsComponent,
        NewReviewComponent,
        EditReviewComponent,
        PaginationComponent,
        DetailViewComponent
],
    imports: [
        BrowserModule,
        FormsModule,
        HttpModule,
        ...sharedConfig.imports
    ],
    providers: [
```

```
        { provide: 'ORIGIN_URL', useValue: location.
origin },
        MoviesService,
        ReviewsService,
        ImagesService
    ]
})
export class AppModule {
}
```

And,

```
import * as Raven from 'raven-js';
import { NgModule } from '@angular/core';
import { RouterModule } from '@angular/router';
import { FormsModule } from '@angular/forms';
import { ToastyModule } from 'ng2-toasty';
import { AppComponent } from './components/app/app.
component'
import { NavMenuComponent } from './components/navmenu/
navmenu.component';
import { HomeComponent } from './components/home/home.
component';
import { FetchDataComponent } from './components/
fetchdata/fetchdata.component';
import { CounterComponent } from './components/counter/
counter.component';
import { MoviesComponent } from './components/movies/
movies.component';
import { ReviewsComponent } from './components/reviews/
reviews.component';
import { NewMovieComponent } from './components/new-
movie/new-movie.component';
import { EditMovieComponent } from './components/edit-
movie/edit-movie.component';
import { NewReviewComponent } from './components/new-
review/new-review.component';
import { EditReviewComponent } from './components/edit-
review/edit-review.component';
import { PaginationComponent } from './components/
utilities/pagination.component';
import { DetailViewComponent } from './components/detail-
view/detail-view.component';
import { MoviesService } from './services/movies.service';
import { ReviewsService } from './services/reviews.service';
import { ImagesService } from './services/images.service';
```

```
Raven
.config('https://7579eaef4acc46bab3ffd87d3d85f3ea@sentry.
io/203240')
    .install();

export const sharedConfig: NgModule = {
    bootstrap: [ AppComponent ],
    declarations: [
        AppComponent,
        NavMenuComponent,
        CounterComponent,
        FetchDataComponent,
        HomeComponent,
        MoviesComponent,
        NewMovieComponent,
        EditMovieComponent,
        ReviewsComponent,
        NewReviewComponent,
        EditReviewComponent,
        PaginationComponent,
        DetailViewComponent
    ],
    imports: [
        FormsModule,
        ToastyModule.forRoot(),
        RouterModule.forRoot([
            { path: '', redirectTo: 'home', pathMatch: 'full' },
            { path: 'movies', component: MoviesComponent },
            { path: 'movies/new', component:
NewMovieComponent },
            { path: 'movies/:id', component:
EditMovieComponent },
            { path: 'movies/detail/:id', component:
DetailViewComponent },
            { path: 'reviews/:id', component:
ReviewsComponent },
            { path: 'editreview/:id', component:
EditReviewComponent },
            { path: 'reviews/new/:id', component:
NewReviewComponent },
            { path: 'home', component: HomeComponent },
            { path: 'counter', component: CounterComponent },
            { path: 'fetch-data', component:
FetchDataComponent },
```

```
            { path: '**', redirectTo: 'home' }
        ])
    ],
    providers: [MoviesService, ReviewsService,
ImagesService]

};
```

Now, my service looks like this.

```
import { Injectable } from '@angular/core';
import { Http } from '@angular/http';

@Injectable()
export class ImagesService {

    constructor(private http: Http) { }
    upload(Id, image) {
        /*return this.http.post('/api/movies/'+Id+'/
photos')*/ //or
        var formData = new FormData();
        formData.append('file', image);
        return this.http.post(`/api/movies/${Id}/images`,
formData)
            .map(res => res.json());
    }
}
```

Fairly simple code! The only point to note here is that the body is **formData** which is the JavaScript object of a key value pair. Again, the key should be the same that is passed in the controller. Hence, I have mentioned **file** as the key here. I have also applied a new syntax instead of the URL concatenation. I have pasted the code snippet for the **detail-view.component.ts** file.

```
import * as Raven from 'raven-js';
import { Component, OnInit, ElementRef, ViewChild } from
'@angular/core';
import { ActivatedRoute, Router } from '@angular/router';
import { Movie } from './../../models/movie';
import { MoviesService } from '../../services/movies.service';
import { ImagesService } from '../../services/images.service';
import { ToastyService } from "ng2-toasty";

@Component({
    templateUrl: './detail-view.component.html',
})
export class DetailViewComponent implements OnInit {
    @ViewChild('fileInput') fileInput: ElementRef;
```

```
        movie: Movie = new Movie();
        images: any[];

        constructor(private route: ActivatedRoute,
        private router: Router,
        private moviesService: MoviesService,
        private toastyService: ToastyService,
        private imagesService: ImagesService) {
        route.params.subscribe(p => {
            this.movie.id = +p['id'];
        });
    }

    ngOnInit() {

        if (this.movie.id) {
            this.moviesService.getMovie(this.movie.id)
                .subscribe(m => {
                    this.movie = m;
                    console.log("Movie:", this.movie);
                },
                err => {
                    if (err.status == 404) {
                        this.router.navigate(['/']);
                    }
                });
        }

    }

    onSubmit() {
        if (this.movie.id) {
            this.moviesService.updateMovie(this.movie)
                .subscribe(x => {
                    console.log(x);
                    this.toastyService.success({title:
'Success',
                        msg: 'Movie Updated!',
                        theme: 'bootstrap',
                        showClose: true,
                        timeout: 5000
                    });
                    this.router.navigate(['/movies']);
                },
                err => {
                    Raven.captureException(err.
originalError || err);
                    this.toastyService.error({
```

```
                            title: 'Error',
                            msg: 'An unexpected error
while updating the record!',
                              theme: 'bootstrap',
                              showClose: true,
                              timeout: 5000
                    });
                });
            }
    }

    uploadImage() {
            var nativeElement: HTMLInputElement = this.
fileInput.nativeElement;
            this.imagesService.upload(this.movie.id,
nativeElement.files[0]).subscribe(image => this.images.
push(image));
            this.toastyService.success({
                title: 'Success',
                msg: 'Image Uploaded!',
                theme: 'bootstrap',
                showClose: true,
                timeout: 5000
            });
    }
}
```

Here, I am using the native element to upload the file. Now, the **files** property is a list here and since we will need to upload one image at a time, I have given **files[0]**.Once done, when I go ahead and upload the image, it will get uploaded in the database and show the toast message as shown below.

And when I see database, it will list both the images against the same movie.

	Id	FileName	MovieId
1	1	75976734-d2ff-491b-8a9b-659ebfb594f1.jpg	1
2	2	2ccb8acf-0d67-4fac-ba3e-c525fc6a1527.jpg	1

100 %   ▼

⊞ Results ▤ Messages

Rendering Images while Uploading

In this section, we will learn how to show an image on the screen while uploading it. It also means that if I already have any image uploaded for any movies, it will render those images as well. Let's get started. Since we are following the Repository Pattern, everything should come from that. Having said this, we need to create the Image repository method in the **IMovieReviewUow** interface as shown below.

```
using MovieReviewSPA.Model;

namespace MovieReviewSPA.Data.Contracts
{
    public interface IMovieReviewUow
    {
        void Commit();
        IRepository<Image> Images { get; }
        IRepository<Movie> Movies { get; }
        IRepository<MovieReview> MovieReviews { get; }
    }
}
```

Now, we will go to its implementation **MovieReviewUow** class and implement the new one as shown below. Here is the code snippet for the same.

```
using System;
using MovieReviewSPA.Data.Contracts;
using MovieReviewSPA.Data.Helpers;
using MovieReviewSPA.Model;

namespace MovieReviewSPA.Data
{
    public class MovieReviewUow : IMovieReviewUow, IDisposable
    {
        public MovieReviewUow(IRepositoryProvider
repositoryProvider)
        {
            CreateDbContext();
            repositoryProvider.DbContext = DbContext;
            RepositoryProvider = repositoryProvider;
        }

        public IRepository<Movie> Movies { get { return
GetStandardRepo<Movie>(); } }
        public IRepository<MovieReview> MovieReviews {
get { return GetStandardRepo<MovieReview>(); } }

        public IRepository<Image> Images { get { return
GetStandardRepo<Image>(); } }
```

```
        public void Commit()
        {
            DbContext.SaveChanges();
        }

        protected void CreateDbContext()
        {
            DbContext = new MovieReviewDbContext();
        }
        protected IRepositoryProvider RepositoryProvider
{ get; set; }
        private IRepository<T> GetStandardRepo<T>() where
T : class
        {
            return RepositoryProvider.GetRepositoryForEnt
ityType<T>();
        }

        private T GetRepo<T>() where T : class
        {
            return RepositoryProvider.GetRepository<T>();
        }
        private MovieReviewDbContext DbContext { get; set; }
        public void Dispose()
        {
            Dispose(true);
            GC.SuppressFinalize(this);
        }
        protected virtual void Dispose(bool disposing)
        {
            if (disposing)
            {
                if (DbContext != null)
                {
                    DbContext.Dispose();
                }
            }
        }
    }
}
```

After this, I also need to modify my Image model. I have pasted the code snippet for the same.

```
using System;
using System.Collections.Generic;
```

```
using System;
using System.Collections.Generic;
using System.ComponentModel.DataAnnotations;
using System.Text;

namespace MovieReviewSPA.Model
{
    public class Image
    {
        public int Id { get; set; }

        [Required]
        [StringLength(255)]
        public string FileName { get; set; }
        public int MovieId { get; set; }
    }
}
```

The reason for adding **MovieId** here is because we want to query images against **MovieId**. Once done, we will go to **ImagesController** and implement the **Get** action. I have pasted the code snippet for the same.

```
using System;
using System.IO;
using System.Linq;
using System.Net;
using System.Net.Http;
using Microsoft.AspNetCore.Hosting;
using Microsoft.AspNetCore.Http;
using Microsoft.AspNetCore.Mvc;
using Microsoft.Extensions.Options;
using MovieReviewSPA.Data.Contracts;
using MovieReviewSPA.Model;

namespace MovieReviewSPA.web.Controllers.API
{
    [Route("/api/movies/{Id}/images")]
    public class ImagesController : Controller
    {
    private IHostingEnvironment _host;
    private IMovieReviewUow _uow;
    private ImageSettings _options;

        public ImagesController(IHostingEnvironment host,
IMovieReviewUow uow, IOptionsSnapshot<ImageSettings> options)
        {
            _host = host;
```

```
    _uow = uow;
        _options = options.Value;
    }
    [HttpPost]
    public IActionResult Upload(int Id, IFormFile file)
    {
        var movie = _uow.Movies.GetById(Id);
        if (movie == null)
        {v
            return NotFound();
        }

        if (file == null) return BadRequest("File not
valid");
        if (file.Length == 0) return BadRequest("Empty
File");
        if (file.Length > _options.MaxBytes) return
BadRequest("File exceeded 10 MB size!");

        if (!_options.IsSupported(file.FileName))
return BadRequest("Invalid File Type");
        var uploadsFolder = Path.Combine(_host.
WebRootPath, "uploads");

        if (!Directory.Exists(uploadsFolder))
        {
            Directory.CreateDirectory(uploadsFolder);
        }
        var fileName = Guid.NewGuid().ToString() +
Path.GetExtension(file.FileName);
        var filepath = Path.Combine(uploadsFolder, fileName);
        using (var stream = new FileStream(filepath,
FileMode.   Create))
        {
            file.CopyTo(stream);
        }

        var image = new Image { FileName = fileName };
        movie.Images.Add(image);
        _uow.Commit();
        return Ok(image);
    }

    //Fetch photos based on movieId
    [HttpGet]
    public IQueryable<Image>[] Get(int id)
    {
```

```
            /*return _uow.Photos.GetAll().Where(m =>
m.MovieId == Id);*/
            IQueryable<Image>[] images = new[] { _
uow.Images.GetAll().Where(m => m.MovieId == id) };
            if (images != null) return images;
            throw new Exception(new HttpResponseMessa
ge(HttpStatusCode.NotFound).ToString());
        }
    }
}
```

This is a straightforward code. I am just passing MovieId and fetching all the images associated with it. Once done, when I go ahead and test the API with URL **http://localhost:35334/api/movies/1/images**, it will appear like this.

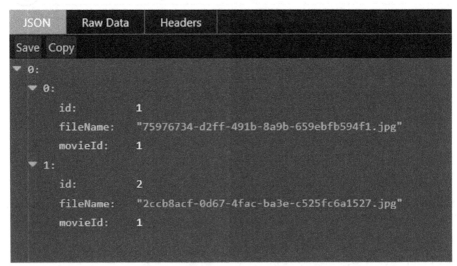

In case there are no images associated, then in that case, it will emit an empty collection. Now, in **images.service**, I have made the following changes.

```
import { Injectable } from '@angular/core';
import { Http } from '@angular/http';

@Injectable()
export class ImagesService {

    constructor(private http: Http) { }

    upload(Id, image) {

        /*return this.http.post('/api/movies/'+Id+'/
photos')*/ //or
        var formData = new FormData();
```

```
        formData.append ('file', image);
        return this.http.post (`/api/movies/${Id}/images`,
formData)
            .map (res => res.json ());
    }

    getImages (Id) {
        return this.http.get (`/api/movies/${Id}/images`)
            .map (res => res.json ());
    }
}
```

Here, I have just created a new method to fetch images based on the movie id. And the corresponding change in **detail-view.component.ts** is shown below.

```
import * as Raven from 'raven-js';
import { Component, OnInit, ElementRef, ViewChild } from
'@angular/core';
import { ActivatedRoute, Router } from '@angular/router';
import { Movie } from './../../models/movie';
import { MoviesService } from '../../services/movies.service';
import { ImagesService } from '../../services/images.service';
import { ToastyService } from "ng2-toasty";

@Component ({
    templateUrl: './detail-view.component.html',
})
export class DetailViewComponent implements OnInit {
    @ViewChild ('fileInput') fileInput: ElementRef;
    movie: Movie = new Movie ();
    images: any[];

    constructor (private route: ActivatedRoute,
        private router: Router,
        private moviesService: MoviesService,
        private toastyService: ToastyService,
        private imagesService: ImagesService) {
        route.params.subscribe (p => {
            this.movie.id = +p['id'];
        });
    }

    ngOnInit () {
        this.imagesService.getImages (this.movie.id)
            .subscribe (images => {
                this.images = images[0];
            });
```

```
        if (this.movie.id) {
            this.moviesService.getMovie(this.movie.id)
                .subscribe(m => {
                    this.movie = m;
                    console.log("Movie:", this.movie);
                },
                err => {
                    if (err.status == 404) {
                        this.router.navigate(['/']);
                    }
                });
        }

    }

    onSubmit() {
        if (this.movie.id) {
            this.moviesService.updateMovie(this.movie)
                .subscribe(x => {
                    console.log(x);
                    this.toastyService.success({title:
'Success',
                        msg: 'Movie Updated!',
                        theme: 'bootstrap',
                        showClose: true,
                        timeout: 5000
                    });
                    this.router.navigate(['/movies']);
                },
                err => {
                    Raven.captureException(err.
originalError || err);
                    this.toastyService.error({
                        title: 'Error',
                        msg: 'An unexpected error while
updating the record!',
                        theme: 'bootstrap',
                        showClose: true,
                        timeout: 5000
                    });
                });
        }

    }

    uploadImage() {
```

```
            var nativeElement: HTMLInputElement = this.
fileInput.nativeElement;
            this.imagesService.upload(this.movie.id,
nativeElement.files[0]).subscribe(image => this.images.
push(image));
            this.toastyService.success({
                title: 'Success',
                msg: 'Image Uploaded!',
                theme: 'bootstrap',
                showClose: true,
                timeout: 5000
        });
    }
}
```

In **ngOnInit**, I have called the API and fetched images. Lastly, we need to add the image tag to the **detail-view.component.html** file.

```html
<h1>Movie</h1>
<div>
        <!-- Nav tabs -->
        <ul class="nav nav-tabs" role="tablist">
            <li role="presentation" class="active"><a
href="#basic" aria-controls="basic" role="tab" data-
toggle="tab">Movie</a></li>
            <li role="presentation"><a href="#photos"
aria-controls="photos" role="tab" data-toggle="tab">Pics</
a></li>
        </ul>
        <!-- Tab panes -->
        <div class="tab-content" *ngIf="movie">
        <!-- Movie tab -->
        <div role="tabpanel" class="tab-pane active"
id="basic">
            <h2>About Movie</h2>
            <ul>
                <li>Name: {{ movie.movieName }}</li>
                <li>Director Name: {{ movie.directorName }}</li>
                <li>Release Year: {{ movie.releaseYear }}
            </ul>
            <br />
            <p>
                <a class="btn btn-info" [routerLink]="['/
movies']">View All Movies</a>
            </p>
        </div>
        <!-- Photos tab -->
```

```
        <div role="tabpanel" class="tab-pane"
id="photos">
            <h2>Movie Pics</h2>
            <input type="file" (change)="uploadImage()"
#fileInput />
            <img *ngFor="let image of images" src="/
uploads/{{image.fileName}}" class="img-thumbnail" style="w
idth:200px;height:200px;" />
        </div>
    </div>
</div>
```

Here, I have just looped the images and rendered them in the image tag. Once done, when I go ahead and check the page, it will appear like this.

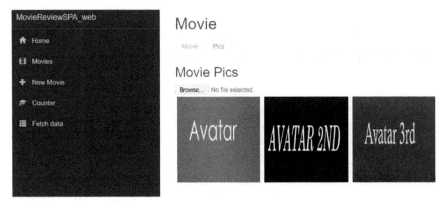

Now, when I browse any image, it will also get listed here and uploaded in the database.

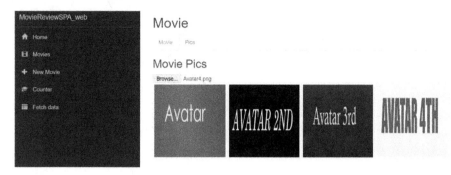

Questions

1. How to add pagination control?
2. How to control page size and page numbers in pagination control?
3. How to create a tabbed view?
4. What to transfer data across views?
5. What are local template references?
6. What is View Child in Angular?
7. What is the difference between @Input() and @Output()?

Summary

In this section, we started a couple of things like adding different capabilities such as paging and filtering control. Then, we created a new tabbed view where in it will present the read-only view of the movie on the first page and on the second page, it will show the movie pics. From the sa me page, you can upload images corresponding to the movie. We also implemented a new Image model, added a new migration and hence implemented a new functionality around the same.

Authentication & Authorization

Introduction

In this section, we will implement authentication and authorization features in our app. Therefore, we will see how we can implement authentication and authorization both in client side and on the server in modern apps. In order to implement the same, we will use JWT (JSON Web Token) and Auth0. We will see how to protect our endpoints, routes, etc. Later on, we will also see how roles work and how to grant or deny access based on the user's role.

Understanding the Authentication Lifecycle

In this section, we will first understand the architecture of MVC Applications like how it authenticates the system and extends our solution. In a typical system, whenever a user logs in, the system validates the user id and password and if they are valid, the system issues an authentication ticket. In this ticket, we often have a User ID and Expiration Date as an encrypted string. Therefore, the system puts this ticket in a cookie and returns the same to the client. Now, this cookie is sent to the server with every subsequent request. Let's say we want to protect an action, and then we simply put the [Authorize] attribute on the action. When ASP.NET runtime receives the request, it checks for the existence of this attribute on the action. Therefore, if the attribute is there, ASP.NET will extract the authentication ticket from the authentication cookie and then it will decrypt the ticket and if it's valid, it will get access to the target action.

We have a very similar architecture when building Single Page App using ASP.NET Core and Angular 4. Here, instead of using AUTH tickets, we use JSON web tokens aka JWT. A JWT is basically a JSON object, which includes some data or attributes about the user. We refer to these attributes as claims or statements about the user. In a nutshell, it's an object with a name value pair and each representing the user. It also has a signature which protects it from being tampered. Therefore, if anyone tries to change any of the values, the signature will no longer be valid and hence authentication will fail. And the only party which can create the signature is the issuer or server as we have the private key on the server which is used to generate the signature. Therefore, the very obvious difference between the AUTH ticket and JWT is that AUTH usually has a user id only, but JWTS can have any number of parameters related to the user. This also means that we don't need to query the database time and again for fetching user values; we can simply extract and read the same from JWT. One point to note here is that none of these attributes in JWT include private and sensitive data. Another difference is that here we don't use cookies. Cookies are only available in browsers. However, if we build other types of clients for mobile devices, then in that case, traditional authentication won't fit. Therefore, we put the JWT in the request header and send it to the server.

Now, in terms of storage, if we are building the browser app, then we usually store it in the local storage of the browser. Therefore, all modern browsers have this local storage which simply stores values in name-value pairs. If you are building any mobile app, then in that case, it gets stored at some other place. Now, building this entire authentication system is a lot of repetitive work. In modern applications, we usually delegate the work to third-party systems so that we can entirely focus on building the application.

Setting AUTHO

In this section, we will set up **AUTHO**. Here, we need to navigate to **https:// auth0.com/** to set up the account first. You can either sign up on their site or via the options shown below.

Auth0

Log In   Sign Up

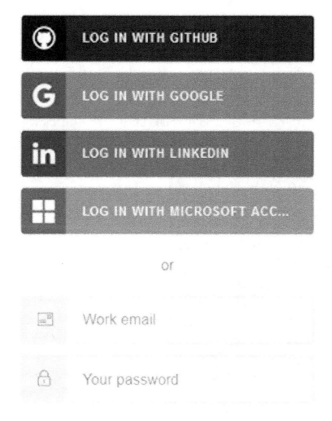

LOG IN WITH GITHUB

LOG IN WITH GOOGLE

LOG IN WITH LINKEDIN

LOG IN WITH MICROSOFT ACC...

or

Work email

Your password

Don't remember your password?

LOG IN ›

I will log in with my **GitHub** account. After logging in, we need to set up the sub domain as shown below. Here, I have given **movie-review**.

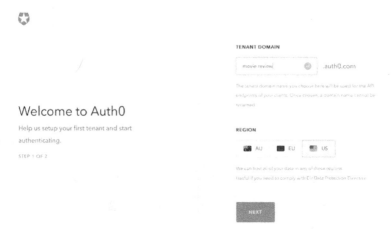

After this, I chose the region as US. You can choose any one of the regions listed here. Then, I need to click on the **Next** button. Here, it shows me the options as shown below. From these options, I chose the developer account.

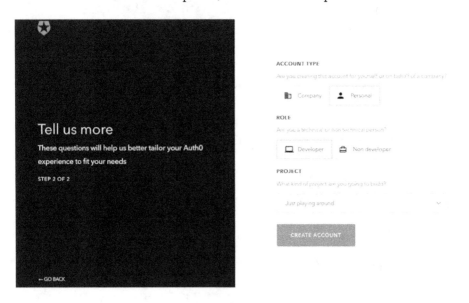

Finally, I need to click on **Create Account**. On successful creation, it takes me to the following dashboard page.

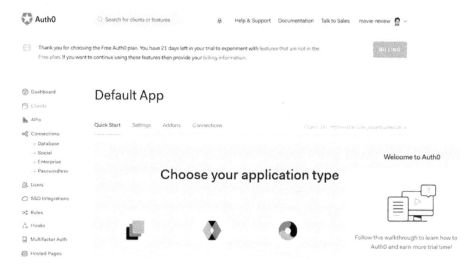

Now, from the drop-down list, we will select settings.

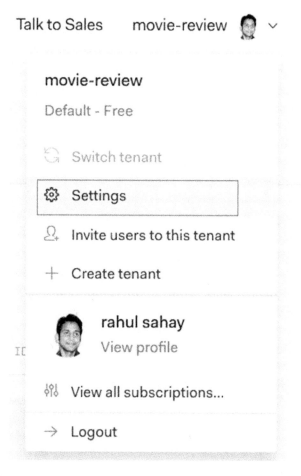

It will display the screen as shown below.

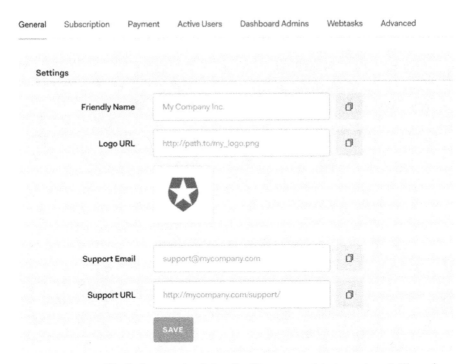

Here, we can fill all the required details. However, this is optional. Therefore, I will go to left menu and click on APIs.

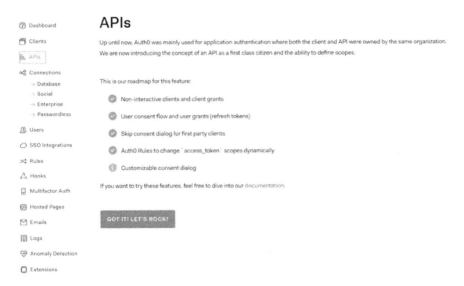

Next, when I click on the GOT IT! LET'S ROCK tab, it displays the nest screen.

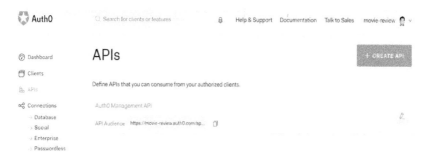

Here, I need to click on the **CREATE API** button which shows the following options.

New API

| Name | Movies |

A friendly name for the API.

| Identifier | https://api.movie-review.com |

A logical identifier for this API. We recommend using a URL but note that this doesn't have to be a publicly available URL, Auth0 will not call your API at all. This field cannot be modified.

| Signing Algorithm | RS256 |

RS256

HS256

CREATE

Identifier is something which is internal to **Auth0**, hence this is not publicly an accessible API. Here, I have selected Signing Algorithm as **RS256** as this is an asymmetric one and more secure than **HS256**. Then, I need to click on the Create button.

Movies

Quick Start   Settings   Scopes   Non Interactive Clients   Test

1. Choose a JWT library

As your API will be parsing JWT formatted access tokens, you will need to setup this capabilities on your API.

You can navigate to jwt.io and choose from there. Remember to pick a library that support your selected signing algorithm.

2. Configuring your API to accept RS256 signed tokens

Configure the library that will validate the access tokens in your API. Validating a token means that you are certain you can trust it's contents.

C#   Node.js   PHP

This page has documentation for different language setups. One point to note here is that this trail version is free till 21 days. Therefore, I may choose to opt for out of paid service at some point of time. This is just for demonstration purpose. From the language options, I need to select the C# tab. This will display the code as shown below.

2. Configuring your API to accept RS256 signed tokens

Configure the library that will validate the access tokens in your API. Validating a token means that you are certain you can trust it's contents.

C#   Node.js   PHP

```
public class Startup
{
    public void Configure(IApplicationBuilder app, IHostingEnvironment env, ILoggerFactory loggerFactory)
    {
        var options = new JwtBearerOptions
        {
            Audience = "https://api.movie-review.com",
            Authority = "https://movie-review.auth0.com/"
        };
        app.UseJwtBearerAuthentication(options);

        app.UseMvc();
    }
}
```

I will just copy this code and paste it in the Configure method under the startup class. I have pasted the code snippet for the same. Once I paste the code, it didn't in **JwtBearerOptions**, as the required dll was not there. Therefore, we need to install the highlighted package from Nuget as shown below.

One point to note here is that I have installed the **1.1.2 version**.

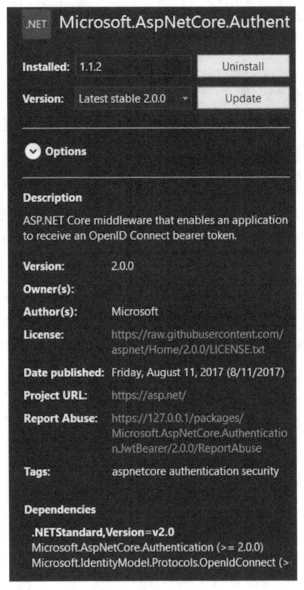

Once done, the DLL reference error vanishes. Here is the code snippet for the same.

```
using Microsoft.AspNetCore.Builder;
using Microsoft.AspNetCore.Hosting;
using Microsoft.AspNetCore.SpaServices.Webpack;
using Microsoft.EntityFrameworkCore;
using Microsoft.EntityFrameworkCore.Infrastructure;
using Microsoft.Extensions.Configuration;
using Microsoft.Extensions.DependencyInjection;
```

```csharp
using Microsoft.Extensions.Logging;
using MovieReviewSPA.Data;
using MovieReviewSPA.Data.Contracts;
using MovieReviewSPA.Data.Helpers;
using MovieReviewSPA.Data.SampleData;
using MovieReviewSPA.Model;

namespace MovieReviewSPA.web
{
    public class Startup
    {
        public Startup(IHostingEnvironment env)
        {
            var builder = new ConfigurationBuilder()
                .SetBasePath(env.ContentRootPath)
                .AddJsonFile("appsettings.json",
optional: true, reloadOnChange: true)

.AddJsonFile($"appsettings.{env.EnvironmentName}.json",
optional: true)
                .AddEnvironmentVariables();
            Configuration = builder.Build();
        }

        public IConfigurationRoot Configuration { get; }

        // This method gets called by the runtime. Use
this method to add services to the container.
        public void ConfigureServices(IServiceCollection
services)
        {
            services.AddEntityFramework()
                .AddDbContext<MovieReviewDbContext>(options =>

    options.UseSqlServer(Configuration["Data:MovieReviewSPA:ConnectionString"],

                    b => b.MigrationsAssembly("MovieR
eviewSPA.web"))));
            // Add framework services.
            services.AddMvc();
            //Initiating Seed Data
            services.AddTransient<InitialData>();
            //DI Setup

services.Configure<ImageSettings>(Configuration.
GetSection("ImageSettings"));
            services.AddScoped<RepositoryFactories,
RepositoryFactories>();
```

```
            services.AddScoped<IRepositoryProvider,
RepositoryProvider>();
            services.AddScoped<IMovieReviewUow,
MovieReviewUow>();

        }

        // This method gets called by the runtime. Use
this method to configure the HTTP request pipeline.
        public void Configure(IApplicationBuilder app,
IHostingEnvironment env, ILoggerFactory loggerFactory,
InitialData seedDbContext)
        {
loggerFactory.AddConsole(Configuration.
GetSection("Logging"));
            loggerFactory.AddDebug();

            if (env.IsDevelopment())
            {
                app.UseDeveloperExceptionPage();
                app.UseWebpackDevMiddleware(new
WebpackDevMiddlewareOptions {
                    HotModuleReplacement = true
                });
            }
            else
            {
                app.UseExceptionHandler("/Home/Error");
            }

            app.UseStaticFiles();

            var options = new JwtBearerOptions
            {
                Audience = "https://api.movie-review.com",
                Authority = "https://movie-review.auth0.com/"
            };
            app.UseJwtBearerAuthentication(options);

            app.UseMvc(routes =>
            {
                routes.MapRoute(
                    name: "default",
                    template: "{controller=Home}/
{action=Index}/{id?}");
                routes.MapSpaFallbackRoute(
                    name: "spa-fallback",
                    defaults: new { controller = "Home",
action = "Index" });
```

```
        });
        //Initiating from here
        seedDbContext.SeedData();
    }
  }
}
```

Now understand what this code is doing. Here, we have the options object with two properties. One is authority, which is the party that generates authentication tokens. The other property is audience which determines who this audience is for? Therefore, the token which this authority uses can only be used by this audience. We cannot use them for different websites.

Testing Movies API

Now, let's go to the Movies controller and put the [**Authorize**] attribute in front of the Movies API.

```
// GET api/movies
        [HttpGet("")]
        [Authorize]
        public IQueryable Get(Pager movieQuery)
        {
            var model = UOW.Movies.GetAll(movieQuery).
OrderByDescending(m => m.Reviews.Count())
                .Select(m => new MovieViewModel
                {
                    Id = m.Id,
                    MovieName = m.MovieName,
                    DirectorName = m.DirectorName,
                    ReleaseYear = m.ReleaseYear,
                    NoOfReviews = m.Reviews.Count()
                });
            return model;
        }
```

Once done, whenever any request comes to this route, our new middleware kicks in and it looks at the request header, and we have an authorization header with a valid JSON web token, the request will pass through it and it will get routed to the Movies action. Having said this, let's open postman and try the URL **http://localhost:35334/api/movies**.

Here, it returns the 401 unauthorized result. And because of this, the Movies page appears as a blank page.

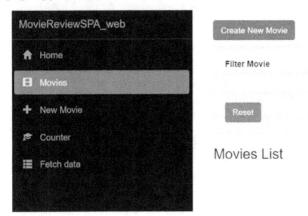

Therefore, we saw how easy and flexible it is to set up authentication. Now, let's see how to get a valid JSON web token. For this, we need to go to the APIs page and select the **Test tab**.

On the same page, if we scroll down, we can see the Response token.

In order to copy the token, we need to click on **Copy Token**, and it will copy the entire string. Now, we need to go to postman. Here, in the Headers tab, we need to add the authorization header.

Here in the Key, I have added **Authorization** and value as **Bearer**.After Bearer, we need to give one space and paste the token and click on the tab. It will appear like this.

Once done, when I click on Send, it will return the result as expected.

However, we should not keep the **[Authorize]** attribute on those APIs which are read-only, which means this is just listing movies or reviews. Rather we should keep an expensive operation like Delete, Update, etc.

Securing Client Apps

In this section, we will learn how to secure client-side apps. Here, we need to click on **Clients**. On clicking, it will display the following page.

Next, we need to click on **Create Client**. This will show the following screen.

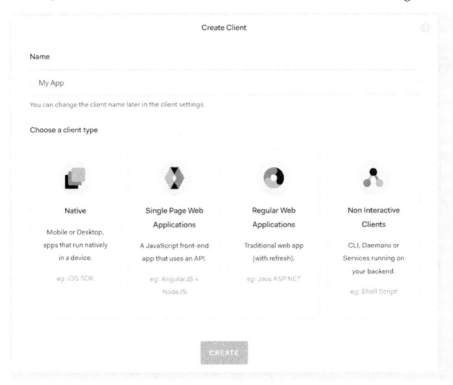

Here, we have got a couple of options. From these options, we need to select the **Single Page Web Applications** option and then click on the Create button.

On doing so, it will show the following options.

Here we need to select the **Angular 2+** option. It will display the dashboard as shown below.

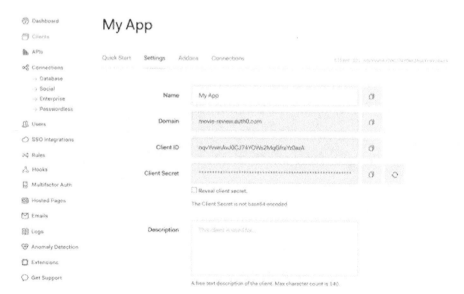

Make sure that the Encryption algorithm is set to **RS256**.

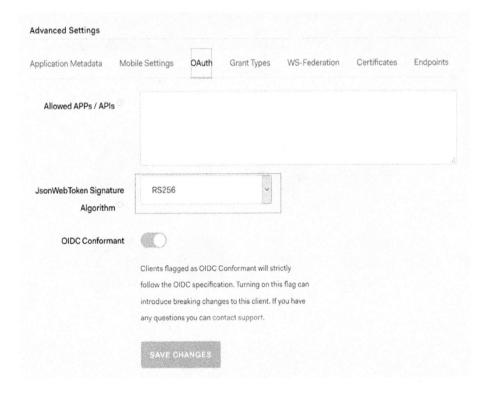

Now, if we take a look at the quick-start documentation, we need to install the following:

Install auth0.js

Integrating Auth0 in your application requires the auth0.js library. Install it using npm or yarn.

```
# installation with npm
npm install --save auth0-js

# installation with yarn
yarn add auth0-js
```

Note: On the Auth0 page, the example is based on auth0-js. But, the example listed out there fails. Hence, we need to use another implementation of auth0-lock. You can find the complete documentation at https://github.com/tawawa/auth0-angular2-lock-sample.

We need to install one more helper library for the Angular 2+ application using the following **npm install angular2-jwt --save** command.

Once this is done, we need to import the packages as well. I have pasted the code snippet for the same.

```
const path = require('path');
const webpack = require('webpack');
const ExtractTextPlugin = require('extract-text-webpack-
plugin');
const merge = require('webpack-merge');

module.exports = (env) => {
    const extractCSS = new ExtractTextPlugin('vendor.css');
    const isDevBuild = !(env && env.prod);
    const sharedConfig = {
    stats: { modules: false },
    resolve: { extensions: [ '.js' ] },
    module: {
        rules: [
            { test: /\.(png|woff|woff2|eot|ttf|svg)
(\?|$)/, use: 'url-loader?limit=100000' }
        ]
    },
    entry: {
```

```
    vendor: [
        '@angular/animations',
        '@angular/common',
        '@angular/compiler',
        '@angular/core',
        '@angular/forms',
        '@angular/http',
        '@angular/platform-browser',
        '@angular/platform-browser-dynamic',
        '@angular/router',
        'angular2-jwt',
        'auth0-js',
        'auth0-lock',
        'bootstrap',
        'bootstrap/dist/css/bootstrap.css',
        'font-awesome/css/font-awesome.css', '
        'es6-shim',
        'es6-promise',
        'event-source-polyfill',
        'ng2-toasty',
        'ng2-toasty/bundles/style-bootstrap.css',
        'jquery',
        'raven-js',
        'zone.js'
    ]
},
output: {
    publicPath: '/dist/',
    filename: '[name].js',
        library: '[name]_[hash]'
    },
    plugins: [
        new webpack.ProvidePlugin({ $: 'jquery',
jQuery: 'jquery' }), // Maps these identifiers to the
jQuery package (because Bootstrap expects it to be a
global variable)
        new webpack.ContextReplacementPlugin(/\@
angular\b.*\b(bundles|linker)/, path.join(__dirname,
'./ClientApp')), // Workaround for https://github.com/
angular/angular/issues/11580
        new webpack.ContextReplacementPlugin(/
angular(\\|\/)core(\\|\/)@angular/, path.join(__dirname,
'./ClientApp')), // Workaround for https://github.com/
angular/angular/issues/14898
        new webpack.IgnorePlugin(/^vertx$/) //
```

```
Workaround for https://github.com/stefanpenner/es6-
promise/issues/100
            ]
        };

        const clientBundleConfig = merge(sharedConfig, {
            output: { path: path.join(__dirname,
'wwwroot', 'dist') },
            module: {
                rules: [
                    { test: /\.css(\?|$)/, use:
extractCSS.extract({ use: isDevBuild ? 'css-loader' :
'css-loader?minimize' }) }
                ]
            },
            plugins: [
                extractCSS,
                new webpack.DllPlugin({
                    path: path.join(__dirname, 'wwwroot',
'dist', '[name]-manifest.json'),
                    name: '[name]_[hash]'
                })
            ].concat(isDevBuild ? [] : [
                new webpack.optimize.UglifyJsPlugin()
        ])
    });

    const serverBundleConfig = merge(sharedConfig, {
        target: 'node',
        resolve: { mainFields: ['main'] },
        output: {
            path: path.join(__dirname, 'ClientApp', 'dist'),
            libraryTarget: 'commonjs2',
        },
        module: {
            rules: [ { test: /\.css(\?|$)/, use: ['to-
string-loader', isDevBuild ? 'css-loader' : 'css-
loader?minimize' ] } ]
        },
        entry: { vendor: ['aspnet-prerendering'] },
        plugins: [
            new webpack.DllPlugin({
                path: path.join(__dirname, 'ClientApp',
'dist', '[name]-manifest.json'),
                name: '[name]_[hash]'
            })
```

```
        ]
    });

    return [clientBundleConfig, serverBundleConfig];
}
```

Now, before running **web-pack**, we need to exit IIS from the taskbar. This is just to avoid getting any weird error from the node modules. Use the **webpack --config webpack.config.vendor.js** command.

Now, we need to run the **webpack** command.

Next, we will create the service for the same. I have created the **auth** service with the name **auth.service.ts** and pasted the above code. Therefore, now my solution explorer looks like this.

I have pasted the code snippet for the same.

```
import { Injectable } from '@angular/core';
import { tokenNotExpired } from 'angular2-jwt';
import Auth0Lock from 'auth0-lock';
/*import { myConfig } from './auth.config';*/

// Avoid name not found warnings
//declare var Auth0Lock: any;
@Injectable()
export class AuthService {
```

```
        lock = new Auth0Lock('nqvYvwnAvJ0CJ74YOWs2MqGfraY
z0azA', 'movie-review.auth0.com');

        constructor() {
            // Add callback for lock `authenticated` event
            this.lock.on('authenticated', (authResult) => {
                console.log(authResult);
                localStorage.setItem('token', authResult.
idToken);
            });
        }

        public login() {
            // Call the show method to display the widget.
            this.lock.show();
        };

        public authenticated() {
            // Check if there's an unexpired JWT
            // It searches for an item in localStorage
with key == 'token'
            return tokenNotExpired('token');
        };

        public logout() {
            // Remove token from localStorage
            localStorage.removeItem('token');
    };
}
```

Let me explain the code here. Here, we have created the authentication service, which will get injected into our components. This service has three important methods. The first is login, which will simply call the auth0 login method. The lock is part of the auth0 lock library. The show method will simply show the login widget. We also have the authenticated method which simply returns true, if it has a valid authentication token. Then, we have the **tokenNotExpired** function, which is part of the Angular-jwt library. Its job is to read the values from the local storage of the browser. Finally, we have the logout method which removes this token from the local storage. Now, we need to add the same to our module file. I have pasted the code snippet for **app.module.ts** and **app.module.shared.ts**.

```
import { NgModule } from '@angular/core';
import { BrowserModule } from '@angular/platform-
browser';
import { FormsModule } from '@angular/forms';
import { HttpModule, BrowserXhr } from '@angular/http';
import { sharedConfig } from './app.module.shared';
import { MoviesComponent } from './components/movies/
movies.component';
```

```
import { MoviesService } from './services/movies.service';
import { ReviewsService } from './services/reviews.service';
import { ImagesService } from './services/images.service';
import { AuthService } from './services/auth.service';
import { ProgressService, BrowserXHRService } from './
services/progress.service';
import { NewMovieComponent } from './components/new-
movie/new-movie.component';
import { EditMovieComponent } from './components/edit-
movie/edit-movie.component';
import { NotFoundComponent } from './components/not-
found/not-found.component';
import { ReviewsComponent } from './components/reviews/
reviews.component';
import { NewReviewComponent } from './components/new-
review/new-review.component';
import { EditReviewComponent } from './components/edit-
review/edit-review.component';
import { PaginationComponent } from './components/
utilities/pagination.component';
import { DetailViewComponent } from './components/detail-
view/detail-view.component';

@NgModule({
    bootstrap: sharedConfig.bootstrap,
    declarations: [...sharedConfig.declarations,
        MoviesComponent,
        NewMovieComponent,
        EditMovieComponent,
        NotFoundComponent,
        ReviewsComponent,
        NewReviewComponent,
        EditReviewComponent,
        PaginationComponent,
        DetailViewComponent

    ],
        imports: [
            BrowserModule,
            FormsModule,
            HttpModule,
            ...sharedConfig.imports
        ],
        providers: [
            { provide: 'ORIGIN_URL', useValue: location.
```

```
origin },
            // { provide: BrowserXhr, useValue:
BrowserXHRService },
            MoviesService,
            ReviewsService,
            ImagesService,
            AuthService

    ]
})
export class AppModule {
}
```

And,

```
import * as Raven from 'raven-js';
import { NgModule } from '@angular/core';
import { RouterModule } from '@angular/router';
import { FormsModule } from '@angular/forms';
import { BrowserXhr } from '@angular/http';
import { ToastyModule } from 'ng2-toasty';
import { AppComponent } from './components/app/app.
component'
import { NavMenuComponent } from './components/navmenu/
navmenu.component';
import { HomeComponent } from './components/home/home.
component';
import { FetchDataComponent } from './components/
fetchdata/fetchdata.component';
import { CounterComponent } from './components/counter/
counter.component';
import { MoviesComponent } from './components/movies/
movies.component';
import { ReviewsComponent } from './components/reviews/
reviews.component';
import { NewMovieComponent } from './components/new-
movie/new-movie.component';
import { EditMovieComponent } from './components/edit-
movie/edit-movie.component';
import { NewReviewComponent } from './components/new-
review/new-review.component';
import { EditReviewComponent } from './components/edit-
review/edit-review.component';
import { PaginationComponent } from './components/
utilities/pagination.component';
import { DetailViewComponent } from './components/detail-
view/detail-view.component';
```

```
import { MoviesService } from './services/movies.service';
import { ReviewsService } from './services/reviews.service';
import { ImagesService } from './services/images.service';
import { AuthService } from './services/auth.service';
import { ProgressService, BrowserXHRService } from './
services/progress.service';

Raven

.config('https://7579eaef4acc46bab3ffd87d3d85f3ea@sentry.
io/203240')
    .install();

export const sharedConfig: NgModule = {
    bootstrap: [ AppComponent ],
    declarations: [
        AppComponent,
        NavMenuComponent,
        CounterComponent,
        FetchDataComponent,
        HomeComponent,
        MoviesComponent,
        NewMovieComponent,
        EditMovieComponent,
        ReviewsComponent,
        NewReviewComponent,
        EditReviewComponent,
        PaginationComponent,
        DetailViewComponent
    ],
    imports: [
        FormsModule,
        ToastyModule.forRoot(),
        RouterModule.forRoot([
            { path: '', redirectTo: 'home', pathMatch: 'full' },
            { path: 'movies', component: MoviesComponent },
            { path: 'movies/new', component: NewMovieComponent },
            { path: 'movies/:id', component:
EditMovieComponent },
            { path: 'movies/detail/:id', component:
DetailViewComponent },
            { path: 'reviews/:id', component:
ReviewsComponent },
            { path: 'editreview/:id', component:
EditReviewComponent },
            { path: 'reviews/new/:id', component:
```

```
NewReviewComponent },
                { path: 'home', component: HomeComponent },
                { path: 'counter', component: CounterComponent },
                { path: 'fetch-data', component: FetchDataComponent },
                { path: '**', redirectTo: 'home' }
        ])
    ],
    providers: [
        MoviesService,
        ReviewsService,
        ImagesService,
        AuthService
    ]

};
```

Implementing Login/Logout

In this section, we will implement the **Login/Logout** functionality. Let's go ahead and refresh the app. As soon as I refresh the app, it gives the following error.

This is because **auth0-lock** is not designed to execute the outside browser at the moment. Therefore, when we refresh this page, server-side pre-rendering kicks in and our first page gets rendered in the server which is inside the node process and outside the browser.

That's why we get an exception here. Now, the work around for this is to disable server-side pre-rendering. It's ok to delete the same as we are not relying on tag-helpers and other server-side related stuffs as we are using Angular as our frontend component. Therefore, we need to go to **Index.cshtml**, and make the following changes.

```
@{
    ViewData["Title"] = "Home Page";
}

@*<app asp-prerender-module="ClientApp/dist/main-
server">Loading...</app>*@
<app src="ClientApp/dist/main-server">Loading...</app>

<script src="~/dist/vendor.js" asp-append-
version="true"></script>
@section scripts {
    <script src="~/dist/main-client.js" asp-append-
version="true"></script>
}
```

Here, I have just commented the pre-rendering line and then replaced pre-rendering tag with src. Now, if we refresh the app, it will display the following screenshot as expected.

Now, let's add the **Login/Logout** link. First, we need to inject the auth service into our **navmenu.component.ts** file. I have pasted the code snippet for the same.

```
import { Component } from '@angular/core';
import { AuthService } from '../../services/auth.
service';

@Component({
    selector: 'nav-menu',
    templateUrl: './navmenu.component.html',
    styleUrls: ['./navmenu.component.css']
})
export class NavMenuComponent {
    constructor(private authService:AuthService){}
}
```

And the corresponding change in the navmenu.component.html file is shown below.

```
<div class='main-nav'>
    <div class='navbar navbar-inverse'>
        <div class='navbar-header'>
            <button type='button' class='navbar-toggle'
data-toggle='collapse' data-target='.navbar-collapse'>
                <span class='sr-only'>Toggle navigation</
span>
                <span class='icon-bar'></span>
                <span class='icon-bar'></span>
                <span class='icon-bar'></span>
            </button>
            <a class='navbar-brand' [routerLink]="['/
home']">MovieReviewSPA_web</a>
        </div>
        <div class='clearfix'></div>
        <div class='navbar-collapse collapse'>
            <ul class='nav navbar-nav'>
                <li [routerLinkActive]="['link-active']">
                    <a [routerLink]="['/home']">
                        <span class='glyphicon glyphicon-
home'></span> Home
                    </a>
                </li>
                <li [routerLinkActive]="['link-active']">
                    <a (click)="authService.login()"
*ngIf="!authService.authenticated()">
                        <span class='glyphicon glyphicon-
user'></span> Login
                    </a>
                    <a (click)="authService.logout()"
*ngIf="authService.authenticated()">
                        <span class='glyphicon glyphicon-
user'></span> Logout
                    </a>
                </li>
                <li [routerLinkActive]="['link-active']"
[routerLinkActiveOptions]="{exact:true}">
                    <a [routerLink]="['/movies']">
                        <span class='glyphicon glyphicon-
film'></span> Movies
                    </a>
                </li>
```

```
        <li [routerLinkActive]="['link-active']">
            <a [routerLink]="['/movies/new']">
                <span class='glyphicon glyphicon-
plus'></span> New Movie
            </a>
        </li>
        <li [routerLinkActive]="['link-active']">
            <a [routerLink]="['/counter']">
                <span class='glyphicon glyphicon-
education'></span> Counter
            </a>
        </li>
        <li [routerLinkActive]="['link-active']">
            <a [routerLink]="['/fetch-data']">
                <span class='glyphicon glyphicon-
th-list'></span> Fetch data
            </a>
        </li>
    </ul>
  </div>
 </div>
</div>
```

Here, I have created one new line element which has a conditional login and logout logic. With the above change in place, when I go ahead and refresh the app, it will appear like this.

Here, when I click on the login button, it will look like this.

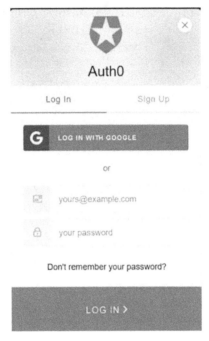

Here, Google is enabled by default. However, we can add other social logins as well. Now, if we try to sign-up with the following credentials, it fails.

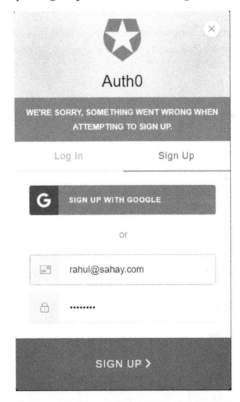

However, if we inspect the browser, it clearly shows the **Access-Control-Allow-Origin** error.

Basically, it's tries the cross domain request and hence it fails. Therefore, we need to add this domain http://localhost:5000 to the Auth0 page. Therefore, we need to go to the Settings page of the client and set two things there. I have pasted the change for this.

Allowed Callback URLs

http://localhost:35334

After the user authenticates we will only call back to any of these URLs.
You can specify multiple valid URLs by comma-separating them
(typically to handle different environments like QA or testing). You can
use the star symbol as a wildcard for subdomains (`*.google.com`).
Make sure to specify the protocol, `http://` or `https://`,
otherwise the callback may fail in some cases.

Allowed Logout URLs

http://localhost:35334

A set of URLs that are valid to redirect to after logout from Auth0. After
a user logs out from Auth0 you can redirect them with the `returnTo`
query parameter. The URL that you use in `returnTo` must be listed
here. You can specify multiple valid URLs by comma-separating them.
You can use the star symbol as a wildcard for subdomains
(`*.google.com`). Notice that querystrings and hash information are not
taking into account when validating these URLs. Read more about this
at https://auth0.com/docs/logout

In-case, you have multiple environments, you will have multiple URLs, which you can seperate by commas. Once done, when I again try to sign-up, the sign up will be done correctly.

Here, it fails again. This is because it expects http://localhost:35334/home.

Hence, we need to add this URL to the callback list and then save the changes.

Allowed Callback URLs	http://localhost:35334,http://localhost:35334/home

After the user authenticates we will only call back to any of these URLs. You can specify multiple valid URLs by comma-separating them (typically to handle different environments like QA or testing). You can use the star symbol as a wildcard for subdomains ('*.google.com'). Make sure to specify the protocol, `http://` or `https://`, otherwise the callback may fail in some cases.

Once done, when I try to log in again, it will login successfully. During the last sign-up process, the registration was done but redirect failed.

The reason is because the OIDC conformant is enabled by default.

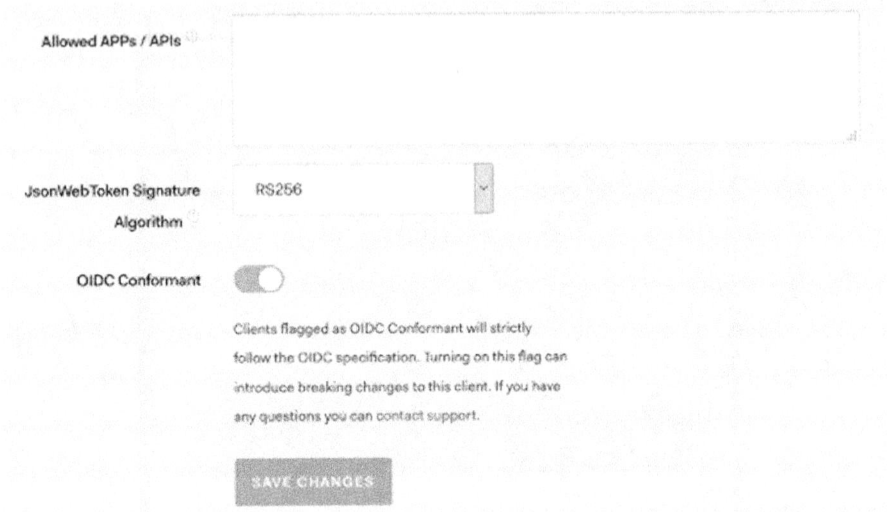

Allowed APPs / APIs	
JsonWebToken Signature Algorithm	RS256
OIDC Conformant	(toggle)

Clients flagged as OIDC Conformant will strictly follow the OIDC specification. Turning on this flag can introduce breaking changes to this client. If you have any questions you can contact support.

SAVE CHANGES

Hence, we need to disable it. This setting is present in the OAuth tab as shown below.

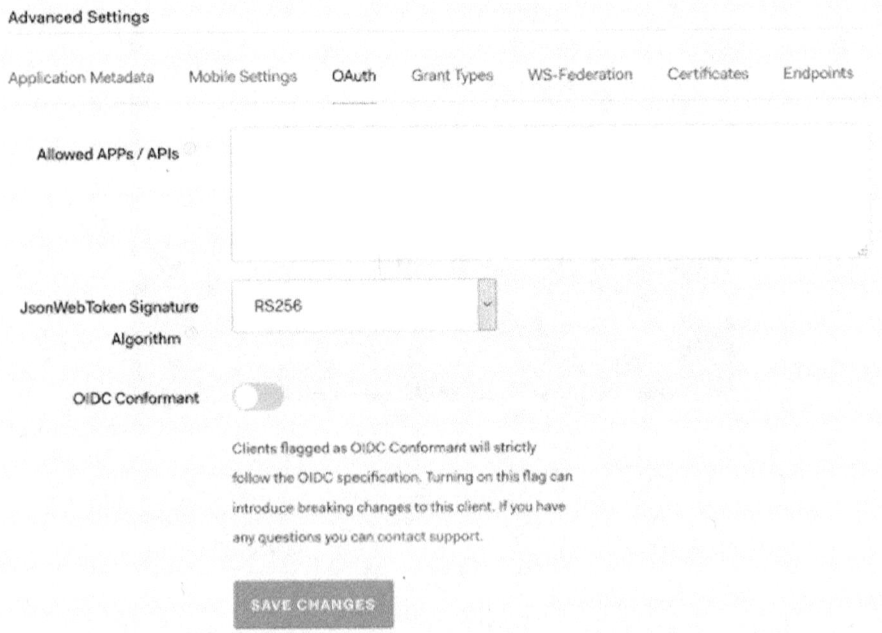

Advanced Settings

Application Metadata   Mobile Settings   OAuth   Grant Types   WS-Federation   Certificates   Endpoints

Allowed APPs / APIs	
JsonWebToken Signature Algorithm	RS256
OIDC Conformant	(toggle)

Clients flagged as OIDC Conformant will strictly follow the OIDC specification. Turning on this flag can introduce breaking changes to this client. If you have any questions you can contact support.

SAVE CHANGES

With the above changes in place, when we try it again, it will get redirected correctly. Also, the Logout link will appear correctly.

Using Custom Login Pages

In this section, we will use the custom login page. Currently, the login page comes up as a pop-up box. In auth0, we have this concept of hosted pages. With this feature enabled, we can redirect the user to hosted login pages. And the benefit of using this is that we can customize the look and feel icon, and it's more secure than what communication is on HTTPs channel.

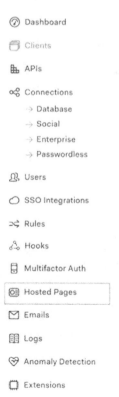

When, I click on this page, the following page will open. Here I need to click on Enable below the highlighted link.

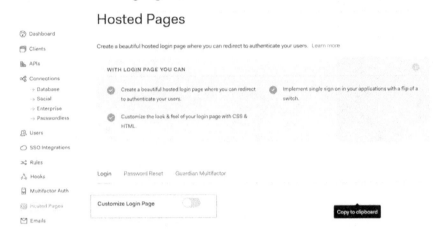

When I do so, of the following HTML will appear. Now, when I click on the preview button, it will render the following beautiful UI.

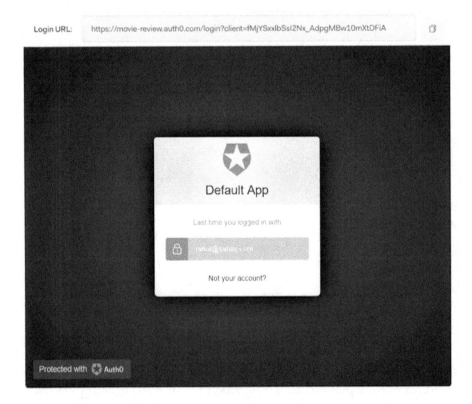

Let me paste the HTML code from the auth0 site.

```
<!DOCTYPE html>
```

```html
<html>
<head>
    <meta charset="utf-8">
    <meta http-equiv="X-UA-Compatible"
content="IE=edge,chrome=1">
    <title>Sign In with Auth0</title>
    <meta name="viewport" content="width=device-width,
initial-scale=1.0" />
</head>
<body>

<!--[if IE 8]>
    <script src="//cdnjs.cloudflare.com/ajax/libs/
ie8/0.2.5/ie8.js"></script>
<![endif]-->

<!--[if lte IE 9]>
    <script src="https://cdn.auth0.com/js/base64.js"></
script>
    <script src="https://cdn.auth0.com/js/es5-shim.min.
js"></script>
<![endif]-->

<script src="https://cdn.auth0.com/js/lock/10.18/lock.
min.js"></script>
<script>
    // Decode utf8 characters properly
    var config = JSON.parse(decodeURIComponent(escape(wind
ow.atob('@@config@@'))));
    config.extraParams = config.extraParams || {};
    var connection = config.connection;
    var prompt = config.prompt;
    var languageDictionary;
    var language;

    if (config.dict && config.dict.signin && config.dict.
signin.title) {
    languageDictionary = { title: config.dict.signin.title };
    } else if (typeof config.dict === 'string') {
    language = config.dict;
    }
    var loginHint = config.extraParams.login_hint;

    var lock = new Auth0Lock(config.clientID, config.
auth0Domain, {
        auth: {
```

```
                redirectUrl: config.callbackURL,
                responseType: (config.internalOptions || {}).
response_type ||
                    config.callbackOnLocationHash ? 'token' :
'code',
                params: config.internalOptions
            },
            assetsUrl: config.assetsUrl,
            allowedConnections: connection ? [connection] :
null,
            rememberLastLogin: !prompt,
            language: language,
            languageDictionary: languageDictionary,
            theme: {
                //logo:              YOUR LOGO HERE',
                //primaryColor:      'green'
            },
            prefill: loginHint ? { email: loginHint, username:
loginHint } : null,
            closable: false,
            // uncomment if you want small buttons for social
providers
            // socialButtonStyle: 'small'
        });
        lock.show();
</script>
</body>

</html>
```

Let me explain the snippet here. One point to notice here is that we are creating the auth0 object here. The first argument to this constructor is client id, which is unique to each client and the second is the auth0 domain which is basically a sub domain on auth0. Now, if I take a look at our application code, you find it very similar to the code that we already have in auth service.

Here, the first two arguments are the same but the third argument we are passing as a blank JSON object. But in this sample code, the third argument has quite a few properties. Now, in order to understand all these properties, you need to see its documentation. One point to change here is the response type property. Currently, it's set to token if **config.callbackOnLocationHash** comes true. However, in our app, this config object will not have this property, in which value of the response type becomes code.

And this means that when we log in via this hosted page, auth0 will return a short code in the query string. But we need a token which is JWT. Therefore, here I will explicitly take this as **token**. I have pasted the changed value for the same.

```
var lock = new Auth0Lock(config.clientID, config.auth0Domain, {
  auth: {
    redirectUrl: config.callbackURL,
    responseType: 'token',
    params: config.internalOptions
  },
```

Once done, let's save the changes and go to the preview tab again. Now, from the client drop-down list, let's select the highlighted client.

Login Page

HTML   Preview

CLIENT ▾

☐ Default App

☐ Movies (Test Client)   //movie-review.auth0.com/login?client=fMjYSxxlbSsl2Nx_AdpgMBw10mXtDFiA   ⎘

☐ My App

Now, you can simply copy this URL and go to **navmenu.component.html**. Here, instead of using the auth service to log in, we can simply paste this URL as shown below. Here is the code snippet for the same.

```
<div class='main-nav'>
        <div class='navbar navbar-inverse'>
          <div class='navbar-header'>
                <button type='button' class='navbar-
toggle' data-toggle='collapse' data-target='.navbar-collapse'>
                  <span class='sr-only'>Toggle
navigation</span>
                  <span class='icon-bar'></span>
                  <span class='icon-bar'></span>
                  <span class='icon-bar'></span>
                </button>
            <a class='navbar-brand' [routerLink]="['\/
home']">MovieReviewSPA_web</a>
        </div>
        <div class='clearfix'></div>
        <div class='navbar-collapse collapse'>
          <ul class='nav navbar-nav'>
                <li [routerLinkActive]="['link-active']">
                  <a [routerLink]="['\/home']">
                    <span class='glyphicon glyphicon-
```

```
home'></span> Home
                    </a>
                </li>
                <li [routerLinkActive]="['link-active']">
                    <a href="https://movie-review.auth0.
com/login?client=HwTjSrCFV320gGkuhZ2KiT861miuXMh1"
*ngIf="!authService.authenticated()">
                        <span class='glyphicon glyphicon-
user'></span> Login
                    </a>
                    <a (click)="authService.logout()"
*ngIf="authService.authenticated()">
                        <span class='glyphicon glyphicon-
user'></span> Logout
                    </a>
                </li>
                <li [routerLinkActive]="['link-
active']" [routerLinkActiveOptions]="{exact:true}">
                    <a [routerLink]="['/movies']">
                        <span class='glyphicon
glyphicon-film'></span> Movies
                    </a>
                </li>
                <li [routerLinkActive]="['link-active']">
                    <a [routerLink]="['/movies/new']">
                        <span class='glyphicon
glyphicon-plus'></span> New Movie
                    </a>
                </li>
                <li [routerLinkActive]="['link-active']">
                    <a [routerLink]="['/counter']">
                        <span class='glyphicon
glyphicon-education'></span> Counter
                    </a>
                </li>
                <li [routerLinkActive]="['link-active']">
                    <a [routerLink]="['/fetch-data']">
                        <span class='glyphicon
glyphicon-th-list'></span> Fetch data
                    </a>
                </li>
            </ul>
        </div>
    </div>
</div>
```

Once done, let's go ahead and try it again. When I click on the Login button, it gets redirected to the new URL and that to on the secure port.

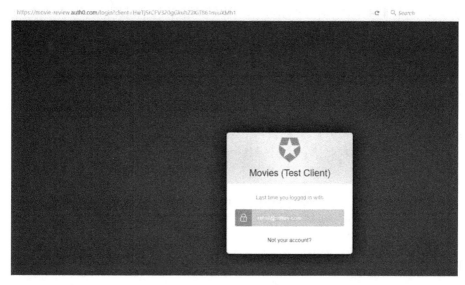

Now, when I click on my email here to log in, it flags the following error message.

This error message is very clear as we have not set up the callback URL for this. Hence, we need to copy this URL and paste this in the callback tag as well.

Allowed Callback URLs	http://localhost:35334/,http://localhost:35334/home

After the user authenticates we will only call back to any of these URLs. You can specify multiple valid URLs by comma-separating them (typically to handle different environments like QA or testing). You can use the star symbol as a wildcard for subdomains ('*.google.com'). Make sure to specify the protocol, `http://` or `https://`, otherwise the callback may fail in some cases.

Now, since I have selected my Movies client instead of the default app, the client Id will be different. Therefore, I need to select the client id from the page as shown below.

Movies (Test Client)

Quick Start   Settings   Addons   Connections   Client ID: HwTjSrCFV320gGkuhZ2KiT861miuXMh1

Name	Movies (Test Client)	
Domain	movie-review.auth0.com	
Client ID	HwTjSrCFV320gGkuhZ2KiT861miuXMh1	
Client Secret	**	

☐ Reveal client secret.
The Client Secret is not base64 encoded.

And replace it with the earlier client id in the auth service file. I have pasted the code snippet for the same.

```
import { Injectable } from '@angular/core';
import { tokenNotExpired } from 'angular2-jwt';
import Auth0Lock from 'auth0-lock';
/*import { myConfig } from './auth.config';*/

// Avoid name not found warnings
//declare var Auth0Lock: any;

@Injectable()
export class AuthService {
    lock = new Auth0Lock('HwTjSrCFV320gGkuhZ2KiT861miuX
Mh1', 'movie-review.auth0.com',{});
    constructor() {
```

```
        // Add callback for lock `authenticated` event
        this.lock.on('authenticated', (authResult) => {
            console.log(authResult);
            localStorage.setItem('token', authResult.
idToken);
        });
    }

    public login() {
        // Call the show method to display the widget.
        this.lock.show();
    };

    public authenticated() {
        // Check if there's an unexpired JWT
        // It searches for an item in localStorage with
key == 'token'
        return tokenNotExpired('token');
    };

    public logout() {
        // Remove token from localStorage
        localStorage.removeItem('token');
    };
}
```

Once done, you are logged in correctly. And therefore, Logout appears. If you don't replace the client id, it will get redirected but the menu won't change.

Audience Setting

In this section, we will take a look at the audience setting with auth0. In auth service, we have already seen that we have subscribed for the lock object event. And this event fires, when the user successfully logs in. At this point, we are logging in at the console and storing the token in the local storage. Therefore, let's take a closer look at what is happening under the hood. As soon as we log in and check the console, it will display the value shown below.

Here we have the access token which is a short string, and we have the id token which is JSON Web Token (JWT). We also have the id token payload with the following properties.

Here, **aud** is the short form of audience which represents the party this token is for. In this case, **"HwTjSrCFV320gGkuhZ2KiT861miuXMh1"** , this string is the identifier which we created for the movies app. Therefore, the token that we got here is valid for this audience. We have the expiry of this token, which is by default 10 hours; you can change this setting from the auth0 settings page.

We have issuer which is the movie review project on auth0.com and sub which is nothing but the user-id. Therefore, here my user-id has two parts. The first part is auth0 and the second is the unique identifier. However, if I log in via Google, then the first part will be Google and the second part will be some other identifier. Now, we need to set the audience in the API from the settings page. Therefore, if we go to the APIs section, we can see the audience URL.

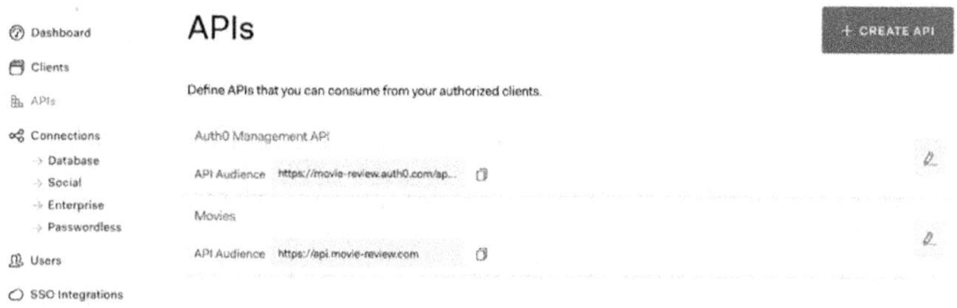
Dashboard
Clients
APIs
Connections
Database
Social
Enterprise
Passwordless
Users
SSO Integrations
APIs
+ CREATE API
Define APIs that you can consume from your authorized clients.
Auth0 Management API
API Audience https://movie-review.auth0.com/ap...
Movies
API Audience https://api.movie-review.com

Now, when we click on Movies, it will show the following screenshot:

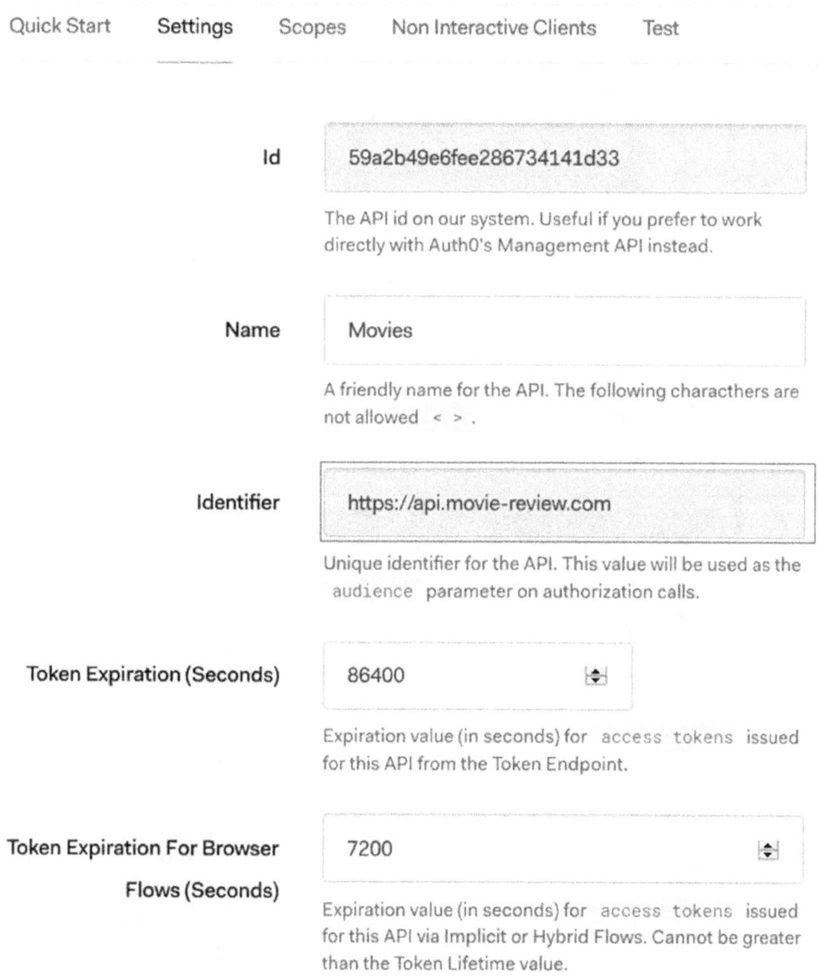
Quick Start
Settings
Scopes
Non Interactive Clients
Test
Id
59a2b49e6fee286734141d33
The API id on our system. Useful if you prefer to work directly with Auth0's Management API instead.
Name
Movies
A friendly name for the API. The following characthers are not allowed < > .
Identifier
https://api.movie-review.com
Unique identifier for the API. This value will be used as the audience parameter on authorization calls.
Token Expiration (Seconds)
86400
Expiration value (in seconds) for access tokens issued for this API from the Token Endpoint.
Token Expiration For Browser Flows (Seconds)
7200
Expiration value (in seconds) for access tokens issued for this API via Implicit or Hybrid Flows. Cannot be greater than the Token Lifetime value.

And from here, we need to copy the Identifier URL. This is just a logical identifier; this doesn't mean that it's a publicly accessible endpoint. Now, we need to add this identifier to our JWT. Therefore, this token can be used to make calls to the API. When we call our API, our JWT middleware will kick in and take a look at this token and see if this token is valid for the API endpoint or not. Now, in order to add this, we need to go to hosted pages, and then in the JavaScript code, we need to make the following changes. Here, I have changed the params value.

```
var lock = new Auth0Lock(config.clientID, config.auth0Domain, {
  auth: {
    redirectUrl: config.callbackURL,
    responseType: 'token',
    params: {
      "audience":"https://api.movie-review.com"
    }
  },
```

Now, save the changes and log in again.

It will prompt a confirmation box as shown below.

On clicking Yes, you will be able to log in. This dialogue is also known as the consent dialog for the first time user. It's just like how you log in via Face book or Google to any third-party app. Now, if you inspect the console, it will show a couple of errors.

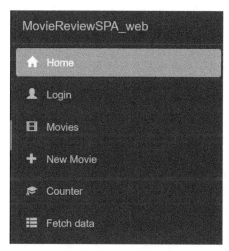

Because of these errors, even after authentication, the login menu does not change to logout.

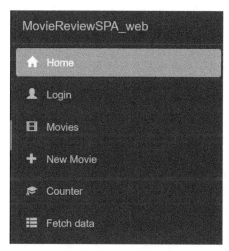

We will fix this in a moment. The access token has a long string; previously it was a short string. Also, we no longer have idToken and payload token property. Therefore, when we set the audience property in our lock object, auth0 behaves in a slightly different way. They call this as OIDC or Open ID connect compliant mode. Therefore, OIDC is an authentication protocol which defines a standard for implementing a single sign on authentication across multiple websites. Auth) embraces Open ID connect. Therefore, when we set the audience property, instead of idToken, it returns an access token which is compliant with Open ID. Now, this exception happens because in our auth service, we are storing this idToken in our local storage and we are extracting this on the authenticated call. Therefore, it tries to extract the value out of something that is undefined and hence it fails. Therefore, we need to change idToken with accessToken as shown below in the snippet.

```
import { Injectable } from '@angular/core';
import { tokenNotExpired } from 'angular2-jwt';
import Auth0Lock from 'auth0-lock';
/*import { myConfig } from './auth.config';*/
```

```
// Avoid name not found warnings
//declare var Auth0Lock: any;

@Injectable()
export class AuthService {
    lock = new Auth0Lock('HwTjSrCFV320gGkuhZ2KiT861miuX
Mh1', 'movie-review.auth0.com',{});

    constructor() {
        // Add callback for lock `authenticated` event
        this.lock.on('authenticated', (authResult) => {
            console.log(authResult);
            localStorage.setItem('token', authResult.
accessToken);
        });
    }

    public login() {
        // Call the show method to display the widget.
        this.lock.show();
    };

    public authenticated() {
        // Check if there's an unexpired JWT
        // It searches for an item in localStorage with
key == 'token'
        return tokenNotExpired('token');
    };

    public logout() {
        // Remove token from localStorage
        localStorage.removeItem('token');
    };
}
```

Now, if we save and refresh the page, we will get the same error in the console but this time, even the Login menu will disappear and it will appear like this.

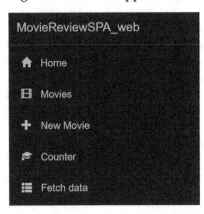

The workaround for this issue is to manually delete the token and then log in again. Therefore, from Chrome developer tools, we need to go to the application tab, and from there, we need to go to the local storage as shown below.

Now, I am going to delete this undefined token and refresh it again. Once deleted and refreshed, the login menu appears on the screen.

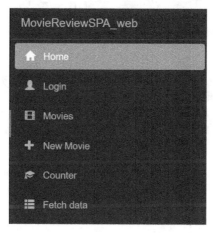

Now, if I log in and check again, I will be able to log in properly. Therefore, after logging in, the logout menu appears on the screen.

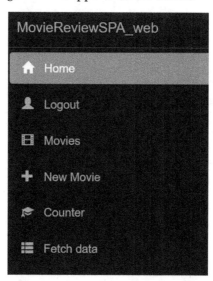

Also, all the errors disappear from the console.

Now, I need to copy this token from the local storage

And, I need to go to http://jwt.io site to decode the same. As soon as I paste the token in the encoded section, it gets decrypted and shows the correct values on the right window. It shows the entire payload and other data. Here, the first part of the audience is the identifier and the second part is the user info. We will use the second part to retrieve the user info in the next section.

Getting User Profile

In this section, we will fetch the user profile information. I have pasted the code snippet for the same.

```
import { Injectable } from '@angular/core';
import { tokenNotExpired } from 'angular2-jwt';
import Auth0Lock from 'auth0-lock';

// Avoid name not found warnings
//declare var Auth0Lock: any;
@Injectable()
export class AuthService {
    profile:any;
    lock = new Auth0Lock('HwTjSrCFV320gGkuhZ2KiT861miuX
Mh1', 'movie-review.auth0.com',{});

    constructor() {
        this.profile = JSON.parse(localStorage.
getItem('profile'));
        // Add callback for lock `authenticated` event
        this.lock.on('authenticated', (authResult) => {
            console.log(authResult);
            localStorage.setItem('token', authResult.
accessToken);
            this.lock.getUserInfo(authResult.accessToken,
                (error, profile) => {
                    if (error)
                        throw error;

                    localStorage.setItem('profile', JSON.
stringify(profile));
                    this.profile = profile;
                });
            });
    }

    public login() {
        // Call the show method to display the widget.
        this.lock.show();
    };

    public authenticated() {
        // Check if there's an unexpired JWT
        // It searches for an item in localStorage with
key == 'token'
        return tokenNotExpired('token');
    };

        public logout() {
```

```
        // Remove token from localStorage
        localStorage.removeItem('token');
    localStorage.removeItem('profile');
    this.profile=null;
  };
}
```

Now, let me explain the snippet here. When the user successfully logs in, we store the token in the local storage and then we call the **getUserInfo()** method. This method takes two parameters; the first one is the access token and the second one is the callback function with two parameters. It takes the error as the first parameter and profile as the second parameter.

If it returns the error, then we simply throw the same else we store the same in the local storage. Since in the local storage, we cannot store JWT, we stringify and then store it. I have also created a profile variable, which I need to set after storing the values in the local storage. With above changes in place, when we refresh and log in again, we can see the stored profile value as well in the local storage. Also, in the logout action, we need to remove the profile from the local storage and need to set the profile variable back to null.

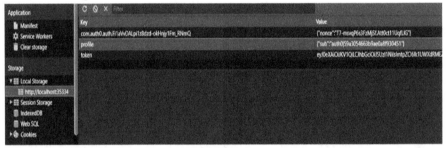

However, currently the profile has only one property which is sub or user-id. We can also save emails here. But for this, we need to specifically ask for the same. In order to fetch them, we need to modify the scope variable in hosted pages in auth0. Now, I need to ask for email as well.

```
var lock = new Auth0Lock(config.clientID, config.auth0Domain, {
  auth: {
    redirectUrl: config.callbackURL,
    responseType: 'token',
    params: {
      "audience":"https://api.movie-review.com",
      "scope":"openid email"
    }
  },
  assetsUrl:  config.assetsUrl,
  allowedConnections: connection ? [connection] : null,
  rememberLastLogin: !prompt,
  language: language,
  languageDictionary: languageDictionary,
```

With the above changes saved, if we refresh our app and log in again, it will show the email as well. Since we have changed the scope, the consent dialog asks permission for accesing emails as shown below.

Once I click on Yes, the email is seen in the console as shown below.

Key	Value
com.auth0.auth.Fi1a...	{"nonce":"T7-msvqP6s3FzMjSf.Att0ct11UqfLIG"}
profile	{"sub":"auth0|59a3054663b9ae0a8f930451","email":"rahul@sahay.com","email_verified":false}
token	eyJ0eXAiOiJKV1QiLCJhbGciOiJSUzI1NiIsImtpZCI6Ik1UWXd XdRMEZCTmpsRlFVXlRVEJHUmppGR05UV

Adding More fields in the Sign Up Form

In this section, I will add more fields in the registration form. Again, we can control this from the auth0 hosted page.

Here, I have added another property in the lock object which is **additionalSignupFields**.We set this property to array, and in this array, for each field, we have an object. Here is a glimpse of the setting.

```
additionalSignUpFields: [{
name: "address",
placeholder: "enter your address",
// The following properties are optional
icon: "https://example.com/assests/address_icon.png",
prefill: "street 123",
validator: function(address) {
  return {
    valid: address.length >= 10,
    hint: "Must have 10 or more chars" // optional
  };
  }
},
{
name: "full_name",
placeholder: "Enter your full name"
}],
```

Here, I have added a couple of fields with placeholder and prefilled values as well. I have also given examples of validators. Once done, when I go ahead and try to sign up, the screen will look like this.

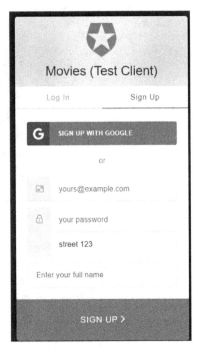

Now, from here, let me register a new user.

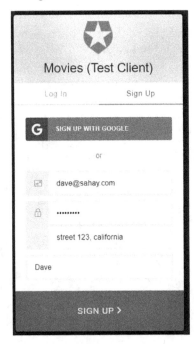

Once a new user is signed up properly, the user needs to log in again. While logging in, it will again ask for user permission to access the email info. Once granted, the user can log in into the application. Now, auth0 also has a complete user management page.

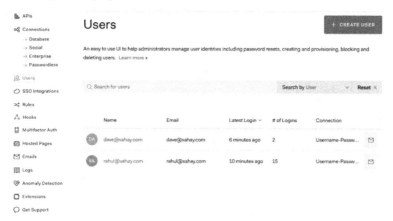

Here you can see all the users, who have registered with your application. This is one of the beautiful things about auth0; you don't need to build all the screens from scratch. When you click on any one of these users, you will get the complete data about the user. Now, let's fetch the user name as well. We can get this from profile. We need to go to the hosted pages link and add profile as shown below.

```
auth: {
    redirectUrl: config.callbackURL,
    responseType: 'token',
    params: {
        "audience":"https://api.movie-review.com",
        "scope":"openid email profile"
    }
},
```

With the above changes in place, when we log in again, we can see that the profile has the complete information.

Now, in order to clearly see the information, we need to log in the console, while fetching the user info. Hence, with these changes, the screen will look like this.

```
▼ {sub: "auth0|59a8194757d70e1088c07c4c", email: "dave@sahay.com", email_verified: false, name: "dave@sahay.com", nickname: "dave", ...} ▮
    email: "dave@sahay.com"
    email_verified: false
    name: "dave@sahay.com"
    nickname: "dave"
    picture: "https://s.gravatar.com/avatar/b288f2a354b18d26f4797b0de08633dc?s=480&r=pg&d=https%3A%2F%2Fcdn.auth0.com%2Favatars%2Fda.png"
    sub: "auth0|59a8194757d70e1088c07c4c"
    updated_at: "2017-08-31T14:34:00.546Z"
    ▶ __proto__: Object
```

Name which appears here is the same as email. We don't want this. In order to fix this issue, we need to pick the name from meta-data.

Adding Rules

In this section, we will set rules. Therefore, in the auth0 page, we need to go to the Rules menu. This will show us the following page.

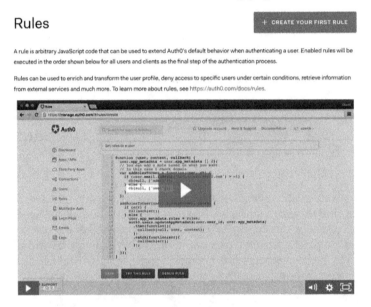

You can check these rules on your own on the auth0 page. However, in a nutshell, rules are very powerful in auth0. Rules are basically JavaScript functions which execute everytime a user logs in. Here, I need to click on Create your first rule button. Next, I need to select a template. Here, I can either select an empty template or select from a bunch of templates as shown below.

Here, I have selected the following one.

Add country to the user profile

```
1    function (user, context, callback) {
2        if (context.request.geoip) {
3            context.idToken['https://example.com/country'] = context.request.geoip.country_name;
4            context.idToken['https://example.com/timezone'] = context.request.geoip.time_zone;
5        }
6        callback(null, user, context);
7    }
```

SAVE   TRY THIS RULE   INSTALL REAL-TIME LOGS

Basically here, we need to check whether geoip is present, or else we need to set the country and timezone properties of the user. Once done, when I log in again and check the console, I can see following GEO settings as well.

```
▼ Object
    email: "dave@sahay.com"
    email_verified: false
    https://example.com/country: "India"
    https://example.com/timezone: "Asia/Kolkata"
    name: "dave@sahay.com"
    nickname: "dave"
    picture: "https://s.gravatar.com/avatar/b288f2a354b18d26f4797b0de08633dc?s=480&r=pg&d=https%3A%2F%2Fcdn.auth0.com%2Favatars%2Fda.png"
    sub: "auth0|59a8194757d70e1088c07c4c"
    updated_at: "2017-08-31T15:19:01.180Z"
    ▶ __proto__: Object
```

Now, we need to fix the name issue. If you see the Raw JSON property of the user, you will get an idea of how to fix the issue. Here is a glimpse of the same.

```
1    {
2        "email_verified": false,
3        "email": "dave@sahay.com",
4        "user_metadata": {
5            "address": "street 123, california",
6            "full_name": "Dave"
7        },
8        "updated_at": "2017-08-31T15:19:01.180Z",
9        "name": "dave@sahay.com",
10       "picture": "https://s.gravatar.com/avatar/b288f2a354b18d26f4797b0de08633dc?s=480&r=
11       "user_id": "auth0|59a8194757d70e1088c07c4c",
12       "nickname": "dave",
13       "identities": [
14           {
15               "user_id": "59a8194757d70e1088c07c4c",
16               "provider": "auth0",
17               "connection": "Username-Password-Authentication",
18               "isSocial": false
19           }
20       ],
```

Therefore, under the rules section, I need to read one more property say name from user_metadata.

Edit Rule

The rule script has been saved

Add country to the user profile

```
1  function (user, context, callback) {
2    if (context.request.geoip) {
3      context.idToken['https://example.com/country'] = context.request.geoip.country_name;
4      context.idToken['https://example.com/timezone'] = context.request.geoip.time_zone;
5    }
6    user.name = user.user_metadata.full_name;
7    callback(null, user, context);
8  }
```

SAVE   TRY THIS RULE   INSTALL REAL-TIME LOGS

Now, you can try this rule here as well or directly test it in the application. Hence, log out and log in again, then it will come properly.

▼Object
  email: "dave@sahay.com"
  email_verified: false
  https://example.com/country: "India"
  https://example.com/timezone: "Asia/Kolkata"
  name: "Dave"
  nickname: "dave"
  picture: "https://s.gravatar.com/avatar/b288f2a354b18d26f4797b0de08633dc?s=480&r=pg&d=https%3A%2F%2Fcdn.auth0.com%2Favatars%2Fda.png"
  sub: "auth0|59a8194757d70e1088c07c4c"
  updated_at: "2017-08-31T15:27:41.507Z"
  ▶ __proto__: Object

Adding Roles

In this section, we will learn how to assign roles to users. The easiest way to do this via the dashboard. Therefore, we need to go to users and under the **app_metadata** section, we need to assign the role.

user_metadata

```
1  ▼ {
2      "full_name": "Rahul Sahay"
3  }
```

Data that the user has read/write access to (e.g. color_preference, blog_url, etc.)

app_metadata

```
1  ▼ {
2    ▼ "roles":["Admin"]
3  }
```

Data that the user has read-only access to (e.g. roles, permissions, vip, etc)

Here, I have assigned myself the **Admin** role. Similarly, I have given the **User** role to Dave.

user_metadata

```
1 ▾ {
2     "address": "street 123, california",
3     "full_name": "Dave"
4   }
```

Data that the user has read/write access to (e.g. color_preference, blog_url, etc.)

app_metadata

```
1 ▾ {
2 ▾   "roles": [
3       "User"
4     ]
5   }
```

Data that the user has read-only access to (e.g. roles, permissions, vip, etc)

[SAVE]

Now, this app_metadata is only known to auth0; it's not part of Open ID protocol, hence it needs to be returned as custom claim. In order to return them to the client, we need to put them in namespace. Therefore, we need to create an empty rule and then add the rule as shown below.

Returning Custom Claims

```
1  function (user, context, callback) {
2    if(user.app_metadata && user.app_metadata.roles)
3      context.accessToken['https://movie-review.com/roles']=user.app_metadata.roles;
4    callback(null, user, context);
5  }
```

[SAVE] [TRY THIS RULE] [INSTALL REAL-TIME LOGS]

Here, the rule is pretty simple; if roles are defined, then only it will go ahead and assign the same under context with a specific namespace. I have used an arbitrary namespace here just to avoid any future name collision.

Showing-Hiding Contents Based on Roles

In the last section, we saw how to return custom claims in a JSON Web Token (JWT). Now, we need to extract this in auth service. I have pasted the code snippet from auth service.

```
import { Injectable } from '@angular/core';
import { tokenNotExpired, JwtHelper } from 'angular2-jwt';
import Auth0Lock from 'auth0-lock';

// Avoid name not found warnings
//declare var Auth0Lock: any;

@Injectable()
```

```
export class AuthService {
    profile: any;

    private roles: string[] =[];
        lock = new Auth0Lock('HwTjSrCFV320gGkuhZ2KiT861mi
uXMh1', 'movie-review.auth0.com', {});

    constructor() {
    this.profile = JSON.parse(localStorage.
getItem('profile'));
        var token = localStorage.getItem('token');

        if (token && token.length>25) {
            var jwtObj = new JwtHelper();
            var decodedToken = jwtObj.decodeToken(token);
            this.roles = decodedToken['https://movie-
review.com/roles'];
        }

        // Add callback for lock `authenticated` event
        this.lock.on('authenticated', (authResult) => {
            localStorage.setItem('token', authResult.
accessToken);
            //Decoding token
            var jwtObj = new JwtHelper();
            var decodedToken = jwtObj.
decodeToken(authResult.accessToken);
            this.roles = decodedToken['https://movie-
review.com/roles'];
            console.log("Roles: ", this.roles);
            this.lock.getUserInfo(authResult.accessToken,
                (error, profile) => {
                if (error)
                    throw error;

                console.log(profile);
                localStorage.setItem('profile', JSON.
stringify(profile));
                this.profile = profile;
            });
        });
    }

    public isInRole(roleName) {
        return this.roles.indexOf(roleName) > -1;
    }
    public login() {
        // Call the show method to display the widget.
```

```
            this.lock.show();
    };

    public authenticated() {
        // Check if there's an unexpired JWT
        // It searches for an item in localStorage with
key == 'token'
        return tokenNotExpired('token');
    };

    public logout() {
        // Remove token from localStorage
        localStorage.removeItem('token');
        localStorage.removeItem('profile');
        this.profile = null;
        this.roles = [];
    };
}
```

Let me explain the snippet a bit. Here, I am decoding token and then I am extracting roles from there. And on logout, I am just flushing the values as well. Now, just to prove the point, I have created a public method which checks the role. Now, in the nav menu, I have just made a new movie accessible to the Admin user only. Here is the snippet for the same.

```
<div class='main-nav'>
    <div class='navbar navbar-inverse'>
        <div class='navbar-header'>
            <button type='button' class='navbar-toggle'
data-toggle='collapse' data-target='.navbar-collapse'>
                <span class='sr-only'>Toggle navigation</
span>
                <span class='icon-bar'></span>
                <span class='icon-bar'></span>
                <span class='icon-bar'></span>
            </button>
            <a class='navbar-brand' [routerLink]="['/
home']">MovieReviewSPA_web</a>
        </div>
        <div class='clearfix'></div>
        <div class='navbar-collapse collapse'>
            <ul class='nav navbar-nav'>
                <li [routerLinkActive]="['link-active']">
                    <a [routerLink]="['/home']">
                        <span class='glyphicon glyphicon-
home'></span> Home
                    </a>
```

```
                </li>
                <li [routerLinkActive]="['link-active']">
                    <a href="https://movie-review.auth0.
com/login?client=HwTjSrCFV320gGkuhZ2KiT861miuXMh1"
*ngIf="!authService.authenticated()">
                        <span class='glyphicon glyphicon-
user'></span> Login
                    </a>
                    <a (click)="authService.logout()"
*ngIf="authService.authenticated()">
                        <span class='glyphicon glyphicon-
user'></span> Logout
                    </a>
                </li>
                <li [routerLinkActive]="['link-active']"
[routerLinkActiveOptions]="{exact:true}">
                    <a [routerLink]="['/movies']">
                        <span class='glyphicon glyphicon-
film'></span> Movies
                    </a>
                </li>
                <li [routerLinkActive]="['link-active']"
*ngIf="authService.isInRole('Admin')">
                    <a [routerLink]="['/movies/new']">
                        <span class='glyphicon glyphicon-
plus'></span> New Movie
                    </a>
                </li>
                <li [routerLinkActive]="['link-active']">
                    <a [routerLink]="['/counter']">
                        <span class='glyphicon glyphicon-
education'></span> Counter
                    </a>
                </li>
                <li [routerLinkActive]="['link-active']">
                    <a [routerLink]="['/fetch-data']">
                        <span class='glyphicon glyphicon-
th-list'></span> Fetch data
                    </a>
                </li>
            </ul>
        </div>
    </div>
</div>
```

Once done, if I am not logged in, then it won't show the new movie menu.

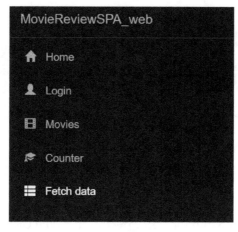

I need to log in with the admin role as shown below.

It will show the new movie menu.

Also, if I inspect the console, it will show the roles as shown below.

```
Angular is running in the development mode. Call enableProdMode() to enable the production mode.
[HMR] connected
Roles:-    ▼Array(1) ●
              0: "Admin"
              length: 1
            ►__proto__: Array(0)
 ►Object
```

I made the new movie menu under admin control, just for demonstration purpose. However, in the actual use case, it's not at all required. We can put the delete operation under admin control.

Route Guards

In this section, we will see how to protect routes. Consider a scenario wherein a user is not logged in. But the user directly pastes the URL as shown below. In that case, in the current scenario, the user can access the page.

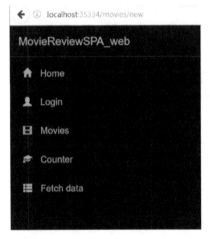

This is the case which we need to prevent. In order to fix this, we need to create another service say **auth-guard.service.ts**. I have pasted the code snippet for the same.

```
import { Injectable } from '@angular/core';
import { CanActivate } from '@angular/router';
import { AuthService } from '../services/auth.service';

@Injectable()
export class AuthGuard implements CanActivate {

    constructor(private auth: AuthService) { }

        //Here, we can check whether user is logged in or
not
        canActivate() {
```

```
        if (this.auth.authenticated())
            return true;
        //else redirect user to login page
        window.location.href = "https://movie-review.
auth0.com/login?client=HwTjSrCFV320gGkuhZ2KiT861miuXMh1";
        return false;
    }
}
```

This is a fairly simple code! Here we are just checking whether the user is logged in or not when he requests for the route. If yes, the user will be redirected to the page else the user will get redirected to the login page. Now, we also need to register this service in **app.module.ts** and **app.module.shared.ts**. Once done, we can apply route guard to the new movie route as shown below.

```
import { NgModule } from "@angular/core";
import { RouterModule } from "@angular/router";
import { FormsModule } from "@angular/forms";
import { ToastyModule } from "ng2-toasty";
import { AppComponent } from "./components/app/app.
component"
import { NavMenuComponent } from "./components/navmenu/
navmenu.component";
import { HomeComponent } from "./components/home/home.
component";
import { FetchDataComponent } from "./components/
fetchdata/fetchdata.component";
import { CounterComponent } from "./components/counter/
counter.component";
import { MoviesComponent } from "./components/movies/
movies.component";
import { ReviewsComponent } from "./components/reviews/
reviews.component";
import { NewMovieComponent } from "./components/new-
movie/new-movie.component";
import { EditMovieComponent } from "./components/edit-
movie/edit-movie.component";
import { NewReviewComponent } from "./components/new-
review/new-review.component";
import { EditReviewComponent } from "./components/edit-
review/edit-review.component";
import { PaginationComponent } from "./components/
utilities/pagination.component";
import { DetailViewComponent } from "./components/detail-
view/detail-view.component";
import { NotFoundComponent } from "./components/not-
found/not-found.component";
```

```
import { MoviesService } from "./services/movies.service";
import { ReviewsService } from "./services/reviews.service";
import { ImagesService } from "./services/images.service";
import { AuthService } from "./services/auth.service";
import { AuthGuard } from "./services/auth-guard.service";

Raven

.config("https://7579eaef4acc46bab3ffd87d3d85f3ea@sentry.
io/203240")
        .install();

export const sharedConfig: NgModule = {
        bootstrap: [ AppComponent ],
        declarations: [
        AppComponent,
        NavMenuComponent,
        CounterComponent,
        FetchDataComponent,
        HomeComponent,
        MoviesComponent,
        NewMovieComponent,
        EditMovieComponent,
        ReviewsComponent,
        NewReviewComponent,
        EditReviewComponent,
        PaginationComponent,
        DetailViewComponent,
        NotFoundComponent
    ],
    imports: [
        FormsModule,
        ToastyModule.forRoot(),
        RouterModule.forRoot([
            { path: "", redirectTo: "home", pathMatch: "full" },
            { path: "movies", component: MoviesComponent },
            { path: "movies/new", component:
NewMovieComponent, canActivate:[AuthGuard] },
            { path: "movies/:id", component:
EditMovieComponent },
            { path: "movies/detail/:id", component:
DetailViewComponent },
            { path: "reviews/:id", component:
ReviewsComponent },
            { path: "editreview/:id", component:
EditReviewComponent },
```

```
            { path: "reviews/new/:id", component:
NewReviewComponent },
            { path: "home", component: HomeComponent },
            { path: "counter", component: CounterComponent },
            { path: "fetch-data", component:
FetchDataComponent },
            { path: "pageNotFound", component:
NotFoundComponent, data: { title: "Page not found" } },
            { path: "**", redirectTo: "pageNotFound",
pathMatch: "full" }
            /*{ path: '**', redirectTo: 'home' }*/
        ])
    ],
    providers: [
        MoviesService,
        ReviewsService,
        ImagesService,
        AuthService,
        AuthGuard
    ]

};
```

Here, I have added another parameter with the **canActivate** property. Once done, when I try to navigate to the new movie link, it will get redirected to the login page as shown below.

Once the user logs in, he will land on the home page and the screen will show the new movie in the menu as well.

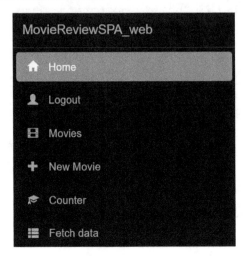

Currently, we have solved the authentication problem. However, in the current scenario, if I log in with any other user who is having any other role, then in that case, also I need to navigate to the new movie page. So, now we need to fix the roles issue. In order to fix this, I need to create a new service with the name **admin-auth-guard.service.ts**. I have pasted the code snippet.

```
import { Injectable } from '@angular/core';
import { AuthGuard } from '../services/auth-guard.service';
import { AuthService } from '../services/auth.service';

@Injectable()
export class AdminAuthGuard extends AuthGuard {

    constructor(auth: AuthService) { super(auth); }

    //Here, we can check whether user is logged in or not
    canActivate() {
        //Called the base class canActivate method
        var isAuthenticated = super.canActivate();
        //If it returns true, then need to check whether
user is in right role
        return isAuthenticated ? this.auth.
isInRole('Admin') : false;
    }
}
```

Again, this code is fairly simple. Here, I have inherited **AuthGuard** and then used the same to check whether the user is authenticated or not. If yes, then I need to check the role. Now, in order to inherit the same, I have modified the constructor in the **AuthGuard** service, where I made the change as protected. Here is the code snippet of **auth-guard.service.ts**.

```
import { Injectable } from '@angular/core';
import { CanActivate } from '@angular/router';
import { AuthService } from '../services/auth.service';
@Injectable()
export class AuthGuard implements CanActivate {

    constructor(protected auth: AuthService) { }

    //Here, we can check whether user is logged in or not
    canActivate() {
        if (this.auth.authenticated())
            return true;
        //else redirect user to login page
        window.location.href = "https://movie-review.
auth0.com/login?client=HwTjSrCFV320gGkuhZ2KiT861miuXMh1";
        return false;
    }

}
```

Next, I have registered the service as providers at both the places viz **app.module. ts** and **app.module.shared.ts** files. Once done, in **app.module.shared.ts** file, I have assigned the admin auth guard here. I have pasted the code snippet for the same.

```
import * as Raven from "raven-js";
import { NgModule } from "@angular/core";
import { RouterModule } from "@angular/router";
import { FormsModule } from "@angular/forms";
import { ToastyModule } from "ng2-toasty";
import { AppComponent } from "./components/app/app.component"
import { NavMenuComponent } from "./components/navmenu/
navmenu.component";
import { HomeComponent } from "./components/home/home.component";
import { FetchDataComponent } from "./components/
fetchdata/fetchdata.component";
import { CounterComponent } from "./components/counter/
counter.component";
import { MoviesComponent } from "./components/movies/
movies.component";
import { ReviewsComponent } from "./components/reviews/
reviews.component";
import { NewMovieComponent } from "./components/new-
movie/new-movie.component";
import { EditMovieComponent } from "./components/edit-
movie/edit-movie.component";
import { NewReviewComponent } from "./components/new-
review/new-review.component";
```

```
import { EditReviewComponent } from "./components/edit-
review/edit-review.component";
import { PaginationComponent } from "./components/
utilities/pagination.component";
import { DetailViewComponent } from "./components/detail-
view/detail-view.component";
import { NotFoundComponent } from "./components/not-
found/not-found.component";
import { MoviesService } from "./services/movies.service";
import { ReviewsService } from "./services/reviews.service";
import { ImagesService } from "./services/images.service";
import { AuthService } from "./services/auth.service";
import { AuthGuard } from "./services/auth-guard.service";
import { AdminAuthGuard } from "./services/admin-auth-
guard.service";

Raven
.config("https://7579eaef4acc46bab3ffd87d3d85f3ea@sentry.
io/203240")
    .install();

export const sharedConfig: NgModule = {
    bootstrap: [ AppComponent ],
    declarations: [
        AppComponent,
        NavMenuComponent,
        CounterComponent,
        FetchDataComponent,
        HomeComponent,
        MoviesComponent,
        NewMovieComponent,
        EditMovieComponent,
        ReviewsComponent,
        NewReviewComponent,
        EditReviewComponent,
        PaginationComponent,
        DetailViewComponent,
        NotFoundComponent
    ],
    imports: [
        FormsModule,
        ToastyModule.forRoot(),
        RouterModule.forRoot([
            { path: "", redirectTo: "home", pathMatch: "full" },
            { path: "movies", component: MoviesComponent },
            { path: "movies/new", component:
NewMovieComponent, canActivate: [AdminAuthGuard] },
```

```
            { path: "movies/:id", component:
EditMovieComponent },
            { path: "movies/detail/:id", component:
DetailViewComponent },
            { path: "reviews/:id", component:
ReviewsComponent },
            { path: "editreview/:id", component:
EditReviewComponent },
            { path: "reviews/new/:id", component:
NewReviewComponent },
            { path: "home", component: HomeComponent },
            { path: "counter", component: CounterComponent },
            { path: "fetch-data", component:
FetchDataComponent },
            { path: "pageNotFound", component:
NotFoundComponent, data: { title: "Page not found" } },
            { path: "**", redirectTo: "pageNotFound",
pathMatch: "full" }
            /*{ path: '**', redirectTo: 'home' }*/
        ])
    ],
    providers: [
        MoviesService,
        ReviewsService,
        ImagesService,
        AuthService,
        AuthGuard,
        AdminAuthGuard
    ]
};
```

Once done, when I log in with Dave who is a normal user, then following screen menus will appear on the screen.

If I try to navigate to the new movie route, it shows a blank page as shown below. Now, rather than showing a blank page, we can show un-authorized page.

This is because we are returning false. In order to improvise it, we need to create a new component for not authorized and return the same from here.

Calling Secured Server-side APIs

In this section, we will call the APIs which we secured initially. However, I have put the [Authorize] attribute now on the Post method as shown below.

```
// Create a new movie
   // POST /api/movies
   [Authorize]
   [HttpPost("")]
   public int Post([FromBody]Movie movie)
   {
       UOW.Movies.Add(movie);
       UOW.Commit();
       return Response.StatusCode = (int)HttpStatusCode.
Created;
   }
```

Now, in order to send the bearer token in the header, we don't need to modify anything at server side. We just need to make use of the **AuthHttp** service. Here is the code for **movies.service.ts**.

```
import { Injectable, Inject } from '@angular/core';
import { Http } from '@angular/http';
import 'rxjs/add/operator/map';
import { AuthHttp } from 'angular2-jwt/angular2-jwt';

@Injectable()
export class MoviesService {

    //In order to use any injectable, pass it via ctor
    constructor(private http: Http, @Inject('ORIGIN_URL')
private originUrl: string, private authHttp:AuthHttp) { }

    getMovies(filter) {
```

```
        return this.http.get(this.originUrl + '/api/
movies' + '?' + this.toQueryString(filter))
            //Once, we get the response back, it has to
get mapped to json
            .map(res => res.json());
    }
    getMoviesCount() {
        return this.http.get(this.originUrl + '/api/movies')
            //Once, we get the response back, it has to
get mapped to json
            .map(res => res.json());
    }
    toQueryString(obj) {
        var parts = [];
        for (var property in obj) {
            var value = obj[property];
            if (value != null && value != undefined)
            parts.push(encodeURIComponent(property) + '='
+ encodeURIComponent(value));
        }
        return parts.join('&');
    }

createMovie(movie) {
    return this.authHttp.post('/api/movies', movie)
        .map(res => res.json());
    }

    getMovie(id) {
        return this.http.get('/api/movies/' + id)
            .map(res => res.json());
    }
    updateMovie(movie) {
        return this.http.put('/api/movies/', movie)
        .map(res => res.json());
    }
    deleteMovie(id) {
        return this.http.delete('/api/movies/' + id)
            .map(res => res.json());
    }
}
```

Here in createMovie, instead of using http.post, I have used the authHttp. post method with the same parameters. Now, this method will automatically add the bearer token to the request header. Apart from this change, we also need to register this service as provider in the app.module.shared.ts and app.module.ts files. But, here we need to register **AUTH_PROVIDERS**. With the above change in place, when I try to create the new movie, it will get created properly.

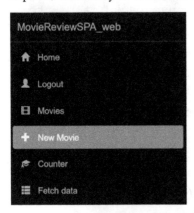

Now, at this moment, when I inspect request headers, I can see the bearer token there.

▼ Request Headers   view source
  Accept: application/json, text/plain, */*
  Accept-Encoding: gzip, deflate, br
  Accept-Language: en-US,en;q=0.8
  Authorization: Bearer eyJ0eXA1OiJKV1QiLCJhbGc1OiJSUzI1NiIsImtpZCI6Ik1UNXdRMEZCEZCTmpsR1FVVK1RVEJHQWpGMlVTFNRVJOTWtSRU1FRkRRVGs1TXpFeVFzqVkJQQ5J9.eyJpc3M1OiJ3
  MC5jb20vIiwic3V1IjoiYXV9a0B4NT1hNzABMY2M2I5YWkwYThwOTM4ODUwIiwiYXh0IjpbImh0dHBzOi8vYXBpLmIvdmmI1UX3IdmI1dy5jb20iLCJodHRwczovL21vdmI1UX3I1dmI1dy5hdXRoWC5jb20vXXX
  yQ02WKzIw28drdkRwRtpVOg2NW1gpdVNkANDEILCJ1eWA1OjE1MDQyODA2TAsIm1hdCIGMTUMDI3MtQ5RCwIc2NvcGU1Oi1JvcGVuaWQgZW1haWwgcGVydfmIsZSIsImh0hRHU:018vtN2amURcwV2aWV1Q
  IFtghFH0Jxh3murA2kgRlbnb1nEO7Zbp8ZO1F13zjtKS_fEkx3vTJ06758pJF6ysLwQQG28IashIUv1V1dK-1SdLQiX11BS8r3C_VP1fKdd1_ydhxrqsvrTUXvDtX8vkIQTXFJ9FS_Y5jm1KLjR_D01W5e
  EwKS4ggG0P19AKUZxn1gL1Frg1TV4jgF2Qq87CcX1B21BVFz7KmICEYeQFLaidWTovuR8eRKHJVT2HLNIToLtIa_vO26s1oH3Ul-_tRtS1H8vEMPFHCuXHH_bH3bQh3p1rFVt10W5yacLu10RoZzFHvQ
  Connection: keep-alive
  Content-Length: 99
  content-type: application/json
  Cookie: _ga=GA1.1.131817057.1494527827
  Host: localhost:35334

Here, for demo; I have enabled it only for the creation of the movie. You can extend this to other endpoints as well.

Resticting API Access

In this section, we will basically restrict the access of APIs to certain roles. In order to implement this, we need to go to the **startup.cs** file and make the following changes.

```
using Microsoft.AspNetCore.Builder;
using Microsoft.AspNetCore.Hosting;
using Microsoft.AspNetCore.SpaServices.Webpack;
using Microsoft.EntityFrameworkCore;
using Microsoft.EntityFrameworkCore.Infrastructure;
using Microsoft.Extensions.Configuration;
using Microsoft.Extensions.DependencyInjection;
```

```
using Microsoft.Extensions.Logging;
using MovieReviewSPA.Data;
using MovieReviewSPA.Data.Contracts;
using MovieReviewSPA.Data.Helpers;
using MovieReviewSPA.Data.SampleData;
using MovieReviewSPA.Model;

namespace MovieReviewSPA.web
{
    public class Startup
    {
        public Startup(IHostingEnvironment env)
        {
            var builder = new ConfigurationBuilder()
                .SetBasePath(env.ContentRootPath)
                .AddJsonFile("appsettings.json",
optional: true, reloadOnChange: true)

                .AddJsonFile($"appsettings.{env.
EnvironmentName}.json", optional: true)
                .AddEnvironmentVariables();
            Configuration = builder.Build();
        }

        public IConfigurationRoot Configuration { get; }

        // This method gets called by the runtime. Use
this method to add services to the container.
        public void ConfigureServices(IServiceCollection
services)
        {
            services.AddEntityFramework()
        .AddDbContext<MovieReviewDbContext>(options =>
options.UseSqlServer(Configuration["Data:MovieReviewSPA:Co
nnectionString"],
                    b => b.MigrationsAssembly("MovieRevie
wSPA.web")));
        // Add framework services.
        services.AddMvc();
        //Initiating Seed Data
        services.AddTransient<InitialData>();
        //DI Setup
services.Configure<ImageSettings>(Configuration.
GetSection("ImageSettings"));
        services.AddScoped<RepositoryFactories,
```

```
RepositoryFactories>();
        services.AddScoped<IRepositoryProvider,
RepositoryProvider>();
          services.AddScoped<IMovieReviewUow,
MovieReviewUow>();

        //Authorization Policy
        services.AddAuthorization(options =>
        {
            options.AddPolicy("AdminRole",
policy=>policy.RequireClaim("https://movie-review.com/
roles","Admin"));
        });

    }

    // This method gets called by the runtime. Use
this method to configure the HTTP request pipeline.
    public void Configure(IApplicationBuilder app,
IHostingEnvironment env, ILoggerFactory loggerFactory,
InitialData seedDbContext)
    {
loggerFactory.AddConsole(Configuration.
GetSection("Logging"));
        loggerFactory.AddDebug();

        if (env.IsDevelopment())
        {
            app.UseDeveloperExceptionPage();
            app.UseWebpackDevMiddleware(new
WebpackDevMiddlewareOptions {
                HotModuleReplacement = true
            });
        }
        else
        {
            app.UseExceptionHandler("/Home/Error");
        }

        app.UseStaticFiles();

        var options = new JwtBearerOptions
        {
            Audience = "https://api.movie-review.com",
            Authority = "https://movie-review.auth0.com/"
        };
        app.UseJwtBearerAuthentication(options);
```

```
app.UseMvc(routes =>
{
    routes.MapRoute(
        name: "default",
        template: "{controller=Home}/
{action=Index}/{id?}");

        routes.MapSpaFallbackRoute(
            name: "spa-fallback",
            defaults: new { controller = "Home",
action = "Index" });
        });
        //Initiating from here
        seedDbContext.SeedData();
    }
}
}
```

Here in the **ConfigureServices** method, I have added one new policy which looks for a claim with namespace **http://movie-review.com/roles** and value **Admin**. If the value is valid, it allows the API access. Next, I need to go to the Movies controller and make the following changes.

```
[Authorize("AdminRole")]
    [HttpPost("")]
    public int Post([FromBody]Movie movie)
    {
        UOW.Movies.Add(movie);
        UOW.Commit();
        return Response.StatusCode = (int)
HttpStatusCode.Created;
    }
```

Once done, we need to be sure that API is accessible to only users with the Admin role.

Questions

1. Explain Authentication Lifecycle in general.
2. What are JWTs?
3. How to integrate Auth0 with application ?
4. How do you secure Client APIs?
5. How to apply Roles?
6. How Route Guards work in general?
7. What are the steps involved in implementing Route Guards?
8. How to Restrict API Access?

Summary

In this chapter, we started with understanding of the Authentication lifecycle and then we implemented it using auth0. We learned how to set up the auth0 account for secured APIs both at client and server level. Later on, we implemented the Login/Logout concept. Then, we extended the same concept via hosted pages at auth0. Next, we saw how to access audience setting and user profiles. We also learned how to customize the sign-up form via auth0. Lastly, we learned how to implement roles and claims.

CHAPTER 10

Introduction to Azure Cosmos DB

Introduction

Cosmos DB is a NoSql database that provides strong consistency. It's schema free, supports SQL-like querying, even has stored procedures, triggers and UDFs (User Defined Functions) written in Javascript. It's really Microsoft's answer to MongoDb, Cassandra, Couchbase and others. According to Cosmos DB, "Azure Cosmos DB guarantees less than 10 millisecond latencies on reads and less than 15 millisecond latencies on writes for at least 99% of requests." With that kind of performance guarantees, Cosmos DB is set to take over the world.

Microsoft also supports a .NET, Node.js, Java and a Python SDK for Cosmos DB. It runs in Azure and is fully managed. It automatically replicates all the data to any number of regions worldwide. It provides a wide variety of consistency levels.

1. **Strong consistency:** This is an RDBMS like consistency. With every request, the client is always guaranteed to read the latest acknowledge write. However, this is slow and in order to use this the Cosmos DB account cannot be associated with more than one region.

2. **Bounded staleness:** This level guarantees that the reads may lag behind by at most x versions of the document or at certain time interval by the client. For example, if the client sets x=2, the user will be guaranteed to get a document no later than the last two versions. It is the same with time. If the time is set to five seconds, every five seconds the resource will be guaranteed to have been written to all replicas to make sure that subsequent requests can see the latest version.

3. **Session:** This is the most popular of all, and as the name suggests, is scoped to a client session. Imagine someone added a comment on a product on an e-Commerce website. The user who commented should be able to see it; however, it will take some time before other users on the website can see it too.

4. **Eventual:** As the name suggests, the replicas will eventually converge in absence of any additional writes. This happens to be the one with the weakest read consistency, but the fastest of all options.

5. **Consistent Prefix:** This level guarantees that the replicas within a group eventually meet even if there is any absence of future writes. All writes will be performed in a particular order and hence reads won't ever see out of order writes.

Architecture

The architecture is very simplistic. The Cosmos DB account has multiple databases. The database can be reached via = Uri [AccountUri]/ dbs/{id} where AccountUri is of the following pattern.

"*https://[account].documents.azure.net*". The database has:

1. Collections: Collections can be reached with the Uri [AccountUri]/ dbs/{id}/colls/{id}. A Collection may have one or more of the following.

   (a) Documents: can be reached with the Uri [AccountUri]/ dbs/{id}/colls/{id}/docs/{id}

   (b) Attachments: can be reached with the Uri [AccountUri]/ dbs/{id}/colls/{id}/docs/{id}/attachments/{id}

   (c) Stored Procedures: can be reached with the Uri [AccountUri]/ dbs/{id}/colls/{id}/sprocs/{id}

   (d) Triggers: can be reached with the Uri [AccountUri]/ dbs/{id}/colls/{id}/triggers/{id}

   (e) User Defined Functions: can be reached with the Uri [AccountUri]/ dbs/{id}/colls/{id}/functions/{id}

2. Users: Users can be reached with the Uri [AccountUri]/ dbs/{id}/users/{id}.

   (a) Users have permissions that can be reached with the Uri [AccountUri]/ dbs/{id}/users/{id}/permissions/{id}

The unit of record is a Document and a collection is just as the name sounds, a collection of documents. Since documents are flat, it's better to think of them as a flat object and not like rows in a table. Coming from the Sql world, there is a tendency to think of collection as table and documents like rows. However, that analogy has more problems than we might fully recognize, especially when it comes to designing the architecture and later implementing it.

Setting up cosmos db in azure: -

In order to provision a Cosmos DB account, database and collection, follow the below steps:

1. Go to https://portal.azure.com

2. Go to New -> Search the marketplace.

3. Type Cosmos DB and it shows up as 'NoSQL (DocumetnDB) -> Create.
4. Select Pin to dashboard so you can access it easily.
5. (SeeFigure10.1)AddID:codemagazine(keepitmindthisisaURLhastobeunique)
   ResourceGroup: CodeMagazine ResourceGroup

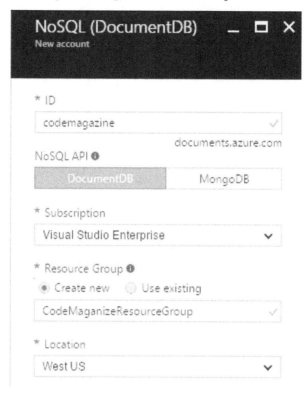

Figure 10.1: Creating a New Cosmos DB Account

Once that is done click Overview (Figure 10.2) and then click Add Collection.

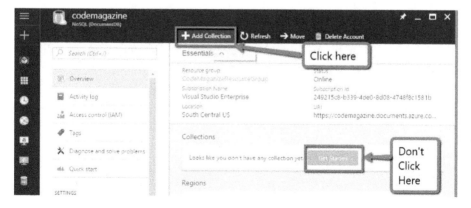

Figure 10.2: Cosmos DB Account

Add these values

Collection Id: Product

Database: MasterDb

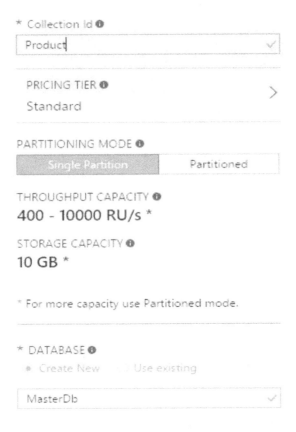

Figure 10.3: Create Collection Form

If you click Browse you should see that both the database and the collection has been created.

COLLECTION ID	DATABASE	THROUGHPUT	PRICING TIER
Product	MasterDb	1000	Standard

Figure 10.4: Browse: Cosmos DB Database and Collection

In order to connect, you will need the URI and the keys. For now, feel free to grab the URI and Primary Key. However, in an actual production environment you are better off using Secondary Keys and even Resource Tokens in order to control access to the database instance. Keys are in Figure 10.5.

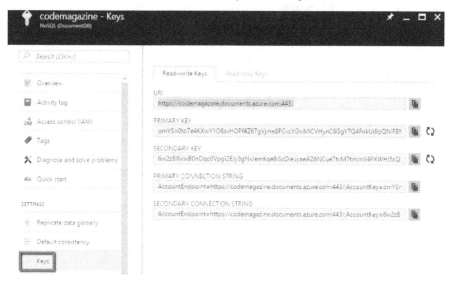

Figure 10.5: Uri, Primary and Secondary Keys

Figure 10.5: Cosmos DB Portal Features

Figure explained

No. 1: Generally speaking, you should avoid clicking on 'Get Started' as this will create a collection ToDo Items, which works with sample code. However, if you want your own collection, ignore this.

No. 2: Default Consistency: When you click on No 2, you will be able to set the default consistency for your account.

No. 3: When you click No 3, it will take you to Figure 10.5 and you can copy the Uri and the keys to connect to the Cosmos DB instance.

No. 4: Browse: When you click No. 3, Figure 10.4 will show the current databases and once you pick the database you need from the dropdown it will list the collections under it.

No. 5: Document Explorer: This is where you can select a collection and explore the documents in entirety.

No. 6: Query Explorer: This helps you to create SQL like queries on the data within Cosmos DB.

No. 7: Script Explorer: Allows you to write Stored Procedures, UDFs and other Javascript scripts supported by Cosmos DB.

Cosmos Db Emulator

While developing on the Cosmos DB Azure instance, you must remember that you will be spending money for both dev and test. However, the good news is that the Emulator comes in handy. You can do most of the things in the emulator and it's free as it runs on your local environment. You do not need an Azure subscription to work on this locally. A few limitations of the emulator are:

1. It supports a single account only (AuthKey and Uri is shared below).
2. It's not scalable.
3. It doesn't simulate any of the consistency levels.
4. It doesn't support multi-region replication.

CRUD using web api and cosmos Db

Now let's create a Web API that does CRUD (Create, Read, Update and Delete) operations on. I'm using .NET Framework 4.5.2.

Go to File -> New Project -> Web -> ASP.NET Web Application and Choose Web API template. We named our solution – CodeMagazineDocDb.

1. Firstly, we need to add the following code in the Web.Config. If you downloaded the emulator the endpoint and the authKey listed below are standard ones and the only way to connect to it for now. If you'd like to target the Azure instance, you can use the Uri and key in Figure.

Web.config file

```
<appSettings>
    <add key="endpoint" value="https://
localhost:8081/" />
```

```
        <add key="authKey" value="C2y6yDjf5/R+ob0N8A7Cgv3
0VRDJIWEHLM+4QDU5DE2nQ9nDuVTqobD4b8mGGyPMbIZnqyMsEcaGQy67
XIw/Jw==" />
    <add key="database" value="MasterDb" />
    <add key="collection" value="Product" />
</appSettings>
```

2. Create class Product.cs and add some properties to it. Decorate it with JsonProperty as we will be using Newtonsoft.Json wherever needed and the data will be passed around as JSON.

Product Code

```
using Newtonsoft.Json;

namespace CodeMagazineDocDb
{
    public class Product
    {
        [JsonProperty(PropertyName = "id")]
        public string Id { get; set; }

        [JsonProperty(PropertyName = "name")]
        public string Name { get; set; }

        [JsonProperty(PropertyName = "model")]
        public string Model { get; set; }

        [JsonProperty(PropertyName = "price")]
        public float Price { get; set; }
    }
}
```

3. We need to install Nuget Package Microsoft.Azure.Cosmos DB. You can use the GUI by right clicking the References tab in your project and clicking Manage Nuget Packages.
4. Create a folder Repositories.
5. Add the following interface. IDocdbRepository.cs

IDocdb Repository Code

```
using Microsoft.Azure.Documents;
using System;
using System.Collections.Generic;
using System.Linq;
using System.Linq.Expressions;
```

```
using System.Text;
using System.Threading.Tasks;

namespace CodeMagazineDocDb.Repositories
{
    interface IDocdbRepository<T> where T : class
    {
        Task<T> GetAsync(string id);

        Task<IEnumerable<T>>
GetManyAsync(Expression<Func<T, bool>> predicate);

        Task<Document> CreateAsync(T product);

        Task<Document> UpdateAsync(string id, T product);

        Task DeleteAsync(string id);

        void Initialize();
    }
}
```

All the methods are pretty standard for a repository and we kept it generic so we can use it for any entity whatsoever.

6. Add the following class. DocdbRepository.cs
7. Once you have the class implement the interface as described in the comments sections below.

```
using Microsoft.Azure.Documents;
using Microsoft.Azure.Documents.Client;
using Microsoft.Azure.Documents.Linq;
using System;
using System.Collections.Generic;
using System.Configuration;
using System.Linq;
using System.Linq.Expressions;
using System.Threading.Tasks;
using System.Web;

namespace CodeMagazineDocDb.Repositories
{
    public class DocdbRepository<T> : IDocdbRepository<T>
where T : class
    {
        //Click IDocdbRepository and press (Ctrl + .).
        //This will implement the interface. Press (Ctrl
+ Shift + B) to compile
```

```
        }
    }
```

Adding Logic

First, we need to add the DatabaseId and CollectionId as shown below.

```
    private static readonly string DatabaseId =
ConfigurationManager.AppSettings["database"];

    private static readonly string CollectionId =
ConfigurationManager.AppSettings["collection"];

    private static DocumentClient client;
```

//Usually this needs to be handled by the IoC container. However, keeping things simple for now.

8. Now we want to make sure we can create a Database inside Cosmos DB. We will try to read and find out if a database exists. If a database doesn't exist at that particular Uri, we will create one. In order to do that we use the DatabaseId from Web.Config and create the Uri by using this code.
   UriFactory.CreateDatabaseUri(DatabaseId)

```
    private async Task CreateDatabaseIfNotExistsAsync()
    {
        try
        {
            await client.ReadDatabaseAsync(UriFactory.
CreateDatabaseUri(DatabaseId));
        }
        catch (DocumentClientException e)
        {
            if (e.StatusCode == System.Net.
HttpStatusCode.NotFound)
            {
                await client.CreateDatabaseAsync(new
Database { Id = DatabaseId });
            }
            else
            {
                throw;
            }
        }
    }
```

9. Similarly, we will create a private method to create a Collection if it doesn't exist.

```
        private async Task
CreateCollectionIfNotExistsAsync()
        {
            try
            {
                await client.ReadDocumentCollectionAsy
nc(UriFactory.CreateDocumentCollectionUri(DatabaseId,
CollectionId));
            }
            catch (DocumentClientException e)
            {
                if (e.StatusCode == System.Net.
HttpStatusCode.NotFound)
                {
                    await client.
CreateDocumentCollectionAsync(
                        UriFactory.
CreateDatabaseUri(DatabaseId),
                        new DocumentCollection { Id =
CollectionId },
                        new RequestOptions {
OfferThroughput = 1000 });
                }
                else
                {
                    throw;
                }
            }
        }
```

10. Once that is done we just create an Initialize method which will be called one time. Later, we will add it to Global.asax.cs.

```
        public void Initialize()
        {
            client = new DocumentClient(new
Uri(ConfigurationManager.AppSettings["endpoint"]),
                ConfigurationManager.
AppSettings["authKey"],
                new ConnectionPolicy {
EnableEndpointDiscovery = false });
            CreateDatabaseIfNotExistsAsync().Wait();
            CreateCollectionIfNotExistsAsync().Wait();
        }
```

11. Now you can call this code from Global.asax.cs. Of course, this code should ideally be added through your IoC container (for a real production environment). However, this is a simplified version.

```
var repository = new DocdbRepository<Product>();
            repository.Initialize();
```

12. First thing we need to do is to create a Product. So, we will implement a method CreateAsync inside the DocDbRepository class. The trick is to understand that the document here is the product object and the Uri appended to it will just have the DatabaseId and CollectionId. Why do we not need the Document Id? Simply, because the document hasn't been created. Once we have the document, Cosmos DB will automatically assign an Id to it. Cosmos DB creates it's own '_ID' which is different than the ID created by the user or application. That '_ID' is unique and is only read only.

```
        public async Task<Document> CreateAsync(T
product)
        {
            return await client.CreateDocumentAsync(
                UriFactory.CreateDocumentCollectionUri(Da
tabaseId, CollectionId), product);
        }
```

13. Now, we need to implement the GetAsync method and in this case, all we need to do is pass in an ID of type string. BTW, Cosmos DB requires the ID to be a string so it's a best practice to create the ID as a string rather than using ToString() on an int field.

    The way the following code works is that it tries to read the Id. However, if the ID doesn't exist it throws an exception and if the HTTP Status Code is 404, that means the resource doesn't exist.

```
public async Task<T> GetAsync(string id)
        {
            try
            {
                var uri = UriFactory.
CreateDocumentUri(DatabaseId, CollectionId, id);
                Document document = await client.
ReadDocumentAsync(uri);
                return (T)(dynamic)document;
            }
            catch (DocumentClientException e)
            {
                if (e.StatusCode == System.Net.
HttpStatusCode.NotFound)
                {
```

```
            return null;
        }
        else
        {
            throw;
        }
    }
}
```

14. GetManyAsync uses an Expression that has a predicate. Predicate is a condition that can be specified by the method that calls this function and in this an object that confers to interface IDocumentQuery is created, uses deferred execution using Linq. This executes inside the while loop in an async fashion and adds the list of results as a range to the results list.

```
public async Task<IEnumerable<T>>
GetManyAsync(Expression<Func<T, bool>> predicate)
    {
        var uri = UriFactory.CreateDocumentCollection
Uri(DatabaseId, CollectionId);
        IDocumentQuery<T> query = client.
CreateDocumentQuery<T>(
                uri,
                new FeedOptions { MaxItemCount = -1 })
                .Where(predicate)
                .AsDocumentQuery();

        List<T> results = new List<T>();
        while (query.HasMoreResults)
        {
            results.AddRange(await query.
ExecuteNextAsync<T>());
        }

        return results;
    }
```

15. Update is very easy. We need to pass in the Id of the document we are updating and the updated product object. Delete is self-explanatory.

```
public async Task<Document> UpdateAsync(string
id, T product)
    {
        return await client.
ReplaceDocumentAsync(UriFactory.
```

```
CreateDocumentUri(DatabaseId, CollectionId, id),
product);
        }

        public async Task DeleteAsync(string id)
        {
            await client.DeleteDocumentAsync(UriFactory.
CreateDocumentUri(DatabaseId, CollectionId, id));
        }
```

16. In order to call this repository, we will create a Web API controller. It will have a route prefix of Products. In the absence of dependency injection or an IoC container, we will use the less preferred option of instantiating the repository inside the controller.

    We will have to create an HTTP Post method. We will need to specify from the body. This is required for model binding between the JSON array that we will send using Postman (It's a chrome utility used to make HTTP calls) and Web API. You can also use curl or fiddler instead of post man.

```
using CodeMagazineDocDb.Repositories;
using Microsoft.Azure.Documents;
using System;
using System.Collections.Generic;
using System.Linq;
using System.Net;
using System.Net.Http;
using System.Threading.Tasks;
using System.Web.Http;

namespace CodeMagazineDocDb.Controllers
{
    [RoutePrefix("Products")]
    public class ProductsController : ApiController
    {
        private DocdbRepository<Product> repository;
        public ProductsController()
        {
            repository = new DocdbRepository<Product>();
        }

        [HttpPost]
        [Route("")]
```

```
        public async Task<Document> CreateAsync([FromBody]
Product product)
        {

            var documentCreated= await repository.
CreateAsync(product);
            return documentCreated;

        }
    }
}
```

Postman Call

Verb: HTTP Post

Url

http://localhost:7345/products

Headers

Content-type: application/json

Body

```
    {
        "id" : "123",
        "name" : "iPhone",
        "model" : "iPhone 7 Plus",
        "price" : "FREE"
    }
```

17. Next, we'll call the GetAsync method. In this case the condition is simple. Since the ID is a string return, every single document that has an ID. This simply means return all records. (Note: You really don't want to use this in production).

```
[HttpGet]
        [Route("")]
        public async Task<IEnumerable<Product>>
GetAsync()
        {
            var products = await repository.
GetManyAsync(x => x.Id != null);
            return products;
        }
```

Verb: HTTP GET

Url

```
http://localhost:7345/products
```

No body or header

18. Rest is easy to follow and if you like to code the rest of the controller logic, the code is there for reference.

```csharp
using CodeMagazineDocDb.Repositories;
using Microsoft.Azure.Documents;
using System;
using System.Collections.Generic;
using System.Linq;
using System.Net;
using System.Net.Http;
using System.Threading.Tasks;
using System.Web.Http;

namespace CodeMagazineDocDb.Controllers
{
    [RoutePrefix("Products")]
    public class ProductsController : ApiController
    {
        private DocdbRepository<Product> repository;
        public ProductsController()
        {
            repository = new DocdbRepository<Product>();
        }

        [HttpPost]
        [Route("")]
        public async Task<Document> CreateAsync([FromBody]
Product product)
        {

            var documentCreated= await repository.
CreateAsync(product);
            return documentCreated;
        }


        [HttpGet]
        [Route("")]
        public async Task<IEnumerable<Product>>
```

```
GetAsync()
        {
                var products = await repository.
GetManyAsync(x => x.Id != null);
                return products;
        }


        [HttpPut]
        [Route("")]
        public async Task<Document> EditAsync([FromBody]
Product product)
        {
                var document = await repository.
UpdateAsync(product.Id.ToString(), product);

                return document;
        }


        [HttpDelete]
        [Route("")]
        public async void DeleteAsync(string id)
        {
                await repository.DeleteAsync(id);

        }
    }
}
```

This was a basic tutorial on Cosmos DB. It covered basic operations of create, agreed, update, and delete. The power of Cosmos DB has already been proven in the MSDN user data store. There is a lot you can do with this amazing database, fully managed by Microsoft and I hope you have a lot of fun working with it.

Summary

In this section, we have discussed Cosmos db in detail. Cosmos db is one of the disruptive technologies which is going to rule the world in future. We have seen in brief working and setup of cosmos db. We have also discussed its architecture in brief. Then, we have seen how to setup the same in azure. After that, we have called it via web api. Then, we have seen how to implement repository pattern via Web API and Cosmos Db.

www.ingramcontent.com/pod-product-compliance
Lightning Source LLC
LaVergne TN
LVHW022333060326
832902LV00022B/4011